HOW TO READ THE BIBLICAL BOOK OF PROVERBS:
In Paragraphs

HOW TO READ THE BIBLICAL BOOK OF PROVERBS:
In Paragraphs

CALVIN G. SEERVELD

DORDT PRESS

Edited by John H. Kok
Cover by Rob Haan
Layout by Carla Goslinga

Printed in the United States of America.

Dordt Press   www.dordt.edu/DCPcatalog
700 7th Street NE
Sioux Center, Iowa 51250

ISBN: 978-1-940567-24-2

Library of Congress Cataloging-in-Publication Data

Names: Seerveld, Calvin, author.
Title: How to read the biblical Book of Proverbs : in paragraphs / Calvin G. Seerveld.
Description: Sioux Center, Iowa : Dordt Press, 2020. | Includes index. |
Summary: "This book is a collection of pastoral exhortations based the book of Proverbs, a careful professional essay that argues for reading the Bible in a scholarly responsible literary way, and various readings from Proverbs – all aimed at helping the reader read Proverbs whole. All of the Scripture passages are translated by the author" – Provided by publisher.
Identifiers: LCCN 2020021185 | ISBN 9781940567242 (paperback)
Subjects: LCSH: Bible. Proverbs–Criticism, interpretation, etc.
Classification: LCC BS1465.52 .S44 2020 | DDC 223/.706–dc23
LC record available at https://lccn.loc.gov/2020021185

Front Cover: "Enlaced: A Burning Bush" by David Versluis (2011)—Dordt University, Sioux Center, Iowa; COR-TEN, H 18 x W 8 x D 8 ft. Used with permission of the artist.

Back cover photograph: by the author

Presented with deep thanks
to the good preaching pastors by whom
my wife and I have been blessed

Dewey Hoitenga Sr. (Revelation)

J.A. Kwint (Isaiah)

François Kouwenhoven

Morris Greidanus

Louis Tamminga

Carl Tuyl

Jack Westerhof

George Vandervelde

Herm van Niejenhuis (Job)

Joel Kok

TABLE OF CONTENTS

PREFACE

My wife Inès, the family Anya, Gioia, Luke, and I moved from Trinity Christian College in Chicago to Toronto in 1972, so I could begin teaching graduate courses in Philosophical Aesthetics at the Institute for Christian Studies. At that time a very literate, charismatic evangelical fellow named Robert Carvill was becoming a leader in the Reformational movement by editing a monthly journal of cultural and societal critique called *Vanguard.* The style of the articles was not to be the hot-rod prose of *Time*, nor the subtle, cultured phrasing of *The New Yorker*, but the writing was to have fresh diction, provocative theses, yet withal be biblically wise, and be directed to the ordinary intelligent reader. One of its issues titled "The American Way of Death" was temporarily stopped at the border of Canada by USA postal authorities. Carvill asked me to write a "biblical meditation" column for *Vanguard* we named *"Take Hold of God and Pull,"* the title of a book I had published in 1966.[1]

So I wrote occasional meditations on Proverbs 25–29 in *Vanguard* from 1972 until 1978, probably because on a sabbatical from Trinity Christian College (1966–1967) I had studied Old Testament with Gerhard von Rad in Heidelberg, Germany (as well as with Claus Westermann and Hans Wolter Wolff). That sabbatical year, 1966–67, was before Professor von Rad had published his important book *Weisheit in Israel* (1970).[2] But while in Heidelberg I read the doctoral dissertations of two of Von Rad's current students—on *Proverbs*: Christa Kayatz, *Studien zu Proverbien 1–9* (1966), proved, contrary to Von Rad's own initial judgment! that Proverbs 1–9 was booked early, and was truly Solomonic. And Hans-Jürgen Hermissson's analysis of Proverbs 10–15, *Studien zur altisraelitischen Spruchweisheit* (1968) was trying to find "collected unities" in the helter-skelter congeries of proverbial sayings in those six chapters.

After I returned from Heidelberg, I was led to examine the collection of *Proverbs* in chapters 25–29, to see what King Hezekiah's "wise counselors" had copy-edited from the Solomon archives (Proverbs 25:1), to give the officials of Hezekiah's administration the godly wisdom they would need for governing Judah outside Jerusalem in the 600s BC. So

---

1   A new revised edition was published in the UK: *Take Hold of God and Pull* (Carlisle: Paternoster Press, 1999). It is still available at *seerveld.com/tuppence.html*

2   Translated in English as *Wisdom in Israel* (London: SCM, 1972).

these particular proverbs, chapters 25–29, on how to rule and administer merciful justice, are very relevant for today, when bearing false witness with "alternative facts" is politically current, and where the ubiquitous "social media" gives easier license for every one to do what is right in their own eyes.

As it turns out, my intuited treatment of those proverb chapters as booked in paragraphs, and my proposal in the 1970s that certain proverbs modified and corrected earlier proverbs in the book, as if the rabbis were teaching younger ones in their pedagogical way of saying, "**Yes**, that may be so, **but** do you realize what really counts?": that intuited exposition is being confirmed today by the best current scholarship on *Proverbs*.[3] Theologians are now finding "clusters of proverbs" and "variant repetitions" in the biblical book of *Proverbs* that show there is likely **literary context** given to the proverb verses, and **edited cohesion**—proverbs are not to be read as if they be loose atoms or disparate nuggets of quotable sayings.

Also, in 1977 I was tempted to break my promise to my Vrije Universiteit professor mentor, D.H.Th. Vollenhoven, not to take time from teaching christian philosophy to be a preacher. A Christian Reformed pastor friend, Morris Greidanus, invited me to bring the Good News to his Brampton Ontario congregation on 20 February 1977. I put on my dark charcoal black wedding suit (1956) for the occasion, and in the Council Room before the service, something fell out of my pocket that looked like a peppermint as it rolled across the Council floor. It turned out to be a mothball. After the service in which I exhorted on 1 Kings 9:1–14, our son Luke reported to me the response of the youth in the congregation. I had set a record! for length of sermon.

Vollenhoven's death in 1978 confirmed, I thought, that I was released from the promise not to spend time foraging in the Scriptures. Now some 40 years later, as a "lay preacher" licensed "to exhort" by the Toronto Christian Reformed Church congregation where we belong and worship, I have come to realize that people nowadays in 2019 AD have a much shorter attention span than Dutch immigrants of the 1970s in Canada, who were hungry for God's Word of disciplining encouragement.

This book is a collection of a couple of early pastoral exhortations, which frame the 1970s *Vanguard* journal treatment of *Proverbs* para-

---

3   Knut Martin Heim, *Like Grapes of Gold Set in Silver: An interpretation of proverbial clusters in Proverbs 10:1-22:16* (Berlin: Walter de Gruyter, 2001); Peter T.H. Hatton, *Contradiction in the Book of Proverbs: The deep waters of counsel* (Aldershot: Ashgate, 2008); and K.M. Heim, *Poetic Imagination in Proverbs: Variant repetitions and the nature of poetry* (Winona Lake: Eisenbrauns, 2013), follow up the pioneering studies of Udo Skladny, *Die ältesten Spruchsammlungen in Israel* (Göttingen: Vandenhoeck & Ruprecht, 1962), and Raymond C. Van Leeuwen, *Context and Meaning in Proverbs 25-27* (Atlanta: Scholars Press, 1988).

graphs, plus a careful professional essay (1998) that argues for reading the Bible this literary way (using Proverbs 10:1–22). There is also an early 1960s reading of *Proverbs* I gave for a business men's retreat in the Chicago area. All biblical translations are my responsibility.

My deep thanks go to the Institute for Christian Studies' former research librarian Isabella Guthrie-McNaughton for helping me retrieve the *Vanguard* articles of the 1970s, and to Nik Ansell, professor extraordinaire of Biblical Theology at the Toronto graduate Institute for Christian Studies for pointing me to the best current scholarship on the Older Testament Proverbs. Also I am again grateful beyond words to John Kok, emeritated Professor of Philosophy at Dordt University, Iowa, who knows my mind, its strengths and weaknesses, for editing without faltering this mélange of sermons, journalistic columns and academic article between two covers. Without these three friends I would probably not have persisted in bringing this book to publication. I thank Carla Goslinga too for the meticulous spacing of verses and the placing of visual material in the text.

The *Vanguard* writings are printed here as originally published. The only change made has been to be gender inclusive and to update a few of the everyday examples. I make no apology for trying to be "fresh" in formulating what I think is a scholarly responsible **literary translation** of the Hebrew and exposition of these biblical passages. One week in August 1978, when I was a featured speaker at the Chautauqua Institute in New York, and met the respected Yale University Professor of Old Testament, Brevard Childs, he examined my *Take Hold of God and Pull* way of hearing Scripture, and told me it was a very good way to bring God's Word to God's ordinary people and to any curious inquirers. So I have been glad to carry on this ministry, and hope it may catch you who read this early discovery of how to read *Proverbs* whole.

Calvin Seerveld
Toronto, 2019 AD

A.

A Spoken Introduction:
Proverbs 1, 3, and James 3

Before considering what God is saying to us today in the first chapters of the book of *Proverbs*, I'd like to explain a few things as we prepare to read a longer section.

> Standing still listening before the LORD
> is a head start in full-bodied knowledge:
> to suppose wisdom and instruction (paideia) worthless
> is a trait of fools. (cs 1:7)

These words in *Proverbs*—"knowledge," "wisdom," "instruction" [NIV "discipline"], "teaching," "understanding," and others—have different shades of meaning, but they all basically point to the same thing: "insight into doing what is right."

If somebody says, "**Food** is on the table," or "**Chow**'s ready—come and get it!" or "**Supper** is served," everybody knows what's being referred to. "Food," "chow," "supper," mean something edible from the earth is ready, like manna, to be eaten for nourishment. Or, a teacher may come into a class and say, "**Girls**— " or "**Ladies!**" or "The **women** have a break first," and everybody knows whom the teacher is referring to—not to the boys. But to call people "girls" is more casual, light-hearted, emphasizing how young they are. "Ladies" is more polite, a little formal, and "ladies" rhymes with "gentlemen." "The women" is more like a biological category, distinguishing "women" from "men."

Well, "**knowledge**" in *Proverbs* means "firsthand, intimate experience of what God wants done"; and "**wisdom**" means "you are able to judge what God wants done"; and "**instruction**" [NIV **discipline**] means "the rigorous discipline of acting according to God's Will."

I mention this so nobody will strain like a Pharisee-scribe to pit one word like "knowledge" against another like "instruction." That room in the church building marked LADIES/WOMEN, girls enter too. Talk in *Proverbs* about WISDOM is not vague nor used loosely. "Wisdom" has its special nuances all right, because *Proverbs* is the true revelation of God in poetic form. But if we can get clear what Wisdom is about, then we shall also have an entrance to the Bible's slant on "knowledge" and "discipline" and "law" and "understanding," because all these matters are fundamentally related, according to God's Word.

"The fear of the LORD is the beginning of knowledge, wisdom, and instruction [discipline]—all of which fools despise."

> Hear, my child, your father's instruction,
> and do not reject your mother's teaching. (1:8) [NRSV]

We need to realize that "my son" includes daughters, and even parents, because every father here has been somebody's son, and mothers have been or still are daughters of grandparents. We should read "my son" in *Proverbs* to be an affectionate way of talking to anybody trying to listen, because to teach this is the way the professional, teaching "wise men" and "wise women" of David and Solomon's day: it's the way the "teachers" of Israel spoke to people in making the will of the LORD known. "My son," my daughter, my child, my student, my disciples, my followers, my younger or older generation of people, hear the Word of the LORD in the story I'm going to tell you now....

This is the way rabbi Jesus, the teacher Jesus, carried on the Older Testament wiseman-proverbs tradition in telling parables and in talking to the crowds. You can read it, for example, in Matthew 9:2:

> And see, they brought to Jesus a paralytic, lying on his bed;
> and when Jesus saw their faith he said to the paralytic,
> "My son, take heart; your sins are forgiven."

Paul referred to Timothy, you may remember, as "my son, in the faith" (1 Timothy 1:2), within the same framework. *Proverbs* is not just discriminating and cracking down on teenage boys. *Proverbs* is also for girls and parents, **for anybody willing to listen...as a child in faith.**

Maybe I should mention here something else for the young people to hear. The Bible says (1:8a): "Hear, my son" [NIV listen]—that means, 'Hear and obey'—your father's instruction."

So, if your father gets mad and says, "Go jump in the lake!" you get on your bike or borrow a car, ride over to the nearest lake and then go jump in, even if you can't swim? Proverbs 1:8. "Hear and obey, my son, your father's instruction"! "My daughter," v.8b, "do not reject [NIV forsake] your mother's teaching." So mother says, "Daughter, that fellow is seriously interested in you; he makes $100,000 a year. Marry him." If the fellow is an unbeliever, should you do it?

What are you trying to do, Seerveld, knock parental authority?

Not at all. I believe the Bible teaches that children should honor their father and mother as father and mother even when their parents are wrong about something—but that's a different sermon. Right now it is important for understanding *Proverbs* to realize that 1:8 says:

Hear [NIV listen], my son, to your father's **godly** instruction,
And don't reject [NIV forsake], my daughter, your mother's **godly**
teaching.

The Hebrew word for "teaching" in 1:8b is __torah__, "the LAW" God gave
Moses. If a mother ever told her daughter to marry an unbelieving boy
because he was nice and had money, the Bible would never call that advice "teaching"—__torah__. It would call it stupidity. And the Bible never
gives fathers carte blanche, absolute authority over their sons so they can
act like tyrants. That's a tragedy in families, "christian" families too, when
parents provoke their children to foolishness because the parents don't
know the difference between Wisdom and a dollar bill, or don't know
the difference between "godly discipline" and Prussian military Macht.

> 1:8 Hear my son, your father's instruction, and
>   don't reject, my daughter, your mother's __torah__,
> 1:9 for they, godly discipline and __torah__, "teaching," the guiding law
>   of the LORD, are [NIV will be] a fair garland [NIV to grace] for
>   your head, and pendants, (that's a big word for [NIV a chain] a
>   necklace) for your neck.

1:7–9 are the introduction to the whole first nine chapters of the book
of *Proverbs*. So we should try to get a good picture of what 1:9 means.

You know those headbands joggers wear, or tennis players have
around the head, to keep the sweat out of their eyes? Proverbs 1:9 means
to say: Son, instead of having Adidas written there, to show you've got
quality sport goods, get the words "Dad's Discipline" inscribed on it, for
when you run around the block or jog through the countryside. And
daughter, instead of that T-shirt with the proverb across the front, "Keep
on truckin'" or the advertisement (in Toronto), "If we don't have it, you
don't need it, Steve's Music Store," or the one some wear in Orange City,
Iowa, "If you ain't Dutch, you ain't much": instead, embroider across
your T-shirt chest, "Motherly Guidance."

What in the world for? 1:9 says: Son, if you wear godly discipline
hand-me-downs from your father, you look good! Daughter, if you are
dressed in the guiding law of the LORD sewn by your mother for you,
you'll be beautiful!

Our apostate media and fashion advertisements say a girl is good-
looking if she's got certain bust-waist-and-hip measurements. Secularized
people say a fellow is sharp if he's got a good profile, stylized hairdo, and
his muscles bulge when he flexes his arm. *Proverbs* says a boy or a girl
or a parent is really handsome and attractive if they are clothed in doing
what's right and wonderful, dressed in the shirt of making whoever they
meet glad to be alive in God's world—of such are the true Miss Universes
made, those are the true models of manhood.

So, do you get a picture somewhat of what 1:9 is saying? "Godly dis-

cipline and the LORD's **torah** are a becoming headband for your head or
two lovely necklaces for your neck. But 1:9 is saying more than Zechariah
14:20 says, where the prophecy is made that someday the bridles of the
horses you drive to work will have engraved on them by, say, the Christian Labour Association of Canada or a Christian manufacturing firm,
PRAISE TO YAHWEH! Proverbs 1:9 recognizes that T-shirts with capital P
T L letters on them (Praise the Lord) could be using the LORD's Name
in vain—for show. 1:9 means that when there is loving concern, joy, and
strong gentleness shining **inside** the very way you feel and imagine, think
and talk, eat and drink, then, O my son and daughter, my parent, you are
a very winsome, lovely creature.

Now we're ready to read Chapter 1 first: 1:10–19 set off against 1:20–33.
You'll notice that vv.11–14 are a speech by sinful men, and vv.22–33 are
a speech by Wisdom, in the first person.[1]

Maybe some of you will be surprised at the kind of language the
Bible uses in 1:12 (cf. NIV footnote), but that's the way sinful people talk,
in four-letter words—Are you ready? This is the Word of God:

10 My son, [my daughter, my parent,] if tricky fellows entice you,
   never go along with it.
11 If they say, "Come with us, let's lie in wait for the kill!
   Let's ambush the innocent, for no reason at all.
12 Let's swallow them alive—hell!—whole!
   like those dropped into the grave.
13 We'll find all kinds of costly valuables.
   We shall fill our houses with spoil.
14 Throw in your lot with us, (fellow,)
   there will be just one purse for all of us together!"

15 My son, my daughter, my parent, never walk along that way with
   them.
   Hold your foot back from their well-beaten paths,
16 for their feet are running toward what is perversely evil—
   they are in a hurry to spill blood!
17 Indeed, "In vain is a bird trap set,
   even when it be within the sight of anything with wings."
18 These fellows lie in wait for their **own** blood.
   They ambush their very **own** lives!

19 **Such are indeed the ways of all those who gain stuff by
   violence:
   it takes away the very life of those who grabbed
   the possessions.**

1   I'll use the RSV footnotes to 1:23, which are correct in my judgment. NIV 1:23 is not
    so good as the RSV, which does not have "heart" but the Hebrew word "spirit" poured
    out. The verse reads: "Respond to my rebuke; see! I will pour out my **spirit** upon you
    and make my words known to you." The King James translation has it right.

Verse 19 is saying: The sinful people who try to ruin others, to catch inexperienced ones in their net like birds or butterflies, shall get caught **themselves**, says Proverbs 1:19.

Meanwhile 1:20–33

20 Wisdom is hollering herself hoarse out in the street!
   She is losing her voice shouting to the crowded squares.
21 There she is, calling out on top of the city walls!
   She is (always) busy speaking her careful sayings at the
      entrances of the gates in the city:
22 "How long, you simpletons! shall you love to have a one-track
      mind?
   Till when, you stuck-up stupes! till when must you keep on
      caressing yourselves by making brutally cheap critique?
   You dense, closed people! Why do you hate genuine
      knowledge?
23 Turn yourselves around toward the correction I am speaking!
   Look now, I shall let my spirit spill out all over you,
   I will make my telling words known to you all—

24 "Because I said, 'Let's meet one another,' and you stood me up;
   I stuck out my hand (to you), and there wasn't the least notice
      given:
25 because you let all my deliberated counsel simply go hang,
   and were never willing to be open to my showing you the right
      way:
26 all right, now I, in turn, at your impending disaster, shall just
      make fun of (you).
   As dread of what's coming starts to steal over you, I shall just
      laugh!
27 as shivering begins to shake you like a turbulent storm,
   and calamity strikes you down like the blitz of a tornado,
   while fear and a closing in constrictive feeling (slowly) stifles
      you....
28 Then when they say to me, 'Let's get together!' I will not show
      that I hear.
   They will look hard for me then, but they shall not find me at all!
29 Because they actually hated knowledge,
   and deliberately did not feel like fearing the Lord God:
30 because they would not accept my directing instruction (יתצעל)
   and spurned all my corrective measures:
31 All right, now they must eat the fruit of their own making,
   and be satisfied with their own concocted plans.

32 **"You can count on it:**
   The turned-away-from-God, back-into-themselves
   posture of people with a one-track mind shall
   bring about their own death; and those who disdain
   getting involved shall ruin themselves by their own

comfortable negligence.

³³ But whoever listens to me, [Wisdom,] shall find a place that is
secure,
where he or she can rest, unafraid from the threat of evil
afoot."

Proverbs is very dramatic.

On the one side you have these crooked fellows in 1:11–14, who
might look quite respectable, in three-piece suits, scheming together, trying to suck in simple toms of younger people who have less experience:
"Come on in with us to make a killing, you can't lose! There's a sucker
born every minute; we might as well cash in on it as anybody else—"

And on the other side you have **Wisdom** in 1:22–33, hollering herself
hoarse, chanting out in the middle of the streets, on housetops, at the city
gates (1:21), where the elders, the "wise men" and "wise women" used to go
sit in David and Absalom's time (cf. 2 Samuel 15:1–6) to speak judgment
when anybody in the neighborhood had a lawsuit or a difficult problem.

Over-all Bible story connection

What—who—is **this Wisdom person** in *Proverbs* that's shouting in
chapter 1? To find out who Wisdom, this personal Wisdom, is, we need
to read a little bit more. It becomes more and more clear as you read these
nine chapters, especially during the longer Wisdom speech of chapter
8, where Wisdom says she was God's originary master artisan playing
around in the beginning, helping God fix ordinances for creatures, having fun! [the "delight" translation of the NIV (2011) makes it sound too
proper], fooling around with humankind! But first let's read in chapter
3:13–20 a short hymn about Wisdom.

¹³ O good! for the man or woman who has discovered Wisdom!
Blessed indeed is everyone who is able to get a certain special
Understanding out into service!

¹⁴ The advantage of apt insight is greater than solid money.
The fruit of God-fearing discernment beats the yield on good
old gold!

¹⁵ That's right: Wisdom is more rare than dark pearls!
The sum total of your most treasured things does not equal the
worth of Understanding what's up—

¹⁶ Wisdom holds in the right hand, as it were, a life whose days
last long,
and in the left hand, riches and honor you can hardly imagine!

¹⁷ The ways Understanding goes to work are kindly, joyful ways;
even the littlest footpath of Understanding walked on
means shalom!

¹⁸ **Wisdom is a Tree of Life for whoever takes hold of it
for support!
Whoever holds on to Understanding continues to
be blessed!**
¹⁹ **Do you realize—
the LORD God set up the earth in its
ordinances with the help of Wisdom!
the LORD God used Understanding to get the heavens
firmly established!**
   ²⁰ It took the LORD God's know-how to have the original flood of
waters break down [into oceans, rivers, springs] and to set
things up so that clouds can trickle a dewdrop rain....

Now do you hear what I hear in this hymn to Wisdom, which sums up briefly what Proverbs 8:22–31 exuberantly explicates, by telling us that the LORD God "possessed" (KJ translation of 8:22 קָנָנִי) the needed Wisdom to lay the earth's foundations, the know-how Understanding to firm up the sky, the firsthand Knowledge to set limits to the deep flooding waters and order manageable creatures like oceans, rivers, springs, and clouds to trickle down rain, mist, and dew. Chapter 3:19–20, next to 3:18 which mentions "a tree of life," echoes verses of Genesis 1:

In the beginning God created the heavens and the earth.
The earth was without form and void, and
darkness was upon the face of the deep;
and the **Spirit of God w**as moving over the face of the waters.

(Genesis 1:1–2)

Proverbs starts to get very exciting when you realize that Wisdom with a capital W, speaking in the first person—"I, Wisdom"—is an Older Testament way of revealing to us God the Holy Spirit! (That's why the translation of 1:23 is so important to me: "I, Wisdom, will pour out my self, my *ru'ah*, let **my spirit** spill out over you; and I will make **my words** known to you firsthand, O my hearing people!"

Then you can read Proverbs 1–9 with different eyes and ears. Then the connection of the book of Proverbs to Genesis and to the Newer Testament gospels, Jesus Christ, Pentecost and after, becomes very close, relevant, and provocative for our living as children of faith ("my child") in North America, in the world of Muslims and pope, militarists, anti-Christs, leaders of nations, and hungry, bewildered people needing medicine … and wisdom.

There are 3 points now: (1) How can you be certain that this Wisdom of *Proverbs,* who was there from eternity with the LORD, almost like the "eternal begotten Son of God" (cf. John 1:1–14, 3:16–17, 1 John 4:9–10), assisting God as the LORD ordained and ordered the sky and the sea and the dry land (Proverbs 3:19–20, 8:22–31), is veritably the Holy Spirit? (2) What are the historical implications of Wisdom speaking in Proverbs 1:23,

"I will pour out my **Spirit** upon you, and I will make my **words** known to you"? and (3) So what, now? Why is this important for us?

Biblical literary support for the interpretation

Point 1: Quite simply, other passages of Scripture explicitly identify the Spirit of God as capital W Wisdom and the Source of anyone's being or becoming wise.

For example: The first paragraph of Exodus 31 tells us that God filled Bezalel, Oholiab, and other carpenters, sculptors and seamstresses working on the tabernacle and the clothes designed for the high priests: God filled Bezalel with the Spirit of God, it says, that is (and the King James translation has it exactly), with **wisdom**, understanding, and the knowledge of putting things together so it pleased the LORD (31:1–11). Carpenters, artisans, and ladies who sewed in ways pleasing to God did so because they were filled with the Holy Spirit—Wisdom. A second passage is the famous prophecy of Isaiah 11 about "the sprout that will shoot out of the stump of Jesse": you can read there these words:

> the Spirit of the LORD God shall rest upon him [that person coming, Jesus Christ],
> that is, the spirit of Wisdom and Understanding,
> the spirit of Counsel and restful Strength,
> the spirit of Knowledge and of standing in awe of the LORD God.
>
> (11:2)

This prophecy of Isaiah was fulfilled in history at the baptism of Jesus by John when God publicly ordained, you might say, the wisdom of God's beloved Son on earth in whom God was well pleased by sending down upon him the Holy Spirit, like a dove, to initiate Christ's ministry (cf. Mark 1:9–13, John 1:29–34).

There's a third passage in Daniel, near the end of the Older Testament times, right at the spot where Belshazzar was scared out of his wits by those heavenly fingers writing a message on the wall telling the banqueters that their days were numbered. The Bible reports that the queen-mother said, "Don't turn pale, O King. Get Daniel who has superior vision and insight on what's right to do because he is indwelt by an (extraordinary) Spirit of the Most Holy God" (Daniel 5:10–12). Those pagans recognized Daniel was a man of wisdom and was in the office of making decisions and judgments to run the Persian kingdom, rightly so, because he was filled with the Holy Spirit.

I don't want to be confusing. I just want to underscore that Exodus 31, Isaiah 11, and Daniel 5 all reinforce reading Proverbs 1, 3, and 8, to make the point that Wisdom with a capital W is the Spirit of the living God, the Holy Spirit.

God's Word and God's Spirit in historical development

Point (2): The combinatorial presence of God's creative Word and the active Holy Spirit in the beginning, along with God the Father's "only begotten Son," has always been in effect for us creatures under the one true trinitarian God. But it is worth noting that historically the LORD God's Word and God's Spirit mentioned together in Proverbs 1:23 have gradually become more "available," you might say, for us human creatures to respond to. Let me explain.

God's creative "Let-there-be" Word, which ordered how and when creatures undergo seed time and harvest (Genesis 8:21–22), God's Word-ordinances which ordain the activity of birds, fire, snow, and the weather (Psalm 104, Psalm 148), God's Word-*torah* which holds for Sabbath rest, for raising and instructing the next generation (Exodus 20:7–11, Proverbs 1:7–9, Ephesians 6:1–4), and for building (or ruining) cities (Psalm 127): these Words of life, which the LORD God spoke in the beginning and communicated to God's special people before the Christ showed up bodily, are open for discovery all around us to this day.

Because Sin entered history, God's commanding Word was also later made incarnate in personal Jewish human flesh (John 1:14), Jesus Christ, to make God self heart-rendingly visible, palpable, especially among God's obstinate people, vulnerable and suffering, in order to turn God's beloved folk away from their self-justifying, seductive idols (Matthew 21:33–41, Galatians 4:4–7, Hebrews 2:14–18).

When that historical act "failed," followers of God's incarnate Word testified so that a new shoot of ethnic nobodies, like most of us, were grafted into God's tree trunk of hacked-off branches (Romans 9:22–26, 11:13–24, 1 Peter 2:9–10). And what God said and wrote down for Moses (Exodus 34:1–9), the true story of God's marvelous deeds from before the flood until after Christ's ascension, got saved, edited, and booked (Luke 1:1–4, John 21:24, Revelation 22:18–19) into our canonic text as God's scripted Word, has the voice-power to cut to life or cut to death those it reaches (Hebrews 4:11–13).

So **God's Word setting creational order** is a reality, and **God's incarnate Word** in the Savior Jesus Christ is historically real, and **God's inscripturated Word**, the Bible, put in human language right in front of us, so anybody can pick it up and read: **God's reliable Word has been and is being ever more fully revealed for us earth creatures to hear and obey, to follow, as invitations to creational shalom.**

Along with God's Word, God's Spirit has also remained divinely the same but has quietly moved historically from the background more up into the foreground.

Originally the Holy Spirit was having fun during God's creating the world, says Proverbs 8:30–31, filling in a little the mysterious note in the first verses of Genesis about the Spirit's moving back and forth over the chaos of water. Maybe that's why Psalm 104 describes one of the tasks special to the Holy Spirit is getting baby whales born and stopping the life of skunks (Psalm 104:24–30).

Later on we are told that when Moses was at his wits end about finding meat for God's disgruntled people in the desert, and needed help to govern the unruly nation of Israelites, the LORD God took some of the Holy Spirit resting on Moses, which gave Moses directing wisdom, and infused 70 elders, especially Eldad and Medad, with the Spirited authority and power to "prophesy," that is, to make God's Word and will known to the people (Numbers 11:24–29).

The Bible also tells us in Judges 14:5–9 about Samson's being overpowered by the Holy Spirit; so Samson grabbed the attacking lion by the jaws and ripped it down the sides like the peel of a banana—enormous strength! The Bible says that judges like Gideon were enabled to judge, lead, and rule because of the Holy Spirit (Judges 6:34), that prophets like Samuel and Nathan, Elijah, Elisha, and Isaiah spoke prophetically, thanks to the Holy Spirit (Nehemiah 9:30, Isaiah 59:20–21).

No wonder the sinner-king David's most piteous petition in Psalm 51 is the shriek, "O God! don't take your Holy Spirit away from me!" (Psalm 51:10–12). That's why pop-song writer David composed a dirge for his predecessor Saul (2 Samuel 1:19–27), because David knew God's Spirit had left(!) King Saul (1 Samuel 16:13–14); so Saul's rule was no longer blessed, and Saul died "consulting" a witch, because God no longer communicated with him (1 Samuel 28:3–7) by Word or Spirit.

So God's Holy Spirit was busy in the creatural world from the beginning, and apparently filled the heart and consciousness of certain selected leaders of God's people with the wisdom, humbled knowhow understanding and discipline, to make God's Words tractable, winsome, concrete, for others to recognize, to follow as directives for living in society on God's earth.

And on Pentecost the Holy Spirit went "democratic," you could say, spreading this grace of holy wisdom further than to a few special individuals. Joel's Older Testament prophecy is now being historically fulfilled, said the apostle Peter in Acts 2:17–18:

> I, [the LORD,] will pour out my Spirit upon everybody: your sons
> and daughters will prophesy; old greybeards will dream dreams;
> full-grown adults will see visions. In those days I will even pour
> out my Spirit upon manual laborers and hired girls…! (Joel 2:28–29)

On that Pentecost post-resurrection, post-ascension of God's Son Jesus Christ, the LORD God finally responded to Moses' plaintive request, "Why restrict giving the Spirit of Wisdom to just 70 elderly men? Would that the LORD would put God's Spirit upon **all** the LORD's people!" (Numbers

11:29). **Now anybody can be filled with the Holy Spirit**—male ditch-diggers and female house-cleaners, waiters and waitresses— says Acts 2 following up Joel 2 explicitly.

And after Jesus Christ went to heaven, it all happened! The Holy Spirit arrived on earth in person, so to speak, at Pentecost, to follow up Christ's work (John 7:39). **All wisdom broke loose!** People heard about the great acts of God in whatever their language was and saw with their own eyes acts of love by disciples of Christ for their neighbors and strangers that turned selfish ways of living upside-down and convicted unbelievers of the Truth. (You can read all about it in Acts 2:1–11, 37–47 and 5:12–16).

Point 2 then is this: both the LORD's Word and the Holy Spirit, in tandem as it were, are more fully evident, accessible today than in past ages, more insistent, if you will, in what the Bible calls "these final days" before Christ returns (Hebrews 1:1–2, 2 Timothy 3:1–5, 2 Peter 3:1–7), more imperative to be minded if we would find God's kind of peace. And **it is God's Words and God's Spirit together that are to lead us**,[2] as the luminous cloud in the daytime and pillar of fire at night over the ark holding God's ten Words led God's people once upon a time in their trek out of Egyptland through the wilderness to the promised land (Numbers 9:15–23, Psalm 99:6–7, Nehemiah 9:12–14). Today God's people need the combined direction-giving of God's Word and God's Spirit on the Way to the new Jerusalem, which is not a piece of politically contested real estate, but an everlasting new earth where there are no more tears, pain, failure, AIDS, the terror of war, or death. God's Word and God's Spirit go together. That's why every time we read Scripture, God's Word, in a worship service, we pray for the special presence of the Holy Spirit, so the Word be fully preached and those listening hear God's wisdom.

Point (3): Why is this important? that God the Holy Spirit is revealed in *Proverbs* as capital "W" Wisdom, and is the source of living wisdom among humans, so they can understand God's words?

Well, it's important for understanding the book of *Proverbs,* for understanding the nature of wisdom, and for realizing what it means to be filled with the Holy Spirit.

---

2 Those who think an "Age of the Spirit" has **succeeded** the "Age of the Word" since Christ returned to heaven, and therefore believe our present "dispensation" allows for extra-Scriptural revelations, and/or force a scheme upon world events that precipitates the final Judgment Day, hold what the apostle Paul warned against—do not go beyond what is written (1 Corinthians 4:6)—and forget Jesus' rejection of presuming to figure out when the eschaton will come—it shall be unexpected (Mark 13:32–37)!

Testing your Holy Spirited wisdom

Wisdom, according to the Bible, is being able to judge what God wants done because you have a Holy Spirited, disciplined understanding of God's Words—the creational ordinances, the biblical injunctions, the call of Jesus Christ to follow his lead.

Biblical wisdom is not a matter of IQ, your student score on SAT tests, your dexterity at numbers, or efficient know-how on getting things done. Holy Spirited wisdom is also not "philosophically contemplative" musing, doing a Monday quarterback analysis of what the government or the army should have done last week—acting like a know-it-all pundit in your armchair before the TV set. And anytime directions on what needs to be done are reduced to an imperative T-shirt slogan—"Support our troops!" "Save the family!" or "Make war on terror!"—one needs to be wary of possible pseudo-wisdom, over-simplified and raucous proposals that foment disorderly partisan, violent stances that can poison societal relationships and falsely promise easy solutions.

The great chapter of Job 28 about Wisdom says you can't go get your gun and hunt down Wisdom or dig for it like buried treasure in your backyard, mine it like precious metal or oil, pick it up at the drive-through liquor store or at Tim Hortons on the way home from church. Only God knows the way to Wisdom, it says in Job, and only the LORD can give Wisdom and will give...the Holy Spirit, says Proverbs 2, to those who repent of their sin and selfishness and plead for forgiveness, and unaffectedly say, "I want to love you forever, my Lord, and obey your Words."

True wisdom comes from an indwelling of the Holy Spirit seasoned by disciplined insight into God's Words, God's will for refurbishing justice, becoming generous, keeping earlier covenants, redeeming brokenness, ending pockets of poverty, forgiving harshness, making peace in deed (Galatians 5:16–6:2). Holy Spirit instilled wisdom is not a matter of knowing certain pious formulae, having certain mannerisms, being very clever while wearing a halo.

Christ promised to send his followers the Counselor who will lead them in the true Way of genuine peace. Not the kind of peacefulness the world pretends to give, an easy life without worries, a rose garden without thorns (remember Proverbs 1:13)—"We'll fill our houses with spoil!" No, the Father and I will send you the Paraclete, the Holy Spirit, says Jesus, who will take up lodging with you, counsel you, stand up for you, teach you all kinds of things, fill you with Wisdom—so you will know what to say when your persecutors publicly make fun of you in court (John 12:8–12), so you will know how to offer your lifetime in a way that makes God smile (Romans 12:1–2), so you'll know how to groan in prayer when you have too much pain, are too mixed up or burdened to formulate a prayer request properly and can only mutter, "Daddy, please let the Lord Jesus come back quick!" (Romans 8:12–17).[3]

If being wise is so tied to being indwelt by the Holy Spirit—as maybe Persian overlord Cyrus once was—an "Anointed One" of God even though he was a pagan (Isaiah 44:28–45:13)!? is that what led Babylonian Nebuchadnezzar to confess his pride (Daniel 4)? what stirred Mikhail Gorbachev to initiate *glasnost* and *perestroika* (1987)? moved F.W. De Klerk (1990) and Nelson Mandela to unite for reconciled ruling (since the Holy Spirit is not a Sanctimonious spirit)? If **being wise for ruling is so tied to being indwelt by the Holy Spirit,** that leads me to conclude not with a breakdown of which political rulers today we need to pray be struck by the lightning of Wisdom, but with a rather delicate question: do **you** know the Holy Spirit? Is the Holy Spirit real to you, or just a vague blur, maybe like a ghost?

I'm not talking about going to church regularly, staying out of jail, being agreeable and "nice," or giving a double tithe as good Pharisees should. I'm asking whether you have heard the cry of Wisdom in the streets and back alleys of your lifetime, and whether you could quietly confess to your neighbor, if we took a five-minute break, "Yes, I have been baptized by the Holy Spirit, as Paul puts it in 1 Corinthians 12:13, into the body of Christ; I know the Holy Spirit, I know how to lead by serving, I am a saint, despite my sin and troubles, God help me. I am growing in wisdom...."

We usually think of the Holy Spirit as being the most elusive member of the Trinity. God the Father spoke and created the world and sits majestically unmoved in heaven in providential charge of everything. Jesus Christ showed up bodily on earth as a Jew and very concretely healed people, argued with opponents, bled and died. But the Holy Spirit works more mysteriously as spirit, isn't that so? You can't pin the Holy Spirit down, it seems. Nobody has seen the wind. Pentecost showed flames of fire, that's right, but they soon disappeared, like halos fading into the atmosphere.

Yes, it's true, the Holy Spirit remains uncanny, just as God the Father stays awful and Jesus Christ remains amazing, to keep us creatures —prone to pride—humble, worshipful, thankfully dependent upon such an almighty merciful Lord and Savior and Comforter who stoops to our weakness but transcends our figuring out.

So how can we give ourselves to the Holy Spirit if we can't track the Spirit down? How can we get the Holy Spirit more live to our conscious-

---

3   The Greek παράκλητον/παράκλητος in John 14:16/26 is rendered so: KJ "Comforter"; JB "Advocate"; RSV "Counselor"; NIV "Counselor," footnote "Helper"; NRSV "Advocate," footnote "Helper." The Jerusalem Bible has a good footnote, which explains that translators choose from all the several connotations of the word to fix on a one-word equivalent: "advocate, intercessor, counselor, protector, support," since *paràklètos* means an intermediating, protective support person.

ness without running into T-shirt slogans or sober looks and dark suits? Will relating the capital W Wisdom of *Proverbs* and the Holy Spirit bring us into a closer relationship with the living God revealed in Jesus Christ?

If you have the wisdom to walk **through** temptation (young people, we older people too—temptations don't slack off as you get older, they just change from sex to self-serving greed or do-gooding prestige); if you know the love to **give yourself** to rescue a troublesome neighbor instead of isolating him or her; if you have insight to **work out redemptively how God has set up** families and government and business and congregations to be compassionate, open-hearted, just-doing communities; if you **know the peace that draws you closer to the Lord in the worst trials**: then you know the Holy Spirit for real.

You know the Holy Spirit personally if the Word of the LORD in Psalm 90 or 89 or Romans 8 or Isaiah 40 or Galatians 6 or somewhere has spoken to you with unutterable comfort when you or your loved one walked through the shadows of the valley of Death and you were still certain the Lord would snatch you and your loved one out of the Pit! You may count as your certain blessing that you have been touched, baptized! by the Holy Spirit, if you as a child or as a grownup, as a woman or as a man, have been wise to the wiles of our godless culture, and instead of joining the fast-moving crowd of Proverbs 1:11–14 and being edged into coveting your neighbors' "state of the art" goods, you gently, sorrowfully but strongly do what pleases God in ordinary things and daily life, cooking up and harboring patches of blessing.

You don't get to know God experientially by staring: **you come to know the LORD by doing God's will, submitting to God's Words**. You don't understand the Bible if you approach the text like a glossary of answers to the hard questions about Evil and "Success" and "how to get to heaven," as if one could rationally square the vicious circles of sin. You hear God's biblical voice when you listen to *Proverbs* on your knees as a guideline with the ears of a faithful follower of Jesus Christ, aware that Romans 12, quoting *Proverbs*! (Romans 12:20/Proverbs 25:21–22), says, "Overcome evil"—political leaders as well as church leaders must listen! —"**Overcome evil not by retaliation and power politics, but by doing good!**" (Romans 12:3–21). You never get to know the Holy Spirit by trying to trace the Holy Spirit in sharp theological outline or by practicing ecstatic rituals, or by celebrating Pentecost once a year. **You come to know the Holy Spirit as you become holy and wise.**

And the Holy Spirit in all the Spirit's intangibility and solid mystery is as close to you as the Scriptures, because the **Bible** is the housetop and city-gate headquarters from which the Holy Spirit operates on earth. **The Holy Spirit particularly hangs out in this booked Word of God.** That means your life depends upon loving to understand the Bible so you can see creation and meet Jesus the Christ!

Wisdom herself stands at your door right now and is knocking. Wisdom is crying out from this lectern, stretching out the hand to anybody who will hear the Holy Scriptures today: Hey! believers, unbelievers? faithful people of God! any stupids present? With me, Wisdom, there is new life, firm hope, a Way out of your and this world's sin and troubles! Sin gives you bad eyesight, makes your tongue thick with the lisp of crookedness; sin leads you into disputes and dead-ends despite its tickle of excitement. But I, the Holy Spirit, will give you guts for withstanding pressure to compromise; I'll give you resurrection power for seeing through what is fake—even in yourself. With me—as you search the Scriptures (not just dabble in them), as you struggle in the presence of enemies, and seek my creaturely ordinances for your tasks, willing to follow Jesus as Savior and Lord—I, Wisdom, shall stand by you in sickness and in health, in good times and in bad times, and promise you the insight for doing the Will and words of the Lord, which shall bring you peace with God and the beginnings of gentle wisdom with the neighbors.

Let's give the discriminating Newer Testament hymn about wisdom in James 3, echoing Proverbs 3, the last word:

> Is there a wise man or woman among you? one who knows what he or she is doing?
>
> All right, let that person **show it by** their **daily deeds, dealing wholesomely with others in the gentleness peculiar to wisdom.**
>
> But if you have ruthless enthusiasm and ambitious rivalry in your heart, do not boast [about your wisdom], do not lie against the truth. Such "wisdom" has not come down from heaven: it is utterly earthbound, emotionalistic, demonic. Wherever jealousy and selfish ambition exist, there you will always find upheaval and every kind of mean skullduggery.
>
> Wisdom from heaven is first of all worshipful; it will also produce shalom. True wisdom is willing to wait, is able to be talked to, is full of mercy and good fruits, not hypocritically hiding something, but open-whole-hearted.
>
> Those who produce shalom (peace), in that spirit of rich wholesomeness, sow the fruit of doing what is right [before God]
>
> (James 3:13–18)

PRAYER: Father in heaven, Jesus Christ in heaven, and O Holy Spirit working in the world at large and at our hearts and in our lives: thank you for giving us encouragement in spite of our cussedness or absorbing sorrows, that you comfort us, help us to understand the Bible so we can hear You call us to be patient, reprimand us in love, and guide us in the Way we should go. Please let your *Proverbs* Word of truth and your Spirit of Wisdom grow strong in our lives, not get choked out by attractions that are really just weeds. We pray for You to give us arms to reach out and hold comfortingly those nearby as well as neighbors far away who are hurt or stuck. Make us quiet bearers of the wisdom that brings the fruit of peace with hope amid disputes and misery, rather than just makeshift bandages. We pray these things, and much more we're not ready to ask about out loud, for Jesus' sake, Amen. (Toronto, 1979)

B.
PROVERBS 7, 8, 9, AND GENESIS 6
WITH REVELATION 18

The Scripture reading here is longer than usual, for a couple of good reasons: so you will get a better idea of how to read Proverbs 1–9, with which we began above, and to hear *Proverbs* in the context of the whole Bible.

We are so accustomed to hurry and to chop up the Bible into short commercials—you get this point? do this / don't do that!—we almost never hear the Bible anymore as one long story, a true story of history from Genesis through to Revelation, filled with poetry, visions, eyewitness accounts, parables, and letters all thrown in and given to us by the Holy Spirit for growing in wisdom.

Let's listen first to a very serious paragraph, just a paragraph from Genesis 6, and then to a terribly sad paragraph from Revelation 18, to give us a fresh sense of the whole story and the setting for understanding Proverbs chapters 1–9.

For me the Bible reading is almost the most important part of a worship service. Sermons are just there to make the Bible reading plain, explaining Scripture so we can hear our Father in heaven talking to us. Can we listen to God talk for a good two chapters' worth at one time?

We will turn first to the paragraphs from Genesis and Revelation— like a Bible story read...to grownup children—and then to Proverbs 7 and 9. These readings are my own careful translation from the original Hebrew and Greek languages of the Bible. I work at translating the Bible as Luther said: put it in the ordinary language and idiom of the people, especially young people, so they may hear God speak, tremble, and believe in joy!

So this is the setting of the true story the Bible tells us: Genesis 6:1–8 takes place after Genesis 3:15 where God said to the snake, I will put enmity between you and the woman, between your seed and her seed; her descendants will bruise your head, and your descendants shall bruise her heel. Genesis 6 takes place after the time of Cain and Abel, several generations before the flood.

Now it happened that when humankind began to multiply itself on the face of the dry land, and daughters were born to them, the sons of God saw the daughters of men that Wow! they were good-looking. So the sons of God took for themselves as wives also some of those good-looking daughters of men among all the women they chose as wives.

Then the LORD God said: "My Spirit shall not struggle in humankind forever now that humankind has gone wrong. Humans are perishable flesh. The most time they'll have from now on [to repent or be judged] is 120 years."

Soon there were the misformed giants [=*nephilim*] on the earth, in those days. There were misformed giants ever after that when sons of God went in to the daughters of men, and they bore children together. That's right! These misformed giants are the mighty men who have become "the Big-Name Men" of old.

And the LORD God saw that the wickedness of humankind was "multiplying" on the earth, and that every single desirous intent of what they concocted in their heart(s) was simply evil, day after day after day. Then the LORD God felt sad that God had made humankind on the earth. The LORD God felt stabbed in the heart.

So the LORD God said, "I'll wipe out humankind, which I have created, from the face of the dry landed earth—from human to animal to creepy-crawly things, and even birds of the sky—because I feel heart-sick that I made them all."

But Noah found favor in the eyes of the LORD God.

(Genesis 6:1–8)

Remember this for later: "sons (and daughters) of God" / "daughters (and sons) of men," and the LORD said (6:3), "My **Spirit** shall not struggle in humankind forever!"—God said that 120 years before the flood.

And now listen to a paragraph from Revelation 18:21–24:

And one strong angel picked up a rock, big as a millstone, and heaved it into the lake, saying,

"That's the way—boom!—the great city Babylon shall get the heave and never be found again. The sound of guitarists and folk singers and flute players and trumpeters shall nevermore be heard in your city: no artist, in any of the arts, shall be found any more in your (great) city. The sound of the mill (stone grinding) shall be heard among you no more forever, and the lamp light shall shine no more among you forever, and the voice of the bridegroom and bride shall nevermore be heard among you, nevermore—your businessmen were the bigshots of the earth!—nevermore, because all the people were misled by your clever artistry!"

They found blood too in that (city), Babylon, blood of prophets and saints and all those (believers) who were butchered to death on the earth....

So that is near the beginning and near the ending of the true story

God tells us in Scripture, and now we come to Proverbs 7 and 9. First, chapter 7 (and I realize some of you may think chapter 7 of Proverbs should not be in the Bible, but it is):

My son, (remember last week—my daughter, my parent,) remember what I am saying: Treat the injunction I am laying upon you as a treasure you want to hold tight! Keep the habit of godly wisdom I am requesting (of you), and you shall live! Take care of the guiding instruction I have been giving, as you would the pupil of your eye. Wear them like a ring on your finger. Engrave them (deep) on the tablet of your heart. Tell Wisdom, "Hey! You are my sister!" and shout to Insight, "O, my blood brother!" so that Wisdom and insight may save you from the Strange Woman, so they may keep you safe from the uncanny woman who caresses you with slippery smooth talk.... .

Let me tell you a story:[1]

Once upon a time, as I was standing at the window opening of my house, from behind my shutters I happened to look down (upon the street), and I saw among the inexperienced fellows—I took note of a young fellow among the boys there, who lacked both brains and guts. He was loafing around on the street not far from "her" corner. Finally, he started to step off the way to her house. It was in the cool of dusk falling, as the day darkles into evening, around the time (of the new moon) when the night is really darkness.

Did you see it? It happened! The woman accosts him.

She wears the fashion of a professional whore, and cunning stealth shapes her every move. She's brassy and catty. She can't keep her feet still inside her own place. For a while she lurks outside between the houses, then for a while it's right out in the open; she seems to be lying in wait near every street corner—there! She has grabbed hold of the boy. Now she kisses clinging to him....

She puts on a bold face and says to him: "(Hello!) I was owing some sacrifices of shalom. Today I paid up all the outstanding vows; so I'm free to feast! That's why I came out to meet you. I've been so looking forward to meeting you face to face, and now I've found you! I've made my little couch all ready with fine tapestries, made it plush with brilliantly colored linen goods out of Egypt! I've touched up my larger bed with sprinkles of myrrh and aloes and cinnamon spices—Come on, let's get drunk the whole night until morning on some red-hot loving! Let's drown ourselves in passionate caresses! The husband's not home, you know; he went on a long (business) trip, took his moneybags with him; he won't be back home until it's full moon...."

This is the way she twists and turns him around by her very persuasive talk. She seduces him by the utterly lovely, pursed move-

---

1   Unfortunately your translation may not let the reader know there is a new paragraph break at v.6. Verse 6 introduces a parable; Proverbs 7:6–23 is an Older Testament parable rendered very directly.

ments of her lips.

There he goes! walking behind her like an ox headed for slaughter, like a dog about to be whipped! The fool doesn't know that his very life is at stake. He's like a little bird flying smack into a trap—he won't know it until (her) jagged arrow splits his liver in half.

So now, children, (– parents, do you hear me? Listen closely to what my mouth is saying): Never let your heart be sidetracked into the ways of the Strange Woman. Never get lost in her well-beaten crossroads! because there is a horde of victims she has prostrated; the most mighty men are among all those whom she has extinguished. The house of the Strange Woman opens the ways to hell! (Follow her, my son, my daughter, my parent, and) you end up sunk in the dark, no-exit rooms of Death!

Chapter 8 then says, "Wait a minute! Isn't that Wisdom crying out loud for us to hear!?" And then Wisdom makes a passionate speech:

22 The LORD God set me up as the starting point of what God was doing,
   the very first of God's great deeds long, long ago;
23 from everlasting, yes—from the very origin, I was officially there,
   even before the beginning of the earth!
24 When there were no whirling pool expanses of water yet,
   I was already broken in
   — even when there did not exist sources of water, springs swollen to flow.
25 In the dawn before the mountains were settled into place,
   in front of the foothills—there I was!
26 The LORD God had not yet made the earth;
   neither the (wild) outdoors nor a beginning on all the dirt (needed) for the continents.
27 When God straightened up the sky, I was right there!
   when the LORD God staked out a horizon for the whole ocean expanse,
28 when God firmed up the thunder clouds so they wouldn't fall,
   when the underground springs swelling the unruly ocean waters started to get too powerful;
29 and the LORD God set God's ordinances for the bodies of water
   so that they would not overstep God's Word,
   when God said, "Let there be—" to the very underpinnings of the earth (I was right there!).
30 Yes, I was God's very own protégé (אָמוֹן).
   And I was enjoying myself day after day, playing around all the time in front of God's face,
31 playing through the hemisphere(s) of God's earth,
   having fun with all of humankind. . . .
32 So now, listen to me, you children
   —how happy it will be for those who walk along the way I give the guidelines for!—

³³ all of you, listen obediently to the paideia [of truth, right, troth,
> gentleness, fear of the LORD—cf. 8:4–21]
>> so that you become men and women with understanding!
>> —don't let it just blow away in the air—
³⁴ That man or woman will be a happy one who really listens to me
>> so that they are daily on the lookout for the door to
>> Understanding.
>> So that they are continually knocking on the doorposts where
>> Understanding is to be discovered:
³⁵ (those persons will be happy ones)
>> because whoever find me has found LIFE!
>> —they shake blessings away, as it were, from the LORD God!
³⁶ But whoever misses me have wasted themselves:
>> all those who disdain Understanding love what is dead.

And now comes the climactic chapter 9 of Proverbs 1–9, with the Wisdom Woman of Proverbs 1 and the Strange Woman of Proverbs 7 summing up the choice for those to hear who are young enough at heart they are willing to listen. Verses 7–12 of chapter 9 are a commentary on the choice, and will be read last.

^(v.1) Most excellent Wisdom has built herself a house and she has
> hewed out seven pillars [before it].
> The fatted calf is slaughtered; the wine is mixed; even the table she
> has set.
> Wisdom has sent her maids out to shout from the most
> prominent places of the city: "Whoever is inexperienced,
> let him come in here!"
> She goes tell the person who lacks brains and guts: "Come,
> eat the meal with me; drink the wine I have all mixed.
> Let your one-track simplemindedness go so that you may live
> and walk the way of insight."

^(v.13)Sheer Foolishness woman sounds off empty-headedly and never is
> ashamed that she has no clue as to what's up—
> She sits at the open doorway of her house in an easy chair,
> at the center of the city,
> and calls to those crossing the street, intent
> on going straightforwardly their ways:
> "Whoever is inexperienced, let him drop in here."
> And to the person who lacks brains and guts she says:
> "Stolen waters are sweet."
> "And a meal of secretly hidden [delicacies] tastes so delicious."
> But [the poor fellow] doesn't know that inside her house there are
> dead men,
> that her invited guests end up in the deeps of Sheol.

^(v.7) Reprimand somebody who is contemptuous of laws and you will
> be made fun of yourself; try to stop a wicked man and **you** will
> get hurt.

So don't persist in setting a scoffer straight lest he hate you [to
death].
Straighten out a wise fellow and he or she will thoroughly love
you.
Give [correction] to a wise person and the wise one becomes
wiser still;
help a right-doing person to firsthand knowledge of [something]
and that person develops still deeper acumen.
**Standing still in awe of the LORD God is the beginning of
Wisdom,
and true insight is knowing intimately what things are holy.**
By me, Wisdom, your days will be multiplied; years of life will
be added on for you;
therefore, if you become wise,
you are wise for your good;
but if you remain disdainful of guidance, you shall have to suffer
your foolishness all alone.

Literary format

The speeches, parable, and poetic paragraphs in chapters 1–9 of
Proverbs provide a clue on how to read and understand this entire book
of collected epigrammatic wise sayings, in the context of the whole true
Bible story.

Remember, in Proverbs 1:20–33 capital "W" Wisdom makes a passionate speech rejecting the foolishness of the fast-buck appeal of **evil
men** in 1:11–14. Today the extended vivid picture of the seductive wiles
of a **strange woman** in 7:6–23 is countered by an even longer impassioned speech by the Woman Wisdom in 8:4–31. Then chapter 9 neatly
sums up the choice everybody faces between Wisdom and Foolishness,
and the wise comment made in Proverbs 9:10 emphasizes the key to
God-fearing knowledge (cf. Luke 11:52), which was highlighted at the
beginning of the book in Proverbs 1:7:

> **Standing still before the LORD God is a head start in wisdom,
> and intimate knowledge of what things are holy (or, knowing
> the Holy One) constitutes understanding.**

Proverbs was booked by the wise men and wise women (cf. 2 Samuel
14:1–24, 20:16–22) God used to lead inexperienced people into the Way
of the LORD. So you tell people stories, ask provocative questions like
6:27a, "Can a man have a fire under his belt and not burn his pants"? or
you honestly present what people on the street are thinking and saying,
their slogans like "Stolen water is sweet!" "Things go better with coke!"
and then the rabbi says, "**Yes, but…**you'll end up like a bloodied ox in
an abattoir" (7:22–23).

The book of Job clearly has this "Yes, but" format of biblical wisdom literature. The long well-sounding orthodox speeches of Job's three self-righteous "friends" have Job constantly responding, "Yes, but," until in the last chapter God says Job's friends got it wrong (Job 42:7–9)—Job did not suffer evil because he was bad, but so that God's great deeds might be revealed in his life (cf. John 9:1–5!).

And remember how rabbi Jesus taught the illiterate crowds reported in Matthew 5: "You have heard it was said, 'An eye for an eye and a tooth for a tooth,' **but I say,** 'Turn your other cheek to be hit too!'" (5:38–41). Then startled people would gather around and start a question and answer discussion with the wise mentor... .

This is the way to understand the literary, poetic book of *Proverbs* in its indirect, back-and-forth "Yes, but" format of teaching us to seek and find the Way of obedient living in God's world, which the Lord can bless. We contrast things, often in pictures, to highlight the right choice.

One needs to appreciate that the Bible is not a traffic rule book you need to memorize to get the heavenly driver's license: "Stop at the red light"; "Pass on the left"; "Do to others what you want done to you!" Instead, the Bible takes the time, for example, by presenting a ten-page chorus of voices to tell us to be faithful in our erotic love, with *The Greatest Song* (*The Song of Songs*) *in critique of Solomon.* And the Bible envelops the command to "love God above all and love your neighbor as you respect yourself" in the intricate fabric of poetic Proverbs 1–9 to suggest you cannot love your neighbor simply by following a formulaic rule (cf. Mark 12:28–34): you need to be indwelt and permeated by, marinated in the Holy Spirit of compassionate just-doing, wisdom.

Historical setting

It also usually helps to get the full thrust of the Bible's message if one can ascertain roughly the historical times in which the given chapters are oriented (if not booked). Proverbs 1–9 and 10:1–22:16 are attributed to wise King Solomon of 1 Kings 1–8 (before he went bad, 1 Kings 9–11), so around 950 BC. And Proverbs chapters 25–29 are Solomon proverbs that the counselors of God-obedient King Hezekiah (c. 725–687 BC) collected and edited under the leading of the Holy Spirit (Proverbs 25:1), because Hezekiah was trying to gather material to help his regional governors and judges outside the capital of Jerusalem be instructed in what it means to serve God justly among greedy people in troubled times.

So the book of *Proverbs* stretches at least from the good-times of Solomon's day (c. 960 BC) to the tough times of Hezekiah's period (c. 680 BC).

Proverbs 1–9 addresses the lives of settled urban dwellers who are fairly prosperous—not nomads in the desert; there is a strong rural farming hinterland whose younger generation is migrating to the big city Jerusalem to make their fortune in the construction boom of Solomon's prodigious 20 year! building program—putting up the LORD's temple, his own fabulous palace, civic buildings, military bases, and much much more (1 Kings 6:1–7:51, 9:10–28). It was like the Calgary-Alberta construction boom of the late 1970s, where Job Fairs in Newfoundland and Ontario (where the fishing and manufacturing industry were slowing down) to tempt people with promises of big money to relocate, with all the upset it causes in lifestyle, faith traditions, loose from your conservative parents, away from the rural hometown and rituals. No wonder the idiom of *Proverbs'* paragraphs is money dealing and fraudulent advisers, sexual temptation, idolatrous overwork, and drive for success.

The later chapters from around Hezekiah's time—when the ten tribes of Israel were being demolished and dispersed by superpower Assyria in 722 BC, and when little Judah, thanks to an army of angels, barely survived the 9/11 invasion of mighty Sennacherib in 701 BC (2 Kings 18–19): later *Proverbs* chapters instruct would-be leaders of God's people in how to be a godly neighbor, a trustworthy business partner (Proverbs 22:17–24:22), a merciful dispenser of justice, even toward enemies (Proverbs 25:21–22, cf. Romans 12:9–21). Wisdom is not playing tiddlywinks: **to be biblically wise is to be able to give good direction, and to be busy settling disputes that bring peace.**

Proverbs was given then in Solomon and Hezekiah's day, and now, to help us discern what is holy and to see through bogus smarts. *Proverbs* fits the hand of our culture, having its good times and its hard times, like a snug glove. God never wants "wise guys," but yearns for youth and older folk who breathe the gentleness peculiar to genuine wisdom (James 3:13–18), which knows the deeds that will bear good fruit (cf. Matthew 7:15–20).

Whole Bible story connection

The passage we read in the first book of the Older Testament, Genesis 6:1–8, lines up two communities: the children of God, the obedient children of Wisdom, next to those estranged from God under the curse of Sin, sons and daughters given to human Foolishness. Abel-Seth: Cain. And whenever the faithful children of God intermarry culturally with the unfaithful children of Stupidity, you get strange miscarriages of birth, says the Bible: enormous giants! eight-foot women and ten-foot men, as big as Goliath (cf. 1 Samuel 17:4), as if their glands ran away with them. These giant kids got a big name, says Genesis 6; they became Big Shots, heroes! superstars on the cultural circuit. Later, even after the flood, city developers like mighty, empire-building Nimrod went the way of all flesh and began a heaven-scraping Babel (cf. Genesis 10:6–14), a "Babylon"!

And in the paragraph we read from the last book of the Newer Testament, the *Apocalypse of Jesus given to John* 18:21–24, there are also two women in its story, just like Proverbs 9: the whore of Babylon on the side of the Dragon versus the woman great with child, waiting to be the Bride of the Lamb (Revelation 17:1–19:10). The successful harlots of the earth: the modest heavily pregnant woman, the true Church, whose bridegroom has not yet officially showed up! She's been left waiting pregnant, shamefaced, but filled with the Holy Spirit. . . .

So the sweep of Genesis to Revelation gives us the horizons to focus down on Proverbs 1–9 as a chapter in the one true Bible story.

The parable of Proverbs 7:6–23 is not just a sordid affair of passion or lustful fornication you could read about in the tabloids, a Hollywood script for a movie scene on seduction. Proverbs 7 repudiates sexual licentiousness all right, just as Proverbs 6:26–35 explicitly condemns adultery. But you and I are not scot free from the bite of these biblical passages if you are old enough and have avoided sexual promiscuity and never touched a man or a woman who belongs to somebody else, because Proverbs 5–6–7 is not merely talking boys on street corners and single girls in bars, along with jealous, cuckolded husbands, but has the *Genesis*-to-*Revelation* dimensions of revealing sons and daughters and parents wedded to Jesus Christ who are busy red-hot loving what is Babylonian and strange to God.

Proverbs is not a collection of handy maxims about the moral P's and Q's of a sanctified middleclass life, but faces us with the simple-complicated all-consuming matter of life-and-death—life **or** death: do you choose to accept the meal of holy Wisdom or want to stay caught in the caress of everlasting Foolishness?

Open appeal of the Proverbs passage.

The summing-up point of Proverbs 9 is vividly clear: it's a choice of eating meals with only one of the two women.

Wisdom is portrayed as a noble, queenly woman who is reserved, rich (she has maids); and she invites especially younger people in to join her for an intimate dinner with meat and wine and candlelight (Proverbs 9:1–6). You can trust her. She also makes strong speeches at major gathering spots in the city (Proverbs 1:20–21, 8:1–3). Her Proverbs address (8:4–36) could be heard at "As It Happens" on CBC radio 1 (if they'd give her equal time). Wisdom is firm, gentle, strong, deeply joyfully certain.

The other woman in *Proverbs* is called "the **strange** woman," "the exotic **foreign** woman"[2] in chapter 2:16–19 (= "foreign **to**

---

2   The "strange woman" (מאשה זרה) [Proverbs 2:16, 5:3,20, 7:5] and "exotic foreign woman" (מנבריה) [Proverbs 2:16, 5:20, 6:24, 7:5] and also "woman bringing misfortune" (מאשת רע) [Proverbs 6:24] are designations carefully kept distinct from both "the prostitute who professionally or occasionally commits fornication" (אשה זונה) [Proverbs 6:26] and "adulterous activity" (נאף) [Proverbs 6:32], which is sexual intercourse with the wife of another man.

God"), the whole of chapter 5, with her tempting talk sampled in 7:14–20. This shady lady almost dominates the first nine chapters of *Proverbs*; she is the antagonist, really, of the Wisdom woman. She reclines before her doorway while making her siren call (Proverbs 9:13–18) where she is revealed as Woman Foolishness, Stupidity, alias Mistress of Hell, alias Sin. You can find her alluring picture in almost any newspaper or magazine advertisement for liquor, tires, jewelry or deodorants found in your living room; or just look on the internet, I've been told.

(1) *Egyptian Coptic woman*, c. 1950

Both women say very attractively, "Come in, eat, drink." And then Wisdom Woman, the Holy Spirit, says (9:6): "Remember and believe; leave your indecisive simple-mindedness behind, my child, so you may live and walk in the Way of Insight. Let your wishy-washy double-mindedness go; choose this day whom you will serve!"

The evil woman, Sarx, has a different tune: "Wouldn't you like to try just a sip of stolen water, my boy, my girl, maybe in secret (9:17)? Has God said not to touch **any** of my delicacies? Let's be merry! Not like those long-faced, goody-goody, straight-laced, stay-at-home, go-to-church, proper 'sons of God' and 'Christ-ladies'! My creed is that stolen water is sweeter, we try harder." (Instead of the cool model in the magazine speaking to you by her or his looks, you should see the dead animal, yourself, if you buy into

---

So the sexual imagery of "strange" and "foreign" is primed to be taken in a deeper sense than "commercial prostitution" and is not identical to the specific evil of "adultery," yet pins down exactly the deepest giving of oneself heartfully and bodily in passionate love…to the LORD or to anything which is **foreign** to the jealous covenanting LORD God (cf. Exodus 34:6–7, Hebrews 12:29).

Given the utter all-consuming, sacrificial intimacy of God's love for the Lord's adopted children, and the almost erotic (Narcissistic!) union of a man or a woman with one's idol, only those who may please God shall escape the wages of Sinful attachment, which is death (Ecclesiastes 7:25–26, Romans 6:20–23).

the come-on, yourself ready for the knives.)

Proverbs 5, 6, 7, 8, 9, is facing us with the fundamental matter Paul

(2) Abbatoir, photographer unknown

describes in his letters to the Romans (8:1–39), Galatians (5:13–6:10), and Ephesians (3:14–19), as the struggle of Spirit, Holy Spirit, against "Flesh," Sin, Mammon, in our daily lives.

It is worth noting that the existential appeal of Proverbs 1–9 even surpasses that of Genesis 6 and Revelation 18. The biblical Older Testament is not out of date: the call to choose Wisdom in Proverbs 1–9 is as wide open and compelling as the gospel of Matthew, which confirms its message.

Genesis 6 reveals an historical case that is closed, the time when certain sons and daughters of God succumbed to the wiles of a strange marriage, and then God agonized, according to Genesis 6:3, "My Holy Spirit is not going to stick around forever and struggle to rule in these monstrous hulks! These are not the creatures I created and that Wisdom played with [Proverbs 8:30–31] when I was ordering, ordaining the blessed limits of things!"

You can almost hear the LORD God sob in Genesis 6 (the way you hear God hurting later in the prophecies of Jeremiah, 2:1–3:5), "Do I have to wipe out the people I made to be hallelujah children of light because they're making monsters out of themselves!?" Oh, no! said God. I'll still give them—I'd be willing to give you too—four generations of time, 120 years, to repent and become holy before I flood them with disaster. I'll send them my manservant Noah to bid them return to my Ways.

Yet people on the streets of Genesis 6 thought Noah was a crank with his own believing construction firm building boats high and dry. So then God had to send the flood once upon a time, long ago.

And Revelation 18 portrays a **final** act in history, where the Strange Woman and all her admirers—plus the blood of prophets and saints! says Revelation 18:24, who got stuck in the grooves of Babylon, that apostate churched culture: in Revelation, the Strange Woman herself goes to hell, and all her bloodied dead victims are indeed finished off forevermore (Revelation 20). There is no more opportunity for the simple-minded and confused sons and daughters and parents still around in the Babylon of Revelation 18 to stop scoffing and hesitating to become holy. That time revealed in the last book of the Bible is the time, ironically, when Sin, as well as Christ's work, is completely finished.

But Proverbs 1–9 is still wide open in its call for us to hear and choose Wisdom today! *Proverbs* has a terrible urgency since the first Pentecost: it is a matter of life **or** death for us in North America—for our sons and daughters who are alive in the apostate twenty-first century AD of preemptive strikes and "preventative wars," and for ourselves who aren't getting any younger. God simply can't stand it when the children of Abel-Seth cohabit with the attractive children of Cain. Shall I withdraw my Holy Spirit, quenched (cf. Hebrews 5:11–6:8), says God, and cancel out the offer of everlasting life and fullness of re-creation? Oh, no! I'll send out Wisdom's maids once more—the Willowdale CRC deacons, the faithful Vanderboor Lighthouse Community Centre stewards, the Vacation Bible School leaders and helpers, Alpha programmers, any young person training to speak truth in and to **reform** the technical media— I'll send Wisdom's maids out into the highways and byways to compel people to come to my meal (cf. Luke 14:15–24)! The blood of Abel's seed is precious to me (cf. Psalm 72:12–14); I don't want the children and parents of my congregation—or any church communion—to be sucked in and butchered by standardized Babylonian barbarians....

Now, wait a minute, you could say. Does *Proverbs* speak that way to **us?** Are we really simple-minded? You don't mean that's a picture of us hanging in the abattoir? I'm not perfect, but I'm not stupid either. I know the difference between Wisdom and a hole in the ground. I know what I'm doing. We know the Heidelberg Catechism. We attend regular bona fide worship services. We don't steal. We don't look at an attractive woman or handsome man who belongs to somebody else lustfully. I don't kill by gossiping. I don't covet the other guy's brand-new Lexus, not really. All God's commandments we have kept from our youth up; we are not simple-minded fools who still need Wisdom!

That's fine, but a person is never done with Wisdom the Holy Spirit by talking about the Holy Spirit. If you as a girl or a boy, a woman or a man, are made holy by the Spirit of God, you will be tempted by the Evil One so long as you live in the world before Christ's final coming. That's the whole bent of Satan and Satan's cohorts: to undermine the faithful children of God (cf. Mark 13:22/Matthew 24–25)—Satan's got the others!—to ruin God's creational environment, desecrate Christ's glory, to make Wisdom a joke and Foolishness the rage. That's why *Proverbs* is certainly speaking to us even if we have never spent a night in a red-light district, been a compulsive gambler, or make love to alcohol. *Proverbs* is speaking directly to us if we can pray the Lord's prayer, "O Lord, deliver me from the Evil one (Matthew 6:13), who isolates a person and makes fools out of saints!"

The pressing point
Proverbs 9 implies and Matthew 6:24 states baldly: You have to choose between the two jealous Women. You **cannot** serve God and Mammon. **Yes,** we do it all the time, **but....**

Let me be as plain as possible. I can talk about what I know first-hand.

My and my wife's household, the Willowdale congregation of believers with whom my wife and I normally worship, and the graduate Institute for Christian Studies where I taught, are as sinful as musclebound Samson I dare say, but these specific communities are not at bottom Goliaths, *nephilim,* I trust. And I pray with all my heart that any communion of sinful saints you are a member of which together is trying to give Wisdom place and speech in the home, in the church, in the school, in the nursing home, in the cultural life, marketplace and public square of society, will be able to grow its hair to full, sanctified **Nazarite** length—not with a modish style cut to current fashions—so that when the roll is called up yonder in Revelation 17–19, my and your name and our communities will be found with Samson and Rahab's names in Hebrews 11.

Proverbs does not say Christians ought to become cultural dropouts or paranoid, especially when our own churchly houses and christian institutions are not in holy array and might sometimes even be a front for "strange" activity, a veritable tiny Babylon under a bushel basket. I've studied at hardcore university butcher shops and learned a lot there about how to cut meat. One should never question the faith of God's children who study or work, teach, lead, or suffer redemptively in officially godless institutions. But the point of Proverbs 1–9 is: **know** what is at stake!

be **wise** to what you are into! develop the **discipline of discernment**. We are enjoined to have Scripture, including *Proverbs*, and certainly the *Psalms*, running subconsciously though our heads and hearts and lives so we know what the score is, who the players are, and whether we are in love with the Wisdom Woman shod with the unorthodox armaments of God—**wielding the sword of the Spirit that is the Word of God**, Paul says in Ephesians 6:10–18—**or**, whether we are playing marbles with a gang of butchers, for keeps.

So when a child of God-Abel-Seth-Bride-to-be-of-the-Lamb, when you have to go study at a humungous Multiversity or work in the office of a misformed Giant Monopoly, when you are tempted to buy a song on the charts out for your blood, or have to try to get out of a grocery Chain store like Loblaws, Buy-Low, Safeway, or Aldi for under $6.66— the Strange Woman is after our very life, everything we've got!—go, study, work, buy if you need to, with Psalm 23 on your lips: "LORD, Jesus Christ, prepare for me a table right in the presence of my enemies. You can do it, O Holy Spirit."

You don't become wise when they hand you a high school diploma. You can have a Th.D., according to the Bible, and still be a fool. And to be a successful business man, banker, or professional woman CEO and also be Scripturally wise and just today is almost impossible, says the Bible—it also adds enigmatically in the account of the same episode, "**but, with God all things are possible**" (Matthew 19:16–30).

How to find the Holy Spirit? who, like "the kingdom of heaven" Matthew 13 talks about, may be "hidden" (Matthew 13:44; cf. Job 28)?

Maybe you will just stumble over the treasure, this incredibly perfect pearl you have been searching for to make sense of things (Matthew 13:45–46): by overhearing someone's offhand remark about "following Jesus," or by being impressed by the steadfast prayer of a quiet woman, or by your seeing what the Scriptures say in Proverbs 7:22, which is the offense of the gospel! since sin is not pretty! "Is **that** the choice!? Dining with the Wisdom woman, **or** ending up a slaughtered ox?! And then faced with the alternatives, with a rush of joy you accept the invitation of Wisdom and offer up everything you have and are, to be integrated in the Way the Holy Spirit through Scripture changes your lifestyle.

That's a simple choice, but it becomes complicated because we sinful forgiven people are complicated. Talking with someone named Oleksly Krivoshlykov last week, he said something like this: "When I was among the Communists in the Ukraine, they told you everything you had to do, just like the Bible. I want to know the difference between Christianity and Communism. I don't want it complicated. I want it simple." So I said: "Jesus loves you, and wants you to be **God's** adopted child. You don't have to do anything, except be thankful." That's simple. It is also the message of Romans to boot.

But to live a God-thanking life today in our predominantly God-agnostic culture is not so easy. Being moved to accept the invitation of the Holy Spirit is simple and joyful: living a converted thankful life is often hard, to become a wise person without fanfare, not by prescription, but simply under conviction in a culture of manifold tempting Foolishness. Then you realize that fast food outlets like McDonald's and political parties in North America are inviting the simple-minded to patronize and join them by saying, "Come in, eat, drink…"—and *you* have to decide which Woman is talking. Then you catch on that it may be foolish to think a song is a song is a song, because some are the siren songs of a roaring lion and some are the drivel of a sentimental gospel, and others are the tough holy songs of Moses and the Lamb that will never wear out; so we come to listen to songs with discernment. Then you may also catch yourself wondering whether Almighty God let God's Son be butchered on earth so we could be beguiled by entertaining talk shows, fabulous millionaire athlete gladiators competing, and Reality TV—is this my "redeeming the time" (Colossians 4:5)?

But…a person's life pulls together when you become wise, when you know the most Holy One, when you have insight into what things are holy (Proverbs 9:10), because your consciousness, says God through Paul in Romans 12:1–2, is made brand **new**, and you can detect what God wants, what the good, pleased, full will of the Lord is concretely for family life, personal life, school life, business life, church life, North American cultural life, and the life of water, plants, and animals.

Proverbs **is calling us to discern the spirits at work in our lives**, in our disappointments and sorrows as well as in our happy times, so that the faithful God of Genesis 6 to Revelation 18, and here in Proverbs 1–9 —the God made fully known in Jesus Christ—shall give us the shelter of God's wings under which to work and play before the night comes (cf. Psalm 61:1–5, Psalm 91, John 9:4), to be together busy redemptively on the earth in the wisdom and comforting staying power of the Holy Spirit.

PRAYER: Father in heaven, Jesus Christ in heaven, and O Holy Spirit working at our hearts:

Thank you, Holy Spirit God, that you give us encouragement, in spite of our sin, that you comfort us, that you help us understand the Bible so we can hear you call us, talk to us, reprimand us in love, and guide us in the Way we should go. We want to confess that your *Proverbs* Word is falling into good ground this day—really, LORD, we want to be good sons and daughters and parents together. Please let your Word of Truth and your Spirit of Wisdom grow strong in our lives, not get choked out by attractions that are really just weeds.

You know, O Triune God, the kind of aches each one of us has. Some of us are unsure of ourselves and would like to grow up in normal, wholesome ways that escape the hardnosed bitterness of so many people we meet on the street or at work or at school. Some of us have discomfort or pain in our arm or legs or back, or it hurts inside our bodily organs and we have to take medicine. Some of us are mixed up and feel as if our life is at loose ends, as if nobody around is really holding hands with us. Some of us, O God, do feel satisfied with ourselves and think we don't have any big troubles because we're walking past the people sitting right ahead of us in the pew who do have troubles.

We ask, Lord, that you will bind up our wounds and that you will teach us what a congregation of fellow believers can mean for our 70 years, more or less, on this earth, until you come back to wipe away all the tears, and to finish off sin in our lives and the lives of our neighbors. Teach us to love one another, even when we get in each other's hair because of our idiosyncrasies. Get some of our young people to become prophetic, and let some of the old grey-haired people dream dreams of your Rule in the land, and give the middle-aged people wisdom to stay out of a rut and to walk with a vision of how you use sinful people, keep us walking on in faith without getting tired or discouraged. Help us to give away all our talents and money and time in wisdom, we pray.

If there are those we know who have heard the Bible story before but have not committed their life to You themselves, work in their heart, Holy Spirit; touch a sore spot or a chord of deep response, so the angels may have a good time in heaven tonight. And when we gather together, O Holy Spirit, please remind us of how things will be when our Lord comes back.

We pray these things and much more we don't dare ask about out loud, for Jesus' sake, Amen.

(Toronto, 1979)

C.
How to Deal Biblically with Enemies

Proverbs 25:21–22 with Matthew 5:43–48 and Romans 12:9–21

When you turn to Proverbs chapter 25, you will notice the first verse tells us that chapters 25, 26, 27, 28, and 29 were old Solomon proverbs copied over and edited together by the educated wise men and women of King Hezekiah's court under the leading of God's Spirit, about six generations after Solomon's time.

Good King Hezekiah was trying to put together God's Word in writings he could send out from Jerusalem into the provinces along with his administrative judges and counselors, so they themselves and the people of Judah they were to lead would better know how to live in society as the Lord God wanted it done.

So these five chapters of Proverbs zoom in especially upon learning the wisdom of God to rule justly, to lead wisely, to do what is right in ordinary life far from the city of Jerusalem, its temple and palace, but where God's will still needs to be done.

Biblical proverbs are probably edited in paragraphs. (The NIV translation does this a little bit with subtitles in chapters 1–9, but hardly ever shows paragraphing afterwards.) I can't go into it now, but my hunch is that the very short "paragraph" of 25:21–22 epitomizes this whole five-chapter section of the book intent upon instructing God's people how to protect the weak and undo the evil of oppressive folk cursing our society in God's world.

Let's read **Proverbs 25:21–22.** You can check my literal translation with the NIV:

> 21 If the one who hates you is suffering from hunger,
>   give that person good bread to eat.
>   If the one who hates you is in thirst,
>   give that person water to drink.
> 22 In that way you will be raking together live coals of fire
>   on your enemy's head,
>   **but** the Lord God shall shalom it for you.[1]

---

1 V.22 has caps = Lord God, Yahweh, your Covenant-keeping God; v.22 "shalom it for you," says the Hebrew, "requite it": NIV has "reward you."

Nobody knows yet exactly what the metaphor means—"raking live coals together so they will burn harder" (Isaiah 30:14) on your enemy's head! If you save your enemy's life, it just makes him or her wild with anger? or (Augustine's take on the metaphor) "burning with shame"? Is that so? NIV has "**and** reward / cs: "**But** the LORD will make it all come out really right."

Before we go to this text let's read a paragraph from the Newer Testament, Matthew 5:43–48. Matthew 5–7 is a little like a collection of proverbs—instructive sayings, warnings, directives—that Jesus was giving his disciples—like Hezekiah's princes—but now in order to **correct** the wrong way the Pharisee scribes had come to teach God's Mosaic law to the people who couldn't read.

> You people have heard it said [by your rabbi's], "Love your neighbor and hate the enemy you have." Well, I tell you, "Love your enemies, and intercede for those who are persecuting you," so that you be children of your Father in heaven. God makes the sun rise on both the wicked and good people, and lets it rain on just doers and those who do injustice. If you [only] love those who love you, what kind of 'reward' do you have? Do not even the tax-collectors do the same thing? And if you only give everyday greetings to your brothers and sisters, what are you doing that 'goes the extra mile' [5:20 beyond the legal 'righteousness' of the scribes and Pharisees]? Do not even the *goyim* do the same thing—[say 'hello' to one another]?
>
> [To sum up everything in chapter 5]: You are to be ["perfect"] whole, without blemish/complete/fully mature/holy, because your heavenly Father is complete/holy. (Matthew 5:43–48)

On Matthew 5:43: The Older Testament clearly says, "Love your neighbor"; but the Older Testament does not say, "Hate your enemy"— we just read the opposite in Proverbs 25:21–22; although many people today still think the Older Testament says, "Hate your enemy."

Apparently, the Pharisees twisted certain Mosaic writings like Deuteronomy 23:3–6, where God says Ammonites and Moabites may not enter the precincts of where God is worshiped because they obstructed Israel's travel from Egypt to the promised land. The Pharisee scribes/rabbi's extended that historical judgment into a dogmatic one: those *goyim* remain enemies of God's people forever.[2]

So Jesus had to correct what the people had been taught by their theological leaders, like the scribe who said to Jesus, "wishing to justify himself.... 'Who is my neighbor?'" (Luke 10:29). It was a hefty controversy at the time whether non-purebred Jews should be considered

---

2 Isaiah 56:1–8 shows that earlier restrictions on foreigners and eunuchs with respect to entering the temple for worship were already modified around the time of Nehemiah.

"neighbors" or not. That is why Jesus told the story of the Samaritan who was a neighbor to the robbed, beaten wayfarer (Luke 10:30–37), to help the "teachers of Israel" understand that the hated Samaritans, former collaborators centuries ago with the occupying Persian troops, were **also neighbors!**

Now we read God's Word Paul wrote down for the congregation of Christ's followers in Rome, where the influx of Jewish believers was twisting the truth of God's forgiveness to sinners into the old legalistic program of work-righteousness.

We sinners are made 'righteous" by Jesus Christ's sacrifice on the cross, writes Paul. That's true for the *goyim* too, who by faith are grafted into the tree of life that began with the Jewish nation (John 4:22).

How are followers of the risen Christ to act?

Romans 12 is also almost like *Proverbs* and Matthew 5–7: a direct teaching on our needing to become living sacrifices (the memorable Romans 12:1–2), to be not conformed to this world's fashions, but to be transformed by having our very consciousness made new so we can discern what is the good, acceptable, "perfect"—there's that word again of Christ's concluding comment in Matthew 5:48—so we can discern what is the complete, mature, holy will of God.

This is the Word of God in Romans 12:9–21:

> Let your love be undisguised. Abhor what is wicked, and cling to what is good. Warmly esteem one another in brotherly and sisterly affection. Give leadership in showing honor to one another. Don't be sluggish in diligence, but be on fire in the Spirit, serving the Lord. Rejoice in hope, keep on bearing up during oppressive pressure, persevere in prayer. Become a partner in the needs of the saints. Strive to be friendly to strangers. Bless those who are busy persecuting: bless and do not curse [them]. [Learn] to rejoice with those who are rejoicing and to weep with those who are weeping.
>
> Be of one mind with one another, not to develop a haughty habit of thinking, but to rub shoulders with those who are poorly off. Do not think you are so smart yourselves. Pay back nobody evil for evil, but prospect for what is worthwhile in the estimation of **all** people. In so far as it is possible for you, be at peace with **all** men and women. You people whom I love: do not spend time vindicating yourselves; instead, leave room for the anger [of God], since it is written [in Leviticus 19:18, Deuteronomy 32:35, Hebrews 10:30], "I will exact just judgment; settling scores is **my** prerogative, says the Lord." No, if your enemy suffers hunger, give the enemy a morsel to eat; if your enemy is in thirst, give him or her a drink. By doing this you are heaping red-hot coals on the enemy's head.
>
> **Do not let yourself be overcome by evil, but overcome evil with good.**

So, now with Christ's paragraph from Matthew 5 on "love your enemies" in our ears, and Romans chapter 12 fresh before us, which quotes our text from *Proverbs*, how do we understand what Proverbs 25:21–22 means for living a christian life in our generation?

We know who our brother or sister in the faith is. We know who our neighbor is—right? Anybody who is nearby, who stands next to you (*plésion*), with whom you are in touch.

Who is my enemy? Do I have enemies? Do you have enemies? If we have enemies, is an enemy my neighbor?

Enemies and hating Evil

In the cultural world surrounding ancient Israel, those you hate, as a people, are the enemy. In the ancient Egyptian, Babylonian, Persian, Greek world the ones you are at war with are enemies. No quarter asked or given: you fight to the death because the hatred is mutual.

In the Hebrew of *Proverbs* the two different words for "the one who hates you" (שׂנַאֲךָ) and "enemy" (אוֹיֵב) are synonyms. But it is significant how God's biblical Word relativizes human enemies under God's eye: Proverbs 24:17–18 says, Don't start to be glad when your enemy collapses, lest the LORD find your gloating evil and turn away God's anger from your enemy! Do enemies also mean something to God?

Already back in Exodus 23:4–5 God had Moses write down this little regulation for God's people to follow: "If you happen to meet the ox or ass of your enemy going astray, you shall bring it back to your enemy. If you should see the ass belonging to one who hates you fallen down on the ground under its heavy load, you shall not leave it stuck, but help it up with the burden."

It seems God cares enough for animal beasts of burden—remember, "Do not muzzle an ox when it treads out the grain" (Deuteronomy 25:4, 1 Timothy 5:17–18)—enough to find unimportant whether the ass is owned by your brother or your **enemy**!

Closer to home on the matter of hating someone, Leviticus 19:17–18 says: "Never harbor hate in your heart for your brother or sister: [frankly] reprove him or her in your company of people [when required], lest you come to commit sin because of him or her. Never take vengeance, and never bear a grudge against a brother or sister of your own people: love your fellow neighbor as you do yourself—I am the LORD God!"

That means, since the LORD God is in charge of things, you may never hate, not even softened to a smoldering grudge, a fellow believer. Such percolating contempt for a neighbor not only damages yourself and does not set the wrongdoer right, but lets you pretend to be angry like God! Only the Lord God is completely holy, to be able to set crooked things straight both inside and outside the covenanted people of God (Deuteronomy 32:35–36; Hebrews 10:26–31).

An enemy according to the Bible is anyone or thing hostile to God. Any creature or power that destroys the life God made good is an enemy, biblically speaking. Death is the final enemy, says Scripture (1 Corinthians 15:20–25). So cancer, multiple sclerosis, AIDS, are enemies in God's world today—they kill living people untimely.

The devil as primal tempter is an outright **enemy**, an adversary of the Lord (Job 1:6–12, 2:1–6). A warped, hardened antagonist like the fake prophet Bar-Jesus whom Paul confronted on the island of Cyprus and called "a son of the devil" is described as "an **enemy** of all just-doing" (Acts 13:4–12, v.10). People whose God is the belly, says Scripture, whose lifestyle is to glory in their shamelessness, whose mentality is utterly earthbound, exist as "**enemies** of the cross of Christ" (Philippians 3:18–19).

Before we were reconciled to God by the death of Jesus Christ, says Paul, we sinners were **enemies** to God (Romans 5:8–11). "Friendship with this world," writes James, "is enmity ("enemy-ship" you might say) with God—you make yourself an **enemy** of God" (James 4:4). Does that mean maybe you could look in the mirror and see an "enemy"!? Could such a possibility be related to the strange remark Jesus once made about a person's enemies being in one's own household (Matthew 10:34–39)?

When you study the Bible about "hatred" and "enemies," it starts to get as complicated as the mixture of temptation by the devil to do evil along with testing by God to strengthen your faith through trials. Before you know it, Scripture implicates you yourself on the "enemy" business in your life's turmoils.

We men and women are supposed to **hate evil**: that is the crux of standing in awe before God (Proverbs 8:13), which is the beginning of becoming wise (Proverbs 1:7, 9:10, 15:33), says the Bible. Psalm 139, which is a favorite of many people (who seem to glide over the fact that it holds a terrible curse for God to wipe out the wicked who make the believing psalmist's life miserable) says: "I hate those who hate the Lord with a pure hatred! They are **my enemies**!" (Psalm 139:19–22) And the most quoted verse of the Older Testament in the Newer Testament is Psalm 110:1, which says: "The Lord God says to my Lord, 'Sit at my right hand until I have put down your **enemies** as a footstool for your feet'"!

How do we rhyme a life of faith yearning for the Lord to extinguish God's wicked enemies so there be an everlasting reign of shalom on earth, rhyme it with the injunction of both the Older and Newer Testaments to care for the enemy's wellbeing (Proverbs 25:21–22), love your enemy

(Matthew 5:44), even bless those who persecute you, says Romans, don't curse them! (Romans 12:14)?

If Proverbs 25:21–22 only means what the Red Cross has always said—"A wounded enemy is your neighbor and needs to be cared for" —okay. But if the Bible is more radical than that, am I supposed to self-lessly love back-alley abortionists, radical ideological feminists, snobbish intellectuals, lukewarm Laodicean churchgoers, those who flaunt a secular gay lifestyle, self-righteous Pharisees, murdering militarists, shameless entertainers—what a bunch! What are you asking for, Jesus?

BUT enemies are still neighbors—so?
As far as I understand it today, I think the Scriptures say: **persons who are enemies of God and God's people are still our neighbors, and the Christ our Lord is asking us to do good to them, cost what it may.**

Let me develop this bold Scriptural message with three points, for your response:

(1) To love somebody whose deeds you righteously hate seems practically impossible to me, like asking a camel to go through the eye of a needle (Matthew 19:23–26). But maybe that's the point: unless our righteousness (righteous anger) goes beyond that of the scribes and Pharisees, you people, said Jesus (Matthew 5:20), shall never enter the kingdom of heaven!

God lets the sun rise over abortion clinic personnel and on young pregnant women who are at a loss (Matthew 5:45). So?—I'm not God. But those who are really children of God will abhor what is wicked, affirm victims in their distress, and try to overcome the evil by doing good (Romans 12:9, 15, 21), for example, by instating laws that protect the weak—before, during, and after a wrong abortion—and by distilling from such hostile persecution of life God's message[3] for us "good" church people who have been sorely delinquent in providing unabusive orphanages and have been ready to ostracize instead of up-building societal support for single mothers (cf. James 1:27).

Evil enemies in action should drive us first of all to plead with God for the extraordinary grace not formally to forgive or excuse and forget those who commit hateful, abusive deeds. Jesus did not forgive the enemies who crucified him; he prayed that **God** would find a way to forgive them in their violent stupidity (Luke 23:32–34). Humans cheapen forgiveness by offering it off the cuff to those who don't want it. Jesus **loved** his enemies, Jesus died for his enemies. The active presence of enemies should drive us to **plead with God for the merciful strength to *will***

---

3   Romans 11:25–32 remarks about how the Jews whose hardened hearts toward the Lord make them enemies of God, nevertheless, are instruments for the salvation of the Gentiles: that is God's difficult message for both Jews and *goyim* in the Jewish nation's forsaking their covenant God.

to love the evil doers—it is not a matter of feelings!—to **decide** to suffer, impatiently perhaps, what is wrong (cf. Luke 6:21–36, v.20!) while
our generation gets behind the evident destruction, **and determinedly
changes** the very springs of evil action, even to touch the heart of persecutors.

God help us muster such love to replace the natural anger, because
deeds of long-range tough love hold congealed the bloody traces of forgiveness being born before we are even able or ready to carry through
on consciously forgiving delinquent sinners…like us (cf. Matthew 6:12,
14–15; 18:23–35; Mark 11:12–26).

(2) Scripture says, "Our struggle is not against (human) flesh and
blood, but against principalities, (demonic) powers, against the world-
controlling forces of this (present) darkness, against the hosts of wicked
spirituality" (Ephesians 6:12). When important people in the government, army, university, business or professional world are driven by the
invisible, evil **spiritual power** of Greed or Fear, Manipulative Control
or Selfishness, for example, it doesn't cut much ice to say, "Love the sinner, hate the sin," because when God-hating forces become systemic in
a culture, built into the very fabric of society so no one flesh-and-bloody
person seems to be the guilty responsible figure, such a perverted setup
contaminates everybody in its grip. And such evil principalities never
seem to suffer from hunger or thirst, but keep on gradually destroying
whatever is good, world without end.

Maybe that's the time when the terrible Scriptural verse is appropriate, "Don't throw your pearls before swine" (Matthew 7:6)? At least in
Nazi-occupied Holland in the '40s, if you saw an SS Gestapo agent coming down the street in the distance, you simply turned a corner to get out
of sight. Sometimes in history a Ruling Power or a Mega-corporation…
or a Church Establishment may be such swinish beasts? hints the book
of Revelation (13, 18)….

However, I hear our text, Proverbs 25:21–22, say to Christ's followers after Easter and Pentecost happened, and we expect the returning Lord: still give the dangerous, embodied Hatred Incorporated enemy
good food to eat and unpolluted water to drink.

That is, if labor relations in the land are ironfisted and corrupt, then
organize a union that witnesses to the integrity of honest work rather
than featherbedding, and to a just wage without under-the-table pay-
offs or sweetheart contracts that entail push-up-profits layoffs. If a school
system systematically tries to keep God absent from its studying, then
appoint teachers in alternate schools who together will let the good news
of the Bible breathe normally in the children's classrooms, hallways, and
playground. If the entertainment industry thrives on sexual sensation or
gratuitous violence with happy endings, we need to find and support
financially artists to write stories, paint paintings, compose songs, and

produce independent cinema that tell the imaginative truth about good and evil in God's world.

If a government—Israeli, Palestinian, Zimbabwean, American, or Canadian—believes revenge by car-bomb, missile, or repressive debt collection is kosher justice, believes lawful ownership and treaties may be ignored, believes "preemptive strikes" that call fire down from heaven like Sons of Thunder upon enemies (cf. Mark 3:17, Luke 9:51–55) are justified by the possibility of worse carnage to us: if human manic governments play god and do wrong, then those who hear the Scriptures have to stand up together and say that warmongering by Muslim Fundamentalist, Zionist Jew, or Evangelical Christian, is simply demonic, that vengeance belongs only to the LORD; and then we **begin** to be peacemakers as God's children by finding ways respectfully to fill the mouths of our enemies and their children with sustaining food and drink that breathes the peace of being cared for and safe.

Christ's followers are called upon to give bread instead of stones, and fresh fish instead of scorpions, warm meals instead of bullets, to one's family (Luke 11:9–13), to neighbors **and** to our enemies. Even if the response is hot ridicule, financial tuition hardship, and persecution that in some countries as an uncorrupted leader may cost you and your family their lives! To love enemies is not a lovey-dovey, you're-not-so-bad, go-ahead-and-walk-over-me kind of charade. Genuine christian love selflessly and passionately has us weak human beings give away whatever peaceable gifts of God we have in our hands—including calling to task, stopping violence we are responsible for, and doing what may be only a twinkle of peaceableness—even if such acts are not appreciated by the enemy and cost us dearly.

We must **pray fervently for the wisdom to return good for evil**, especially by persevering in "preventative medicine," as it were, to reform the far-reaching, breaking-down culture of loose, cynical violence we inhabit.

(3) The third clinching point of our text, that "the LORD God will shalom it for you" [the NIV's "reward you" is a bit simplistic as translation], "make it come out completely right for you," is found also in Romans 12:19. "Do not spend time vindicating yourself; instead leave room for the anger [of God], since it is written, 'I will exact just judgment ["vengeance"]; settling scores is my prerogative, says the Lord.'" [That's half-quoting Leviticus 19:18 and Deuteronomy 32:35.]

No matter what the enemy does to you, never say, "Wait till payback time, fellow!" (Proverbs 24:20). Other Proverbs paragraphs (20:22) and both Romans (12:17) and Philippians (4:4–7) reinforce this final thrust of our text: never attempt to repay evil with evil; let your forbearance be known to all people—the LORD is nearby to judge and to bring help. And believe it! **the LORD God shall somehow shalom this evil**

matter for you! That means, as happened to Job (Job 42:10–17), I the LORD God shall redeem you from your affliction with surprising blessing you cannot even imagine now—deepened wellbeing, matured wisdom, healed hurt, fortified trust, a peace that passes human rational understanding (Philippians 4:4–7).

Our natural tendency in hateful struggle with others is to try to get even with those who hurt us. Like Shakespeare's Shylock, the kind of justice we want is to sue for the "pound of flesh" we have coming to us for the wrong suffered. But such unholy, self-vindicating machinations only breed anger, animosity, and the grudge.

Our text proffers a diametrically different approach: **wait expectantly upon the LORD for your vindication during hard times, O steadfast believer, as you pray for those persecuting you.** And if the faithful become holy enough to take on their lips the curses of the Older Testament psalms, the prayers for the Enemy Incorporated may become intercessions pleading with the LORD to stop the evil once and for all! (cf. Psalm 137:7–9, Revelation 18). That would be living faithfully in a vibrant hope that realizes the LORD God's exacting retribution is more patient and inscrutable than that of us who like Job's friends have quicker answers. The LORD's "perfect" "rewarding" is sure to be incredibly just, merciful, surprising, a refining fire overflowing with goodness (cf. Hebrews 12:12–29, Matthew 25:31–46).

If we do not have any enemies to love, to learn to love under the tutoring of God's Holy Spirit, I am afraid our faith life could grow flabby, introverted, and comfortable. You don't have to go out and make enemies: you just have to recognize with the eye of faith their presence, and remember, even with our own hateful blemishes, to do good to them in the firm expectation **to upset the evil** thrown our way in persecution.

Even if one's life were not to have a happy ending, as was true for the many saints mentioned in Hebrews 11, God's children can still, with those women and men of Hebrews 11, "win strength out of weakness" (Hebrews 11:34). Our life need not lose joy. It's just that the saint's joy has grit for the three points I mentioned: we be enabled by God's Spirit (1) **to will to love the persecutors,** (2) **to give good for evil**—which may not be taken well—and (3) **to anticipate the LORD's overflowing restorative justice and shalom a-coming,** maybe even tangible at times here and there in Christ's body on earth....

PRAYER: Dear LORD, this matter of "enemies" is a slippery thing. We hear the Word that enemies are also neighbors, worldwide as well as those within touching distance. We often feel too weak to love those who hate us, who are out to destroy our very lives—culturally, economically, politically, in our testimony of your unspeakable grace.

By your Holy Spirit surprise us, O Christ, with the will, the vision

— How to Read Proverbs —

and wisdom and fortitude to disarm evil people, if possible, by doing what is good for them. And teach us, please, Lord, to trust more surely in your promise to cover our chintzy responses of love toward those doing wrong, cover our awkward, thin deeds of troubled love with shalom.

We believe, Lord, but help us practice what we believe. We ask this for our sake and our enemies' sake, in your world, in Jesus' name, Amen.

Be Just in Judgment, Fair to All

Text: Leviticus 19:15–18; vers. Calvin Seerveld, 1985
Tune: Calvin Seerveld, 1985; harm. Dale Grotenhuis, 1986
Text and music © 1987, Calvin Seerveld

86 86 4
TORONTO

(3) Bible song, Leviticus 19:15–18, Calvin Seerveld, 1985

Postscript
Enemies are a severe temptation, testing one's faith (Matthew 6:13–15).

PRAYER: Dear Lord, we know we live in your good creation, but there is so much bad going on in the world. We would really like to retreat once in a while from all the problems the media keep on pushing in our faces: government cutbacks, strikes and protests, economic uncertainties, horrendous famine, catastrophic massacres of children, youth, women, and men around the world. It's hard to know what to focus on or where to begin to be Christ's followers.

We pray that you let us begin at home, that You discipline us to forgive those who sin against us because **and so that** You, Lord, can forgive

–42–

us (Matthew 6:14–15). Please help us not to be "holier" than the neighbor, but to be holy enough to let You finally shalom the hurts of neglect, injustice, abuse, and hateful deeds some of us have undergone.

And we dare to ask, Lord, that You **stop the enemy** of pain and cancer and undiagnosed sickness that tries to undermine the life of more than one among us, and people we know far away. It's not right in your world, Lord, for evil to triumph and to let your children be hurt so much! We will try to do good to those who do us evil, but your adversary Satan and his cohorts of pain need to have their power broken! Could You not maybe come back a little quicker, Lord?

We confess that there are often things we omit doing that would show love to a neighbor, and we can slide by without looking evil, like walking by on the other side of the road. Please forgive us for not seeing needs we could tend to in your Name.

We thank you today for your work among all those who help behind the scenes and in daily leadership with grace and stamina and insight to make the love of Jesus known to those who are not so well aware of the riches of your saving our lives.

We pray now for much grace to permeate your people, laying these matters and much more before you, confidently in Jesus' name, Amen.

(Toronto, 2001)

Proverbs 25–29 and 30–31

1. Uncover Wrong to *Heal* Things Straight

2 If it is the burdened glory of God to hold back from uncovering something,
   it is the burdened glory of kings to ferret out what's going on

3 (not that you can get to the bottom of the heart of kings
   as you search out the span of the heavens or deepest pits of the earth):

4 when impure metal is removed from silver,
   the refiner starts to get something sound;

5 well, when the underhanded wrongdoer is removed from where the king rules,
   then his seat of kingly authority starts to get truly established
   by the doing of what is straight!

6 [But] don't ever push yourself forward to get kingly authority,
   and don't try to get standing room in the place where important people meet;

7 better they say to you, "Wouldn't you like to come up here?"
   instead of their putting you down in front of the prince.

   [Do you understand?]

8 Don't hurriedly bring whatever your eyes have seen out into the open for judgment
   lest you can't do a thing as the affair comes to its final crunch
   when your man or woman confounds you!

9 Go ahead, fight out your lawsuits, dispute things with your neighbor,
   but never, never betray the intimacy or confiding trust another shared with you.

10 Otherwise, whoever hears it will distrust you,
   and your calumny shall never stop beggaring you!

23 Add to that:
   it's simply never good to play favorites
   when you are called to judge what is right and just.

24 People come to detest whoever says to an underhanded wrongdoer,
   "In my judgment, what you're doing looks all right";
   people come to really despise those who judge what's crooked

as if it be straight.
²⁵ But it goes well with those who call evil to account;
the blessing of genuine wellbeing covers those
who search out what is wrong to heal things straight....
(Proverbs 25:2–10, 24:23b–25)

When this proverbial paragraph of Solomon, copied over by the wise-men of Hezekiah's court (25:1), says "king," "kingly authority," "important people," and "prince," read "anyone with governing authority," "anyone who must oversee men and women," "anyone who is ever responsible for leading and ordering other people." That is, this passage speaks not just for kings and queens and princes, but for anyone who rules somehow in society. People in political office, business men and women, school teachers, parents, leaders of a church, journalists, any adult who judges others and has ruling power of sorts over his neighbor. Proverbs 25 calls them to root out what is undercover and ruining God's order if they would expect to receive blessing. But with all your uncovering, says Holy Scripture, respect the God-given identity of the other person, so that new life can begin.

Only God can really dispose of things, finish off something—either by destroying it or bringing it to completion. That is why it is the peculiar glory of God to hold back (25:2), to wait, to give people and creatures time to repent and change their ways before God Almighty says, "That's it, now." An enormously patient and inscrutable Mercy characterizes the just dealings of the Holy One with humankind.

Isaiah 49–55 notes near the end: so highly contrary to your thoughts is my way of doing things, says the LORD (55:8–9): it is the glory of God that God held back from uncovering Israel's sin till the servant of Yahweh might suffer, so they could by faith enter into a new covenant of Grace. At the end of Romans 9–11, Paul bursts out with, "How inscrutable are God's judgments! How unable to be figured out are God's ways!" (11:33). It is the glory of God that God waited with final judgment till God provided for us pagans to be saved as well as God's chosen people. It is the almost unbelievable, burdened glory of God the Holy One that God stoops to our weakness, forgives sinners, and actually straightens out things, historically!

Our human responsibility
Now it is the burdened glory of those who call the shots in the courtroom, in the living room, schoolroom, corporate executive room, broadcasting, consistory or press room—each within the bounds of one's God-given authority—it is the burdened glory of those who must take care of something till the Lord returns (cf. parable of Matthew 25:14–30) to get their metal pure, to not live with wrong as if it's right, to get their

terrain pleasing to God so the LORD will want to establish it. And do it, says Proverbs 25, with a careful and compassionate reluctance to judge people. Let it be your human burden to get to the bottom of things, to get people walking in the light rather than doing things in the dark (cf. 1 John 1:5–10), not just to "set things straight," but to **heal** things straight.

Do not act as if you be God, or Jesus Christ throwing out the moneychangers. Do not judge evil in a pushy way lest you too be judged without mercy yourself (Proverbs 25:7c–10, Matthew 7:1–5). God holds back executing justice upon wrongdoers. Well, let your human prosecution of what is underhanded and violating the LORD's ordinances also be godly, without glee. Never treat a man-on -the-street, a woman, a child or student or assembly line worker, parishioner or interested observer who is a thief, disrespectful, a cheat, lazy, a gossip or covetous person, as if he or she be your footstool. Stop the evildoers in their tracks, right! and give him or her what they need (not "deserve"). Remember, it is the LORD who will finish things off for you with shalom, if possible (Proverbs 25:21–22).

Guiding vision

To understand Proverbs 25–27 it is important to realize that 25:21–22 dominates the whole section. If you show compassion in your dealings with neighbor, and even enemy, then the LORD God of heaven and earth will complete your deed with the fullness of blessing and peace. That promise holds for all of a believer's daily life, when he or she is unjustly attacked (let your forbearance be known among people—Philippians 4:4–7), or when one is normally at work (Matthew 5–7—the meek are blessed!)

Proverbs 25:21–22 is the key to understanding 25:2–10 too, because it makes clear our passage is not just biblical tips for political life or etiquette at diplomatic dinners (e.g., 25:6–7, cf. the parable in Luke 14:7–11 and its point 14:12–14). Our passage is also not therefore just some scattered admonitions to display fruits of the Spirit, understood in general, moral, or devotional terms. Because what "kings" do daily reflects on the LORD God, Proverbs 25 and appendix to 24 give specific guidelines, direction for ruling life activities:

Probe to the end what should be probed to the end (the curse of evil-doing), and keep covered what should be kept covered (the intimate center of your neighbor's life, which can change). Don't hunt witches and don't let sleeping dogs lie; don't play God and don't excuse or hide sin. But unhypocritically (= identifying with the hunted and oppressed, the evildoer and wicked) **get rid of evil to set up healing**; bring re-direction and Jesus Christ's straightening out Rule to bear upon the crook and profligate, the proud and guilty rich, so they become jealous and desirous of shalomic order rather than embittered, hardened, and wasted in their sin.

Difficulties to obey

There are two difficulties with our understanding this Word of the Lord:

(1) Most of us living in this century are so secularized we act as if there be only two alternatives: you either mollycoddle criminals or pin them to the wall, you either get your pound of flesh or get taken for a ride, you either spank kids into submission with the rod or give them the run of the house and school, you either applaud governmental muscling in on industry or champion laissez-faire market speculation. It seems to be either we "good guys" against those "bad guys," or because we all live in glass houses, one cynically throws no stones at all, affirming the status quo.

But Proverbs 25 repudiates both such abstract alternatives. Evil doing must be stopped, but "the good guys" are just as evil if they denature God's creatures and make healing impossible. It's true, you pull an abscessed tooth to heal your mouth. But it takes more than pulling out a crooked politician and putting him behind bars to heal government, if it was done only so we can get on with our North American standard of living. And journalists out to scoop the truth and set things straight, who treat people in crises like natural catastrophes, push microphones in front of those trapped in their guilt as if they be earthquakes, photograph Solzhenitsyn as if he be a forest fire, turn Kissinger's bride into cheesecake, or trump the repented sin of AACS-ICS[1] and Toronto up into the Land of Mythic Monsterdom—secular journalism always hunts human heads, despite its good intentions, and affords no healing balm in Gilead…or Philistia.

(2) It is a measure of our unbelief and stunted biblical vision that so many of us Christians would prefer to have Proverbs 25 and appendix to 24 give us a recipe for reforming untruth, injustice, and evil. As if the letter of *Proverbs* would save us and get us to please God.

But Proverbs 25 calls us who exercise authority of any kind, to repentance in our daily action. *Us!* not somebody else (cf. Psalm 130:3). And promises all those who stop the old way of doing things and judging people, to speak the truth in love while building up the body of Christ (Ephesians 4:1–6:9), who re-form the wicked patterns of this secular world so that men and women can discern what pleases God (Romans 12:1–2), who uncover wrong so that the Holy Spirit may heal things

---

1 The initials stand for The Association for the Advancement of Christian Scholarship, which was the lay society raising prayer and financial support for the graduate Institute for Christian Studies in Toronto, a "free-standing" educational institution, begun by a few Dutch immigrants in Canada in 1967, which was vilified by many fellow Christians for the untempered critique it was known to utter about the Church and its conservatist activities. Cf. C. Seerveld, "A Modest Proposal for Reforming the Christian Reformed Church in North America" (1970) in *Biblical Studies & Wisdom for Living* (Sioux Center: Dordt College Press, 2014), 233–262.

straight: of such workmen, judges, schoolteachers, parents, salesmen and journalists are the Kingdom of Heaven.

[*Vanguard* May–June 1974, 30–31]

Think of it as the prodigal son (and the older son) returning repentant to the Father God who, with **prodigal love**, went naked in Jesus Christ to reclothe us to cover our shame.

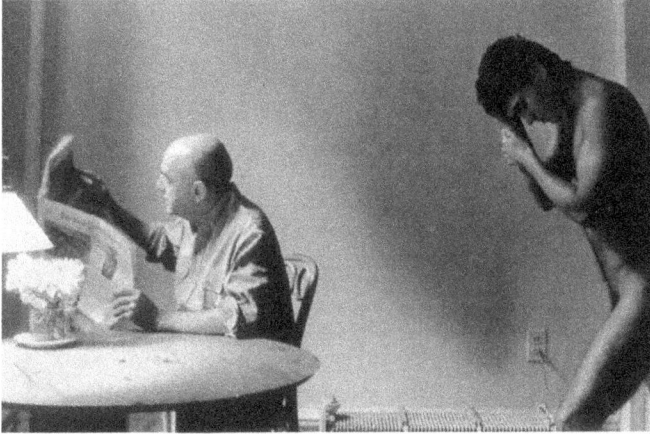

[4-1] Duane Michals, *The Return of the Prodigal*, 1982

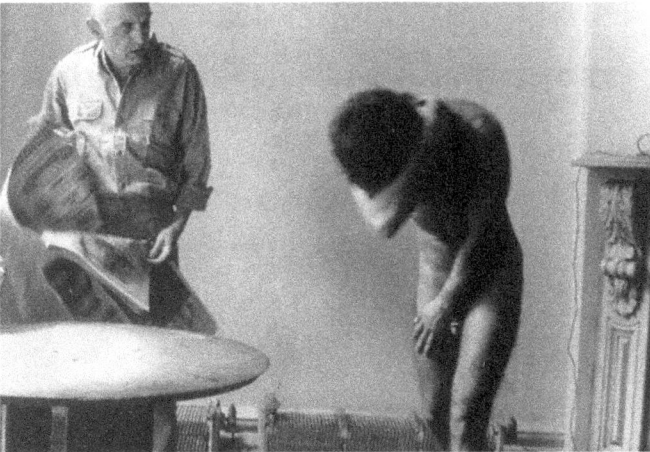

[4-2] Duane Michals, *The Return of the Prodigal*, 1982

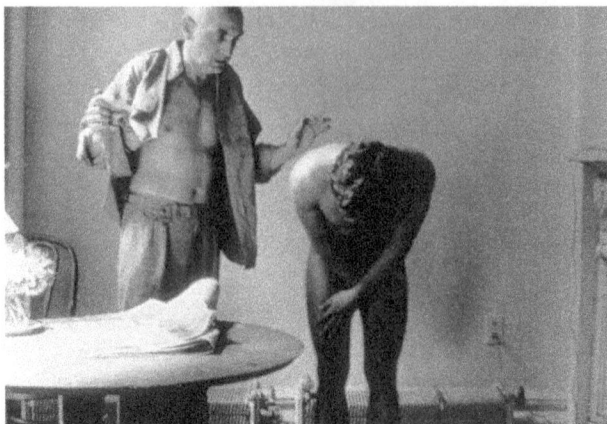

[4-3] Duane Michals, *The Return of the Prodigal*, 1982

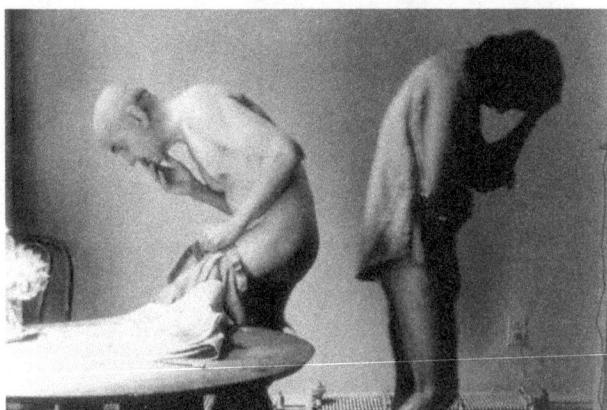

[4-4] Duane Michals, *The Return of the Prodigal*, 1982

[4-5] Duane Michals, *The Return of the Prodigal*, 1982

2. Your Speech Betrays Who You Are

It says in the first verse of Proverbs 25 that the wise men and women at Hezekiah's court copied over some of the "artful comparisons" Solomon had made in his day. Since these careful sayings are the Word of God, it is important for every person to hear their instruction.

¹¹ A word spoken at the right time and place:
> just like gold apples stand out in silver art works!
¹² Like a gold earring, a pure gold jewel!
> appears the correcting word of wisdom to the ear straining to hear.

¹³ To have an envoy you can trust to send
> is like a snow-cold drink on the day of cutting harvest:
> it perks up a master's spirits again.
¹⁴ But a man who boasts of gifts he will never deliver on
> is like wind and fog, with never a shower of rain.

¹⁵ Remember:
> by holding off a long time from snapping back
> you can convince those who must judge;
> **a gentling tongue breaks to stillness the bone (of anger).** . . .

²³ Suddenly unconcealed wind chokes out a flash shower:
> just so, secretive tongue-talk can whiplash persons' faces.
²⁴ It is better to while away time secluded on the roof somewhere
> than spend it with a bickering wife and a household of companions.

²⁵ Hearing supportive good news from a faraway land
> is like (a cup of) cold water to a wearied-out fellow who is faint;
²⁶ but polluted well water, a dirtied spring of water
> (is talk about) an upright man stumbled by someone wicked.

²⁷ More and more when eating honey is not good,
> but going all out to get to the bottom of difficult, weighty matters is something splendid!
²⁸ However, a man who cannot curb his driving spirit
> is like a city that is ruptured, without protective walls
> —never forget it!

(Proverbs 25:11–15, 23–28)

Talk is cheap, but it is also deadly. So with a tongue in everybody's mouth you have a worse problem on your hands, says the Scriptures, than a loaded gun in every home. People by nature can't stand to have others get ahead of them, and nothing is more tempting than to shoot down a neighbor or a stranger, your colleague or an enemy, with a word or two.

All it takes is a touch of knowledge, a little breath, and enough malice to get your hatefulness on the road. Perfectly legal. If you can ruin the work of someone else by talk, just a secretive, misleading remark, you stand to gain yourself (we think).

But God says *false witness* shall be cursed. As the LORD of Truth,

> God self hates especially
> > haughty eyes,
> > a tongue you can never count on,
> > a heart that thinks together strategies to do what is wicked;
> God outright hates!
> > feet all set to run after evil doing,
> > anyone who whispers deceptive things,
> > false witness,
> > or who keeps bickering going on among those who are close to
> > > one another. (Proverbs 6:16–19)

That means: backbiters, people with a tricky tongue, those who twist information out of normed contexts into gossip, go to hell. And whoever says he or she knows God, but undermines the life of one's fellow man or woman with false witness is a liar, says the scriptures (read through Paul's letter to Titus), and grieves the Holy Spirit.

But Proverbs 25 has more for us to hear: testimony that remains unfulfilled, and passionate speech that knows no ego bounds, is also good for nothing! Such testimony and fiery speech, even if it be Jesus-talk, is only *spilled witness.*

For a man who constantly makes promises and does not come through with the goods mocks the fact that a word is a deed, and if his word-deed is not trustworthy it is useless, like spilled milk. To tell a man that Jesus Christ is the answer for all his life problems, and when he believes it you walk away without showing him the goods, is an instance of spilled witness. Like wind and fog it befuddles rather than refreshes, says our passage.

Worse still is the untempered speech of the zealot too full of oneself in his cause to check one's bottomless commitment with the gentling discipline of "if the Lord will, let it be so." A clarion call to repent and reform in Christ's Name is prophetic if it convicts and rallies people together by making them jealous of God's mercies upon those following God's Way. But if the revival appeal is compulsive, and the sloganeering tongue unbridled, then instead of genuine prophecy you have vanity and a rupture on your hands (cf. James 1:26 and chapter 3).

However, a word of wisdom spoken at the right time and place, says Proverbs 25, is the norm for *true witness* in God's world. Concern for clarity and logical consistency in language can sometimes block one's awareness of the confessional dimension to speech, that talk needs to be holy, impassioned, and certain, as well as clear. Above all, what comes out of the mouth

(5) "Someday we will all die"[1]

of God's sons and daughters should be timely and wise, that is, show what kind of response concretely in all sorts of affairs would make God happy. And timely, wise words must be spoken in the right place to be true witness.

That means, in our day, we who confess Christ are called to get our testimony off the street-corners and into the courts, as Christ intended (Matthew 10:16–20). We Christians must shut up our false witness, and get straight that testimony for our individual neighbor's benefit falls short of the Scriptural mandate: we are to testify *for Christ's sake!* not our neighbor's sake (Matthew 10:26–39). Believers who wish to act within the full biblical dimension must press the claims of the Lord before the secular magistrates and the leaders of our culture (as Paul and the apostles did), get the Truth live before the heads of families and shaping education, with the vision of Christ's building a royal priesthood of generations of believers (1 Peter 2:1–10).

True witness happens with a meek sureness that no one shall mistake for timidity. And it is done today not particularly as church men and church women, but as people of God, trustworthy envoys in all walks of life, from distant and nearby lands, who have heard and will obey Proverbs 25.

[*VANGUARD* March–April 1972, 5, 34]

---

1   "Someday we will all die" is often attributed to Charles M. Schulz of *Peanuts* fame, but Peanuts Worldwide informed us that this image is "an unofficial meme that has been available over the internet but never appeared in the Peanuts strip nor was authored by Charles Schulz."

3. Proverbs 25 Again: A Call to Wisdom

It is wrong to read the biblical proverbs as if they were something like Benjamin Franklin's *Poor Richard's Almanac*—advice to men and women of common sense on how to get ahead (spiritually). The Bible is never a manual for success, prescribing routines that, if followed to the letter, bring you inside heaven's gates. That is a mistake Pharisees have always made.

Instead, Scripture is here to tell us the Great Things the Lord has done and will do, and the kind of obedient order Yahweh wants to show up in our daily life. The Bible brings specific life-direction. Not handy answers. That means we must read Proverbs 25 as *a call to wisdom with the Lord*, and not treat it like a collection of pithy, worldly-wise instructions.

The "artful comparisons" Solomon formulated, and Hezekiah's wise men copied over under the leading of the Holy Spirit, have a packed, epigrammatic terseness. They must be read very slowly, like lyric poetry.

16 If you find some honey, eat your fill,
    but no more,
    lest over-full you get stomach sick,
    and make it vomit.
17 Likewise, inside your friendly neighbor or colleague's house
    set a chary foot,
    lest bored weary with the visits
    he loathe your very sight.

18 A club for mauling, a thrust-through dagger, a sharpened arrow
        that pierces flesh:
    a man or woman who answers for his neighbor with the
        meaning slightly twisted.
19 A crumbling, rotten tooth and stumblebum leg:
    that's how the trust you put in a double-dealing person shows
        up when the hard times come.
20 To strip off clothes on an ice-cold day, pour vinegar on lye:
    that's what singing songs at a dejected, cranky old soul is like.

21 **When the one who hates you, your enemy, is suffering**
        from hunger,
    give that person good bread to eat;
    when the one who is out to get you is terribly thirsty,
    give that person some water to drink.
22 **It's true, in that way you will only be raking together**
        the smoldering embers burning on top of your enemy's
        head,
    but the LORD God shall finish it off for you! and give you
        peace.

(Proverbs 25:16–22)

The "honey-neighbor" paragraph here is *not* an appeal for moderation in all things, followed by the maxim "familiarity breeds contempt." That cynical view of intimacy, and old Aristotelian lie about the lukewarm reasonableness of a good, practical life, is foreign to Holy Scripture. Paul asks believers not to be rationally temperate, but to be athletically tempered by the Holy Spirit to persist in the race of everlasting life (1 Corinthians 9:24–27). The Newer Testament designates a holy passionate order as the Christian lifestyle (cf. Romans 12:1–2), and rejects the corseted habit of pick-and-choose reproof practiced by spiritually minded people who have a bad conscience (1 Timothy 4:1–5). *Proverbs* here too calls for a life of disciplined intensity, not one of measured correctness—eat your fill! It just notes for ears to hear that the sweetest pleasures God gives go bad when used without insight.

As for the "tricky talk" couplets, the "two faced," double-minded, rub-it-in grouping of proverbs—we all know that, right? That to be misrepresented, left in the lurch, or made fun of, is like getting a swift kick in the groin?

At the Benjamin Franklin level maybe. But do we know it as revealed, biblical truth? That is, is our consciousness drenched with the awareness of the fact that to alter a man's meaning in public, or to laugh at those who are weeping, is to bludgeon them to pieces? Do we know existentially that to violate the Word of the covenanting Lord—be a reliable witness of your neighbor and to him or her (Exodus 20:16)—to violate that Word is to kill! To betray your neighbor, however slightly and politely, is not a mistake, one-upmanship, or even simply breaking troth; but murder is the name of the game.

Those who know this truth and still practice the evil, ruin…themselves! says the proverb Word of the Lord.

And our passage takes this double-edged Good News about disciplined passion and reliable witness all the way, just as Christ did, bringing its blessing even to those who don't respond in truth. Love your enemies, says the Older Testament Proverbs 25, doing what pleases God.

Again, Scripture is *not* picturing the epitome of man-to-man virtue that every believer should struggle to attain. **To be able to love your adversary is a pure gift of the Holy Spirit, not something a man or woman can do oneself.** But the biblical proverb here, reinforced later by Christ (Matthew 5:38–48), framed in the horizon of Romans 12 (12:9–21 and 13:8–10), is directing us to the way of Shalom on the earth.

Do not let the evil of those who hate you trap you into hate. Paying back people who do you unjust harm belongs only to the Lord—thank God! Let your forbearance be evident (not flabby tolerance) as you speak the truth in love (rather than kowtow to the bluff and lies against Christ's Rule). Pray for those who spite you! Serve the needs of those who undermine your very existence! Be openly charitable to those who work out of a different spirit—do not fake love, but simply act without guile! Your protection as a child of the Lord is to be utterly God-serving! (cf. Ephesians 4:14–15, Philippians 4:4–7).

That is the final Word of Proverbs 25 to all those who are oppressed and hemmed in for Christ's sake, and want saving direction: God's Will is this, that you by doing what is right shut up the abysmal ignorance of foolish people (see 1 Peter 2:15–17). And the LORD God shall give you peace.

[*VANGUARD* May–June 1972, p. 5]

4. Never Respect a Fool

The original Hebrew text has an almost sonnet-like constellation of lines instructing us in the will of the LORD about fools.

1 As snow does not belong to summer, and rain ruins grain-cutting time,
just so ill-fitting is the honor of authority matched to a stupid fool!

2 (It's true, like a sparrow aflutter, like a swallow darting hither and yon,
an undeserved curse does not hit the mark;

3 but a whip for a horse, bridle for a jackass,
you need a clobbering stick to get through to the back of a fool.)

4 **Do not respond to a fool dealing with his stupidity
lest you become like him, you too [working with
what's stupid]:**

5 **respond to a fool as his stupidity deserves,
to stop him from seeming to be wise in his own eyes.**

6 That man hacks off his feet and shall have to swallow an uproar
who tries to get messages across by means of a stupid fool:

7 **like a lame man's legs dangle helplessly loose,
just so treacherously undependable is proverbial wise
talk in the mouth of a fool.**

8 That man is tossing away jewels onto a heap up of stones
who gives in to credit the honor of authority to a stupid fool:

9 like a dagger thorn gotten stuck in the fist of a drunk,
just so wildly dangerous is proverbial wise talk in the mouth
of a fool.

10 Again and again everything gets messed up
when you hire a fool (like hiring a chance passerby [for a job]),

11 because like a dog goes back to what it's vomited up,
a fool repeats and repeats his same old stupidity.

12 Note this too:
if you find a man who persists to seem in his own eyes
to be wise,
you can even expect more from a plain old fool
than from such a self-assured somebody....

(Proverbs 26:1–12)

The key point of the passage is this: never respect a fool! Do not listen to a fool as if his or her stupidities made sense; do not think fools can be of use—they only gum up the works. God says: never credit a fool with authority! or you court disaster.

This damning revelation comes on so strong, there is a parenthetical type remark to say: indeed, undeserved curses flap in the air, but nothing except the strongest rebuke and beating can start to get to the treacherous, closed mentality of a fool!

Fools are so serious to God because they are closed creatures, shut down to the development of God's creation. Outrightly stupid! People without the insight or will to respond to the LORD's ordinances! Fools are men and women who have buried their talents in holes in the ground, or prostituted their gifts with pontificating emptiness. Backward-looking demagogues, professionals of trivia, talkative dullards of hot air....

Somewhat different than the Psalms where "fool" is synonymous with a position of frank godlessness, here Proverbs 26 appropriates the designation "fool" to spotlight the deadened *Dummheit* inhabiting certain people, which sets God's teeth on edge. If such fools are honored as leaders, says Proverbs 26, with all the enlightening Grace of the Holy Spirit: if such stupid fools are accorded authority! it spells ruin.

And God's booked Word does not lie. Stupid foolishness is ruining us.

That means, since Proverbs 26 holds even more forcefully for us today than it did when Solomon was led to compose these "artful comparisons," that the stupidity we honor with TV talk show banality, the foolishness we credit with authority because it comes out of the mouth of sports idols or artistic performers getting paid several $100,000 a year, the unimportant minutiae we give serious attention because some political bureaucrat issued a press release: the whole web of wasteful stupidities we North Americans politely consume is ruining us as people! The endless parade of kings without clothes, leaders without insight, cultural formers without godly perspective—stupid fools! to whom we normally listen and bootlessly follow, along with the sexually spiced ads on mass media to which industry and travel agencies and auto corporations return again and again like dogs to their vomit, is the very mess Proverbs 26 is cursing.

And to follow stupid fools is of special temptation to Newer Testament Christians. Maybe because it is a devil trick to keep Christ's followers so alert for sin reduced to immorality and heresy, that they unwittingly get sucked into honoring stupidities that seem so innocent. But when evangelical organizations adopt stupidly successful, secular fundraising techniques for their causes, Christ's name on their lips, or when clerics and institutional church officials promulgate counter-historical solutions to current problems, because they have lost the key to the Scriptures or lack insight into the creational ordinances of God—Bible texts and proverbial wise talk in their mouths notwithstanding—we believers are led by fools and the "Christian leadership" is blather.

Or when students on Christian campuses stake out "gray areas" and license for themselves booze and dope in the name of using God's gifts (and because their parents take prescribed drugs, tranquilizers) or deal capriciously and immaturely with troth relationships as the right of Christian liberty, such a travesty of biblical direction is pure foolishness at work.

Don't condamn,[1] but ignore the fools

It's true, no one is to go about condamning wholesale those believing brothers and sisters as fools, as if we escape complicity ourselves (Matthew 5:17–26); but Scripture does not temporize any more than it does not moralize. God's Older Testamented Word says forcefully that such stupid fools do not deserve to be taken seriously as people with a mission in God's kingdom; do not hold them in honor; they are frauds for all their slogans of reform or Christian concern or orthodoxy. Shun that vomit stupidity like the plague!

Sin is one thing, and can be repented of and forgiven. A self-assured stupidity is another thing, and can be a hardened form of sinfulness in anti-Christ sheep or wolfs clothing (cf. Hebrews 6:4–8).

Nobody can give biblically fruitful leadership who is not painfully holy.

Also, just because a person's doctrine and life look clean does not mean that person is insured from being a blasted fool, evilly stupid and closed.

We are commanded ironically to be fools of faith for Christ's sake (1 Corinthians 1:18–25, 4:9–13): that is, against the stream we are to seem naive and a joke to sophisticated unbelief in disclosing Jesus Christ's healing lordship over our whole life. Proverbs 26 deepens that imperative by exposing, straight to our faces, the opposite: a crass, God-damned, foolish stupidity that presumes to lead, but is regressive, blindered, dead.

Let all those with ears in the body of Christ, and men and women at large, hear this Word of the LORD in Proverbs 26, and obey. Otherwise all hell will break loose instead of shalom.

[*VANGUARD*, August–September 1972, 20–21]

---

1 "Condamn" is a neologism, halfway between "condemn" and "damn."

5. Will You, O sluggard, Be a Joke to God?

Did you know that the Bible tells at least one joke about sluggards, and quite openly pokes fun of the slothful who "lack heart"? It says that they "lack faith-guts"!

¹³ **The sluggard says,**
   "A roaring beast is out in the street!
   There's a lion outside somewhere in the square!"
¹⁴ [Like] a door creaks slowly open on its hinges
   is the way an indolent man turns over again in his bed;
¹⁵ the sluggard buries his hand deep into a bowl of food,
   but it just about exhausts him to get it back up to his mouth
      again.
¹⁶ Yes, the idle fellow thinks himself to be more wise
   than any seven people who can give you an intelligent answer.
                                        (Proverbs 26:13–16)

³⁰ I was walking past the field of a slothful man, that is,
   up to and around the farm of somebody who simply lacked
      guts;
³¹ and would you believe it!
   the whole works was overgrown with prickly weeds
   —a kind of bramble underbrush covered whatever you could
      see,
   and the stone wall was a broken-down [rim].
³² I looked at it all, I did, quite closely, and took it deeply to heart.
   I stared at it [till] I could catch on to whatever it was that would
      pull me back into line:
³³ "Just a little more sleep, just a tiny little more lullaby sleep!
   only a little more twiddling-thumb-de-dum time hanging
      around,"
   [is what the fellow had said]....
³⁴ then this impoverished disintegration you deserve
   drops in on you like a vagabond tramp,
   and the whole gamut of bankrupt void you have coming
   accosts you like a man with a gun!
                                        (Proverbs 24:30–34)

A genuine sluggard can think up the most fantastic rationalizations for not getting on with one's work—"I can't go outside! There's a lion out there that will eat me alive!"

Slothful people, says the Scriptures, waste time, are stupidly selfish, smug, and shirk doing the dirty work that needs to be done, till doing nothing finally does them in. When you grow into idleness, says *Proverbs*, suddenly the LORD will surprise you like a tramp or an armed stickup man in the night, and confront you with the empty nothingnesses on your hands. And what then?

It would be a bad mistake to think the joking here is indulgent. As if we're all a little bit lazy—who doesn't procrastinate and want to sleep past the alarm now and then? Just let things go till you are in a mess—deadlines are made for humans and not humans for the deadlines—but O.K., you've made your New Year's resolutions to be more prompt, diligent, and energetic. Thanks for the tip, Solomon....

No. Such a reading misses the terrible life-or-death dimension to the irony and *paideia* of the joke and parable before us. Proverbs 26 and appendix to 24 is not just pointing out the faults that bug the so-called "Protestant work ethic," as if sloth is what ruins the equation of

> Early to bed, early to rise,
> makes a Man healthy, wealthy and wise.

No, you miss God's Word if all you hear is a condemnation of those who lack industry as defined by the all-American, get-up-and-go activity normally crowned by success. Then *Proverbs* would be inviting a self-righteous smile on the face of every middleclass citizen. After all, we hardworking people are not sluggards, are we?

I have seen them

I have seen them. I have seen them in government offices shuffling papers and passing the buck. The drones of chic-dressed secretaries in banks and functionaries idling with their spoons at the holy moment of the coffee break. I have watched middle-aged bureaucrats in their highrise business offices go through an everlasting routine, and seen professional persons busy busy answering the minutiae of jangling telephones, treading water. Subway commuters at rush hour pressed like zombies toward exits and factory workers with the spark gone from their eyes make way for the next shift. And their lives were all overgrown with prickly weeds! Brambles of discontent and a broken-down, dogged dullness—waiting for the promotion, hanging on till the pension comes, or dumbly, trapped, half-willingly going through the motions of the tedium, in disrepair, twiddling one's thumbs.

Teachers can a course and repeat it for a decade. Preachers use old sermons to make time for counseling, administrative duties, or golf. Potboiling artists and professional performers use their one successful gimmick again and again: respectable...sluggards! sloth undiluted! Because they lack guts, says *Proverbs*, lack the heart of faith to turn their closed, parasitic, oh! so safe, horizontal life into an open adventure of responding ever new to the call of the LORD **in** their daily work.

You do not avoid idleness, as the Bible understands it, by putting in a solid five or six-day workweek. **The point is: did your routine today reach out with healing that the Holy Spirit could establish for the coming of Jesus Christ's Rule upon the earth?** Else your activity was as idle as the one who stayed abed.

(6) Peter Smith, *Leaving*, 1984

Lion-sized excuses

Too many professing Christian sluggards come with their lion-sized excuses: "You don't expect me to fight the whole bloody, giant corporation myself, do you?" (cf. 1 Samuel 17). "My identity crisis is not yet resolved!" (cf. John 3:1– 21). "I can't talk with those pros…" (cf. Exodus 3–4). "I've just married a wife and gotten a new house with an enormous mortgage—what can I do?" (cf. Luke 14:16–24). "I knew you were a hard man, Lord, and that you wanted a safe return on your investment in me; so I went to church regularly, tithed, led a decent life, didn't get into trouble, and here is your whole talent back as it was."

"O, to hell," says the Lord (Matthew 25:14–30), you sluggard! You never got past watching the ant (Proverbs 6:6–11) in its animal industry. You mistook Paul's rejection of freeloaders in the Christian community, those who don't pay their bills by sweat but absolve themselves by "visions from heaven" on their specialness (2 Thessalonians 3:6–12): maybe you mistook that to mean moonlighting is a saving virtue? Or you thought that by imitating Christ's foot-washing at least, by joining a do-gooding civic organization in the community you could cover up your basic indolence?

No deal, says God Almighty. If you lack the guts of faith to build up My special Rule upon the earth in your daily activities, then your basic, bankrupt condition shall be exposed by Me like a thief in the night, and you shall lose, with shame, everything you have piled up for yourself.

Will you be a joke to God?

The antidote to sloth, whose end is destruction, is not to work yourself to death (cf. Psalm 127:1–2; Proverbs 10:22), but first of all to convert your deed into action that Yahweh self will want to finish off with shalom (Proverbs 25:21–22). And then (on pain of apostasy!) not to settle down sluggishly into a milk-fed Christian life, but become mature, "start acting like people driven by faith and a confident forbearance, hanging on to inherit the riches of what God has promised!" (Hebrews 5:11–6:12). Only then will your life not be a joke to God.

[*VANGUARD* January/February 1973, 15, 30–31]

6. A Kiss Smack on the Lips

Solomon debated the proverb-makers of Egypt in his day like anybody else, and the overpowering insight of his "artful comparisons" spread abroad the name of the LORD (1 Kings 4:29–34, 10:1). The fact that Solomon's wisdom was a special gift from God and not just the reflections of a perceptive, experienced king in Israel must shape the way we read what has been collected and edited in chapters 25–29 by Hezekiah's wise counselors (25:1).

Solomon certainly saw through the flattery and calumny at his court and had to deal constantly with the scheming infighting of his courtiers (e.g., 1 Kings 2:13–25); but his proverbs—even the ones about conniving deceit—are not a laconic, worldly-wise bible of personnel management for your business, congregation, circle of acquaintances, or neighborhood. Proverbs 25–29 is not comparable to the horizontal advice of lovelorn columns, directives by the district manager, or bulletins from governmental offices. Bible proverbs always confront you directly with God!

So the LORD used King Solomon, before he went bad, to reveal the truth of the matter that straightforward answers, petulant talk, and sly winks are manifestations of fundamental God-and-neighbor love **or** acts of sin, with their terrible potential for finality. Unless we hear this awful dimension of *Proverbs*, we read right past what is written in them for teaching us hope (Romans 15:4).

17 A passerby who meddles in a quarrel that's none of his or
   her business
   is like a person grabbing a dog by the ears [who will bite].

18 Like someone half mad throwing around deadly firebrands and
   arrows
19 is that person who has deliberately undercut the neighbor
   and then says, "I was just joking, fellow, wasn't I?"

20 When the wood is up, the bonfire goes out:
   when there's no more slandering around, bitter dispute stops
   still.
21 It takes live coals to stir up a red-hot glow, and wood to make a
   fire:
   it takes a *zanikend* [nagging] crank to keep a bitter argument
   going....
22 Words breaking down other people are tasty tidbits:
   such gossip glides down [a listener's throat] to his innermost
   belly.

23 A cheap piece of clay glazed over with a film of silver:
   that's what sweet-talking lips are like, hiding a double-crossing
   heart.
24 The one who hates you feigns [niceties] with the lips,

but deep down he or she is already concocting treachery;

25 when such a person talks so graciously, don't you trust them at all,
for there's a seven-headed, dirty-dealing scheme inside [behind the facade].

26 Maybe hatred can be covered over with plausible deceit,
but its ruinous evil shall surely show up
when the faithful meet together as a whole.

27 Whoever digs a grave [for somebody else], will be self laid to rest in it.
Whoever rolls a stone up [into position], will have it fall back on oneself.

28 A lying tongue works hatred upon those already beleaguered!
And the gossipy, insinuating mouth boomerangs with ruin all around.

24:28 Never be a falsifying accuser against your neighbor
so that you have misled [others] and betrayed him or her with your lips.

29 Don't you ever say, "Just as he did to me, so I'm going to do to him and her;
I'll pay them back according to their deeds!"

24:26 **A straightforward answer setting things right is a kiss smack on the lips.**

(Proverbs 26:17–28, 24:28, 26)

To speak a word, according to the Older Testament, is like dropping a stone into a pond. Its vibrant sound keeps on working good or ill like concentric ripples reach to the farthest shore. Words are deeds. Words are things that **do** something. Speech can visibly strengthen a human (like vitamins), or even kill somebody (like poison). Lips and tongue and mouth are more than sensitive parts of the anatomy; they are active openings for real blessing and for actual damning to hell (read James 3:1–12).

When the Bible says gossip is

(7) Saul Steinberg, drawing, 25 November 1961

murder, it is not talking metaphorically. Talk that cuts people down to size, usually a notch lower than yourself, is wielding a knife! Unkind words have the solid consistency of blocks thrown in front of people for them to stumble over. As back talk is a slap in the face, and one-way harangue **is** torture, so falsifying accusation—no matter how noble your intention—is HATRED in action.

And those who hate their neighbor, says the Scriptures, do not inherit the kingdom of God (1 John 2:9–11; Galatians 5:13–6:10).

Hateful, loose talk is playing God

Human talk becomes falsifying, evil, and hateful, when it breaks something down, unwilling to assume responsibility for the wreckage, and presumes the prerogatives of God—holy innocence and a kind of absolute judgment.

It can be the premeditated lie. When a man or woman betrays a confidence to one's own advantage and then acts surprised at the harm done, you have something devilishly cheap going on. When a man or woman acts uncommonly gracious, courteous to a fault, meanwhile watching for a vulnerable spot in order to hurt someone there, you have the old, paradise snake-cunning afoot that brings disruption and a shattered world. Whenever there is guile and the double cross among people, says Proverbs 26, especially to get even with somebody, there is cursing at work! And cursing never builds up. Cursing also is always more serious than mere improper human conduct, because men and women who curse play God.

People who have to have the last word in an argument, play God too. Constant bickering in a marriage (Proverbs 25:24), in a family (Ephesians 6:4), in the professional philosophy journals, our tradition of political diatribe, and church disputes that never end, with charges and countercharges: at the core, it is all a matter of face-saving and face-smashing, communications of hate, a cursing that plagues all involved. Such obstinate verbal murder comes about because each party will not admit its own complicity in the trouble, and cannot rest with the fact that the Lord is at hand! and after the truth is spoken firmly in love, the LORD will judge the things not seen too, whether they be good or evil (cf. Philippians 4:4–7, Ecclesiastes 12:13–14). To keep on and keep on jabbering about how right you are and how wrong the other fellow is, *Proverbs* reveals what it is: falsifying accusation—even if you are technically correct. Such pride in speech God Almighty does not brook, and cannot bless.

Loose talk and meddlesome critique are more of the same—so commonplace it is respectable for passing the time of day. Christians, too, often seem to specialize in easy answers for other people, berating even their fellow believers for shallowness of vision (instead of making every man or woman jealous for a full life in Christ, covenanted to God in God Almighty's creation; cf. Romans 11:11). But judgment *en passant* is still manslaughter, whose roots is a humanism that assumes for man an undefined authority, self-righteously certain and unattached.

Whenever critique is spoken out **not** within a definite office as magistrate, parent, pastor, friends, business associate, student, or whatever, limited by and relevant to exercise of that office, you get the kind of critique Jesus Christ forbids—Do not judge lest you yourself be judged, you false god (Matthew 7:1–5)! That means: when church pastors pontificate on styles of art, outside of preaching with aesthetic normativity, and students demonstrate to right political evils, while letting their studies slide, and theoretical philosophers have nostra for social ills, but no shalom in their theories, then you have a meddlesome theatre of the absurd on your hands that can bring no healing insight, because the critique is cheap! Men and women playing god rather than being obedient in their calling.

The Spirit of Humanism, in the name of Humanity, wipes out orderly clusters of creatural authority and would have "the people" solve "world problems"; it encourages every woman and man on the street to settle every problem on the street, especially by talk. And this nonsense, says our passage, bloats the tongue with indiscriminate speech that can only lead to dogs biting hands that grab at them. No follower of Christ should get sucked into such godless trouble-making, grave-digging, with the ruin that inescapably shall boomerang all around....

The kiss of loving, insightful speech

Instead, the direction Proverbs 26 and appendix to 24 posits is this: let your speech and critical judgment (every sensation, really; cf. Philippians 1:9–11) be straightforward, that is, straightening, setting straight what is crooked, a tempered, genuine kiss of love that seals your neighbor to the norms of the Lord. Let your talk lead others in what is right without the compulsive nervousness of pseudo-godly needing to be the absolute authority. Speak "yes" and "no," discriminate what is wrong and what is pleasing to God, using language that is existentially aware it is not emotional persuasion, logically boxing someone into a corner, or banging a table into submission that counts, but that one's words must be talk through which the Holy Spirit can convict people's hearts. Only then does talk become an unhypocritical, holy kiss on the lips.

The gladsome hope Proverbs 26 brings believers is that they are freed from making falsifying accusations to defend themselves, freed from weasel words, bombast, slippery answers, and vengeful responses. God takes care of liars, and we do not need to save the world. Children of God who hear this Proverb passage may exult that their calling is neither the lukewarm tolerance, fearful of saying "Thus says the LORD!" nor the positivist's barefaced "honesty" that blurts out facts like a Judas-kiss to expose your neighbor and kill the possibility of fruitful relationships. The Holy Spirit will lead Christ's followers to testify of God's ordinances in ways that reconcile, if we are contrite at heart (cf. Luke 12:1–12, 2 Corinthians 5:17–19, Matthew 5:3–9).

The Newer Testament "Amen" to our passage is very clear:

If a man seems to be so pious but never holds his tongue in check, that fellow is fooling himself: his pious concern is hot air! Rather, uncorrupted and undeformed piety before God the Father is this: to look out for the fatherless and unmarried, take care of them in their oppressed circumstances; to hold yourself guardedly uncontaminated by the world. (James 1:26–27)

Uncontaminated by the violent, meddlesome, loveless, raping language of current secularity, with all its meanness and death. Openly alive to giving your neighbor a holy spirited kiss on the lips, smack from the richness of Scripture.

[*VANGUARD*, April/May 1973, 24–25, 31]

7. Tomorrow is a Gift of the LORD

If you are willing to turn this small volume into a study exercise: before you continue, first read through Proverbs 27:1–11 in your favorite translation and write down in your own words what you think the verses mean. Then compare your own digest to what is presented here, and maybe write me what you think.

Please read the following passage out loud, very slowly, listening to its intonation. As Buber said, the Scriptures are meant to be heard.

¹ **Don't start congratulating yourself on the fact that tomorrow is coming up,**
   because you don't really know, do you? what your tomorrow will bring.

² [Better] let somebody who doesn't belong to your kind say how good you are, not your own mouth –
   yes, let "the strange fellow" glory in your accomplishments, not your own lips!

³ Stones don't give, and wet sand hangs heavy [on your feet],
   but the unresponsive obstinacy of a godless fellow is more burdensome than both.

⁴ [Never forget:] the cruelty of raging anger and the rush of overflowing scorn [gradually subside];
   but who could ever stand up to the jealousy [of God]!

⁵ **A love that can openheartedly set things straight**
   is much better than one that stays all choked up.

⁶ You can trust the bruising caused by someone who really loves you,
   but all the kisses of one who hates you are superfluous.

⁷ A person who is completely filled will turn up the nose at the sweetest honey,
   but to a man or woman who is hungry, even what is bitter tastes sweet.

⁸ Like a stray bird fluttering distractedly far away from its nest,
   so bewildered is the person who wandering around has lost their place.

⁹ Sweet-smelling oils and lighted incense make you merry deep down;
   so does the sweetness of a person's close friend, because of his or her heart-to-heart talk and counsel.

¹⁰ [So] don't let your fellow friend down; don't leave your friend of the family in the lurch,
   and then run over to your brother's house when your own day of trouble comes:
   a neighbor who is close to you is better than a brother hard to reach.

¹¹ Do become wise, my child, and make my heart joyful!
    so that I may have the word to counter the one
      who taunts me....

                                 (Proverbs 27:1–11)

Too many of us, I am afraid, have been brainwashed into reading Scriptural *Proverbs* like a commonplace book of pithy observations that ring true to life once you stop and think about them. And often, if we happen to be orthodox believers, we are very happy to have these insights in the Bible, because they are so handy for proving a point you want to make; after all, who can argue with a proverb backed up by the Holy Spirit's infallibility.

But to use Scripture unwittingly this way, I believe, has lost us its special revelation and deeply reforming dimension. Even if you show how a given text here and there ties in directly with Jesus Christ's gift of salvation, such a method of reading *Proverbs* has ripped to pieces the imperative seam of Scripture and made its rich directive and healing comfort powerless ("of none effect," says the King James translation). Like a hypocrite then, one is apt to teach earnestly the "traditions of men" as the commandments of God (read carefully Matthew 15:1–9).

The Older Testament *Proverbs* are *not* a collection of atomic protocol sentences that formulate the folk wisdom of Israel about ordinary life and punctuate, for our edification, its common-sense realism with pious pledges of allegiance to Yahweh. No. Instead, as Scripture itself says, these clusters of "artful comparisons" (*meshalim*) composed by the LORD's servant Solomon (Proverbs 1:1, 10:1, 25:1) and other learned wise men and women (22:17, 30:1, 31:1) is of a piece with the rest of Scripture, which is a true account of *magnalia Dei,* the Great Deeds of the LORD! and is a way the very begotten Wisdom of Almighty Yahweh calls to Life whoever has ears to hear (8:22–36, 1–21; 1:20–33). That is, the fear of the LORD and the understanding of God's workings, which *Proverbs* itself says is its point (1:2–6, 7; 22:17–19), must be the key to our actual listening attention. Otherwise the compelling (kerygmatic) texture and claim of its storied narrative unravels into propositional fact and advice.

For example, one could hear the verses of Proverbs 27 something like this: Do not count your chickens before they hatch, since a man's hubris is dealt with severely (27:1). Modesty becomes a man, and humility is a virtue (27:2). The pigheadedness of a fool is worse than obdurate sand and stone (27:3). Jealousy is even more difficult than anger to cope with; so stay out of any triangular love affairs (27:4), etc.

To read Scripture this way seems to me to be the most pitiable of all undertakings. Where is the hope and the joy and the judgment of hearing one's Creator or heavenly Father talk to you?

Proverbs is God speaking directly to us

Rather, one should read the four-verse paragraph beginning chapter 27 while hearing Proverbs 25:21–22 ring in the back of your mind, which sounds the dominant note for the whole large section of chapters 25–27: the Lord God will finish things off! Yahweh shall shalom your broken deeds! **The Covenanting God will make complete and whole the witness, work, and speech of God's people!**

And this glorious promise of 25:22 gets its vibrant pulse from 1:7, which sets the tone of the whole book: unconditional recognition of God Almighty's faithful Rule (= fear of the Lord) is the starting point of wisdom; and to scorn such disciplining is the mark of a fool (= godless man or woman).

Read the verses in paragraphs

So when you pick up chapter 27 and start reading, you hear the Good News: I, the Lord God Yahweh, attend you with daily bread and establish the work of your faithful hands or, with a sorrowful anger, pick up the pieces of your wasted life. Don't take your cue from those who are strangers to my jealous love that hovers over you, Israel, day by day! Don't think you can go it alone if you calculate carefully, make conservative estimates, and plan for tomorrow's success.

Those who go it alone perish alone, as fools. You need not worry about tomorrow's evil, my people, and cut out that self-reliance that creeps every day into your business. I am the same yesterday, today and tomorrow, and hold you tightly by the hand so that the good works I set for you to walk in shall indeed take place. . . .

And then our passage continues with Solomon's literary artistry as mouthpiece for the Lord: your setbacks, my children, are not accidents —pour out your heart to me!—but are the cords of my love, believe me! (27:5–6). You will not be able to hear my voice if you are trying so hard to take care of yourself, but stop it! find out what your appointed service as my adopted son or daughter is so that you will be at home in my world. (27:7–8)

Get past treating friendship like a hedonist frill, and build up your communion of fallback trust beyond your blood relatives: a neighbor of kindred spirit and a friend who sticks closer than a brother is the beginning of a peoplehood of Wisdom. And I want you children of believing Abraham to be children of Wisdom, so I may *show* the Accuser of my Rule straightened-out life (= righteousness) at work (27:9–11).

Overhear the God-focus

Nothing less than God's impassioned speech comes at us in Proverbs 27: God's Name is at stake in how we live. Every phrase is freighted with the cosmic-historical, critically-redemptive faithfulness of God's love command to obedience.

TOMORROW in Scripture (27:1) is "the day that the Lord has made" (Genesis 11–2:3, Matthew 6:24–34), not just another neutral twenty-four hours. *STRANGER* in Scripture (27:2) is somebody strange-**to-God**, ignorant of God's creational-covenantal love bonds, prone to perversity (e.g., Proverbs 5:15–23 and cf. Galatians 4:1–7), not just somebody you are unacquainted with. *FOOL* in Scripture (27:3) is not just some joker or coxcomb able to make you laugh, but is a dreadfully serious offence— anyone who pretends God is not there (for example, compare Romans 1:18–25 and Psalm 14). *JEALOUSY* in Scripture (27:4) is not just some petty, bitchy fickleness, but reveals the terrible, almighty, constant, se-lective edge to Yahweh's love for God's people (Exodus 20:1–7, Song of Songs 8:6–7, Hebrews 12:18–29). And so on.

You have debased the Bible if you think it spends time just piously informing us that quarreling lovers should get things out into the open (27:5) and parental use of the rod is good for us (27:6), that hunger is the best cook (27:7), and displaced persons or homesick people are like lost birds (27:8). That makes a farce of the Bible God has put into our hands.

Passages in a chapter of *Proverbs* are often commentary on other passages

Proverbs 27:5–8 is God-breathed commentary on 27:1–4 and tells us to be responsive to God's leading, not foolishly unresponsive like stones and dirt, but to go ahead and plead with the LORD familiarly, to take hold of God and literally pull God around to face your needs (cf. Luke 18:1–8) because truly, whom God sometimes touches with hard-ship God loves with an everlasting love (Proverbs 3:11–12, Hebrews 12:4–11). If you are satisfied with yourself, closed and hardened to the fact that your food is manna from heaven and your work is meant to be a calling in the King's royal service (1 Peter 2:1–10), then "tomorrow" and even any success will be an everlasting distraction, ruining you, turning you into a creatural fugitive.

That is, the focus of Proverbs 27:1–4 and 5–8 is the wonderful do-ings of the LORD! a revelation of the presence of the LORD's Kingdom Rule right among us, if we only get the eye and ear of faith to receive it (cf. Luke 17:20–21).

Likewise, 27:9–10 is not a brief disquisition on "friendship-in-gen-eral" as Aristotle, Cicero, and Francis Bacon might attempt, a "moral discourse" on how leisurely, confidential talk between staunch friends, with wine and candlelight, ennobles your quality of life. Again, No! Al-ready in Proverbs 27:9–10, at the time of Solomon's expansive business deals with Hiram of Tyre (1 Kings 5) and his luxury trade with Egypt (1 Kings 10:14–29, cf. forbidden, in Deuteronomy 17:14–17), the LORD was sounding a little note against the Jewish racist pride of Abrahamic blood that later grew into such a stumbling block to Christ's ministry and growth of the early Apostolic church (Matthew 3:7–12, John 8:30–47, Acts 6:1, Galatians 2:11–21): troth cemented in Wisdom is thicker than blood—I want you to become *wise*! (27:11)—and is a model for the responsible brotherhood and sisterhood and neighbor-love that shall flow freely from those who know that Yahweh is absolute LORD of the morrow (1 John 2:9–11, Mark 12:29–31).

A Reformational in-depth christian reading of Scripture

Now it is this "Wisdom-focus" of Proverbs 27:1–11, and the intrinsically coram Deo, proclamatory grabbing of the reader to face its special, direct-from-God *(theopneustos)* bite, which the biblical writings have as a whole, that my Toronto colleague, James Olthuis at the Institute for Christian Studies, calls "the confessional focus" of Holy Scripture. He is not saying the Bible is simply a human confession about God's dealings with humankind in history.

Olthuis means that the biblical Word has as its defining character the power to redirect and inform our sinful lives not by giving us bits of information, but by **republishing, with full and total authority primed for confessional response, the Certain Way of Life.** God's biblical Word tells us again how the Almighty God of heaven and earth wants us to walk as God's creatures with God. And Scripture does that by opening our human eyes, made new in accepting Jesus Christ as Lord, to the confessable reality of the LORD God's reconciling Rule of historical creation (cf. 2 Corinthians 5:17–19).

For example, in plain language: the Older Testament Song of Songs reveals the meaning of man-and-woman love as God creationally ordered it to be. God spoke that book for us in a setting critical of Solomon's faithless debauchery (cf. 1 Kings 11:1–13), and had the book artistically composed, almost like an oratorio, to do justice to the nuances of a sexually matured woman and man's betrothed attachment on earth (cf. my *The Greatest Song* [Tuppence Press, 1967]).

The Song of Songs is not a typological tract about Jesus Christ any more than it is a manual of sex education for engaged couples. The biblical Song of Songs proclaims that the to-be-married love bond is God's doing! God's ordinance of bodied troth (among those eulogized by Psalm 119) is what we are called to gratefully live within, exploring the delight of our sexual creatureliness (or disintegratedly die within). And there should be no doubt in anybody's mind, especially in our day of perverse eroticism, that to have the rich normality of a concrete marriage is a Great Deed of the LORD! as big as getting the Israelites through the Red Sea on dry ground, centuries ago. The biblical Song of Songs gives us such specific life-direction.

Tomorrow—

And *Proverbs* too is pregnant with such comforting, challenging Wisdom (remember chapter 8!). Chapter 27 says: **Tomorrow is a gift of the Lord!**

Let no one say that such a reformationally Christian reading of Proverbs 27:1–11 empties the words of confessable! factual meaning, and leaves one with formulae or generalities. *Tomorrow* is as specific and real as the weather when you wake up, and *strangers* are as concrete as your gimmick salesmen on TV; *fool* is as relevant as the man or woman who believes their daily paper gives them news! and *jealousy* is as factual as the twilight of western civilization—if you have biblically tuned ears. That tomorrow is literally a gift of the jealous Lord is simply astounding good news for those who take God at God's Word in the presence of the millions of strangers and fools in North America.

It is the stilted poverty of our devotions (can you hear God talking in Proverbs 27:5 above without crying!?), the self-pitying lament at our difficulties, the terrible pseudo-assurances we take from purposeless routine, and the deep bewilderment we often have at what's happening to the dollar, old-fashioned decorum, and the world situation that stops us from being re-formed to hear and believe this Good News of Proverb 27: **tomorrow is a gift of the Lord!** Tomorrow is not a matter of positivist fact. To have a tomorrow is a Christian faith-reality (cf. refrain in Proverbs 23:17–18, 24:14, 20), and to pick up tomorrow with a confession of genuine thanksgiving is our happy task.

> You people who keep on saying, "Today or tomorrow we're taking off for this or that city and we're going to stay there for a year, do some business and make some money"—don't kid yourself! What do people like you know about tomorrow! and what sort of life will be yours? Actually, you are just a breath of hot air that shows up briefly and disappears.
>
> Instead, come to say, "If it please the Lord and we are alive, we shall be doing this or that...." But now, you are showing off self-certainty in your thoughtless claptrap! And all such self-certainty [about tomorrow] is living in sin.... (James 4:13–16)

Tomorrow is not something you must have mastered, says the Word of God, and is not something you can presume to case. **Tomorrow is a gift of the Lord!** for you, discouraged on your sick bed, or business man with your airplane ticket, student hesitant about a new year of study, craftsman laborer with too many bills to pay, woman uncomfortably filled with child, young person in the bloom of health—Proverbs 27 declares that tomorrow is a gift of the Lord! and that Good News is utterly certain. All we need do is hear it confessingly, and pick it up trustfully, with obedient fear and trembling joy.[1]

[*VANGUARD* August 1973, 24–26]

(8) David Versluis, Enlaced: A Burning Bush, 2011

---

1 Maybe some of you think I'm making it difficult to read the Bible. You mean I can't just pick up Proverbs 27 and start reading it! Do I have to read Proverbs 25–27 first, learn about the centrality of Proverbs 1:7, the subordinate focusing character of 25:21–22, think about James 4 etcetera before I'm done? Good night, I'll need a specialist like a theologian, at least a priest or a preacher, to do all that. Where would I get the time?—I have to earn a living! Are you saying I have to *search* the Scriptures in this Reformational Christian way before I know what they are saying?

(1) Now please reread the translation of Proverbs 27 above. This passage has grown on me as I struggled to hear *its* message in the chorus of the entire book, the Older Testament, and the whole Bible. That takes time. (2) The leaders of God's people, whose professional task it is to *open up the Scriptures* rather than close them with an uncritically inherited, positivistic theory of knowledge hidden behind the club of a Victorian ethic, will have to make their own account with the Lord. (3) You who have taken the time to follow me this far should realize the seriousness of what we are doing and take heart, for it is true, also in reading the Bible: "Whoever knows what the good is and doesn't do it—that business has become sin for them!" (James 4:17).

8. Don't Play Savior for Your Neighbor

To understand the pinpointing yet large significance of Proverbs 27:12 you need to recognize that 27:13 is a quote referring to a long-standing counsel of Wisdom against being guarantee for a stranger, or even your neighbor.

> ¹² **The cautiously wise fellow sees bad, wasteful trouble coming**
> **and hides himself, gets out of the way:**
> **unexperienced people, however, walk right on into it**
> **and pay the price.**
> ¹³ [Remember:]
> "Take his clothes if he stands surety for a stranger;
> if he makes the pledge for a strange woman, grab *him* as the
> bail." (27:12–13)

That forbidding directive quoted to make the point about "wisdom" and "inexperience" recurs in the various sections of *Proverbs*:

> ¹¹:¹⁵You will really suffer serious evil and trouble if
> you have gone bond for a strange fellow:
> but if you shun such offhand pledges of trust,
> then you may live with a quietly reliable certainty.

> ¹⁷:¹⁸ A man who binds himself with a handshake
> to be substitute security for his neighbor
> simply lacks faith-guts.

Even association with those who try to cut corners and are free and easy with their pledges of security is appealed to:

> ²²:²⁶ Don't become one of those glad-handers
> who stand guarantee for a shady loan:
> ²⁷ suppose you can't pay up?
> why have them take your bed from underneath you?

And if you unfortunately were rash, and did not avoid the entanglement of becoming the bond for somebody who is defaulting:

> ⁶:¹ Listen, my child,
> if you ever become the bond yourself for your neighbor,
> if you have given your hand to be security for somebody else,
> a stranger,
> ² gotten tripped up by your own tongue,
> that is, caught by the words of your mouth:
> ³ get busy, my child, so you get yourself out of it!
> for you have come to be completely in the power
> of your neighbor, the "other" person!
> Go sweat it hard! wear your fellow neighbor out!
> ⁴ don't let your eyes shut in sleep—don't let your eyelids
> drowsily blink—
> get yourself out of hock!

⁵ like a gazelle slips out of the [hunter's] hand
  or a bird escapes the clutches of the bird-catcher....

The fervor of Proverbs 6 for getting yourself out of this bind, and the unqualified judgment (17:18) upon those who substitute their own selves to be responsible for the plight of their neighbor—"that person simply lacks faith-guts! (= heart, insightful wisdom)—may strike the modern reader as quite strange. Aren't we supposed to love our neighbor? give to him or her whatever they need? (Luke 6:27–38), go to bat for the neighbor? walk the second mile? (Matthew 5:38–42). Is this Proverb's reproof about bond and bail, surety, security, standing guarantee, not simply a tradition of civil law the Israelites had, reported to us in the "old" testament, and no longer really authoritative for children of God in the "new" testament era? Is not this reluctance to vouch for a bad risk neighbor the kind of Jewishly shrewd business sense Christ freed us from! Why, we evangelical Christians should be ready to die for our drowning, unsaved neighbor, shouldn't we?

There is more than one way to close the book of *Proverbs* to understanding. You can read it like an infallible *Poor Richard's Almanac* of aphorisms, and pick and choose those nuggets that strike your fancy for certain homilies, killing the overwhelming, compelling hope the book gives. But you can also make *Proverbs* a dead letter simply by assuming its *authority* is dated. Then you soon walk around with less than half a Bible, and inevitably come to misunderstand and misrepresent the "Newer Testament" message too. Proverbs 27:12–13 is the Word of the LORD for today as much as it ever was (cf. Psalm 119:105). And only if its older covenanting call is heard can we hear the rich force and directing comfort of, say, Matthew 10:16 with which Jesus Christ sent out his first twelve disciples.

Godly limits to good intentions

But what does *Proverbs* mean by "cautiously wise fellow...gets out of the way" and, do not be surety for another person?

It is a mark of the graciously judging mercy of Almighty God that when God gave Moses on Mount Sinai the light for God's people's pathway, the LORD specified: if you take a poor man's cloak as pawn for the debt he owes, you must return it to him for the night; otherwise, what would he lie on or have with which to keep himself warm (Exodus 22:25–27). The LORD's intense compassion for men and women in their broken histories shows up too in God's disallowing millstones, a man's means of livelihood, from being put in hock as the pledge of making good on a loan, for then you have enslaved the man's life (Deuteronomy 24:6). That is, Yahweh limits what a (powerful) man or woman may demand from their neighbor as security.

And the same covenanting LORD God reveals through Solomon that there are limits to one's pledging allegiance for one's neighbor: you are a presumptuous fool asking for serious evil if you make yourself a possible forfeit for another person's deeds. So men can buy and sell you as slave instead (cf. 2 Kings 4:1). Who are you to pledge so absolutely that you will make good and atone for what another man or woman, neighbor or stranger, fails at!? To act, somewhat thoughtlessly, as if *you* can set things straight, signing your life on the promissory line, as if *you* should assume the office of surety, is not some noble, human gesture but a bankrupt unwisdom. Something inexperienced people do: overcommit themselves to others, often in the flush of good intentions, forgetting that *God* is at hand and directly at work with the Holy Spirit's presence.

Beware of heroics

Proverbs 27:12–13 is getting at something deeper still than suspect business deals and rash alliances, which also cripple God's people so they cannot walk publicly in the light (cf. 1 John 1:5–10). God's Proverb Word here on wisdom, about not selling yourself out as surety for an-other—that is *not* what the LORD requires of you! (cf. Micah 6:6–8)—is a hint, in mirror script, about the One coming who will be the pawn to end all pledges, who shall indeed be able to substitute his life as security to make good for another. Meanwhile, you human, the Good News is: you don't have to guarantee tomorrow: it is a gift of the LORD! (27:1–11). And in all your daily doings, remember, *you* are not to play the savior! *Yahweh* shall finish things off! (25:22).

The Proverbs 27:13 quote sums up the covenanting LORD God's protecting God's people from heroics. Worse than bad deals are commit-ments made to other persons wherein you grandstand (22:26–27), enact it lightly for the nonce (11:15), or where, like an Atlas god, you take all the responsibility on your own broad shoulders (17:18). Counter to ev-ery pagan (and secular) code, such security-giving people, says the Bible, lack guts, are deeply unwise. God takes no more pleasure in "heroic love" than he does in the well-turned leg of a man (Psalm 146:10–11). Yahweh calls us to neighbor service that respects the neighbor as you would your very self, and goes all the way up to giving even your enemy food (Prov-erbs 25:21) so long as you do not preempt the neighbor's hoping in the LORD to redeem him or her from their misery, or waylay yourself into the godless position of being final security for an other man or woman.

This means that Judah was not an early type of Christ when he of-fered himself as bond for Benjamin (Genesis 43:1–14, 44:18–34) but, rather, a desperate man trying to make good for an earlier evil in a way our *Proverbs* passages warn you should try to escape as importunately as the widow pleaded before the unjust judge (Proverbs 6:1–5, Luke 18:1–8). It means that John 15:13 is not recommending we should be prepared to lay down our life for our friend if we really love him: that would be reading Scripture like a Humanist who has never heard that Proverbs 27:12–13 is in the Bible, and foists off on unsuspecting innocents abroad, in the name of New Testament Christianity, a humanitarian type love that knows no limits, that puffs 70x7 confessional forbearance into a religion-ethic with no cutoff points, where *you* must be the expiation for your neighbor on pain of lovelessness.

But, No, says *Proverbs. Christ!* through God's foolishness (which is wiser than any human's calculation) went in hock for us (Hebrews 7:22), so that Christ's followers need not emulate his example and play mediator in daily life; but, as a forgiven people securely preach and practice the healing love of forgiveness among men and women (John 15:9–17). Making-things-whole (giving shalom), as well as vengeance, belongs only to the Lord (Proverbs 25:22, Romans 12:9–21, Philippians 4:4–7). It is redeemed wisdom, not to play god, also not to act like a Christ toward your neighbor; but when things "strange-to-God" like temptation, shaped as a lion or as an angel of light, or whatever is ominously beyond the limits of your calling, appears, it is redeemed wisdom to get out of the way. To face such matters as angels fear to meet, and figure you will walk in, shoot from the hip, and let the chips fall where they may, does not honor the Lord. That is what simple Simons do.

Circumspect discernment

Do you mean Proverbs 27:12–13 supports the cautious conservatism of never sticking out your neck or putting yourself on the line for your neighbor and God?

Not at all. That clever excusing of oneself from the passion of faith is built on the old, well-known legacy of *prudence,* which has artfully covered up the old pagan heroics with a pragmatistic sense of win-rather-than-lose, in the name of Christ, of course. And such worldly-wise "prudence" kills biblical obedience.

The circumspective discernment and tempered action that pleases God, according to Proverbs 27:12–13 and Matthew 10:16, is this: Be as non-Messiah-like as a snake in your prophetic enacting of the Rule of the Lord, and be as innocent as a dove in living the Christian life, exercising forgiveness toward men and women (cf. Matthew 10:5–11). Such selfless, seasoned and trustworthy wisdom, patiently waiting on the Lord while working hard to claim the Lord's blessing, is the mark of a Christian who has Proverbs 27 in one's Bible. The Way of shalom is not to be warring and standing bail for your neighbor, but to practice forgiveness, build up God's people, and praise the Lord—even if it costs us our livelihood and life like sheep among wolves.

Note:

The cautiously wise fellow sees coming so many shopping days before Christmas and goes in hiding (although it is difficult to find even a catacomb or a church free from co-opted advertisement about Christmas cheer and putting Christ back into Christmas). A person's inexperienced kids, however, may walk right on into the trap of getting presents, and pay the price.

If you and your children stand surety for the Madison Avenue economy, if you pledge your Christmas break to "whetting the whistle," or are quite content with the Robert Shaw Chorale's singing "Silent Night" with the six o'clock news, the Lord will grab *you* as the bail.

Christmas means Christ went in hock for us so that we and our neighbor need not be sold down the river. It will take some imaginative preparation in our evil, secularized age to celebrate that fact with a birthday party of joy. That is what advent is for.

[*VANGUARD* December 1973, 30–31]

9. Do Not Kill Dead Horses, But Love Your Neighbor Face to Face

Proverbs 27 again:

14 The booming voiced "God-bless-you-neighbor!" fellow
    who does it eager beaver much too early in the morning,
    should know it counts like a curse coming from him.
15 And a woman who keeps on, keeps on bemoaning her point
    is like the dribbling drivel of a leaky roof on a day of pounding
        rain:
16 to stop it up would be like holding back condensing moisture—
    dirty globs of vapor is all your hand makes contact with.

17 **"Iron gets sharpened by scraping with other flinty iron,"**
    but let a man's face be sweetly joined to that of his neighbor.
19 **As in the water faces mirror faces sheer,**
    just so let the hearts of men and women reverberate
        when near.

20 The grave and hell never get fed up with destroying things;
    neither do the eyes of man or woman ever get tired of desiring
        more and more.
21 Well, a melting pot takes care of silver, and a blast furnace
        dissolves your gold,
    and a human vaporizes before the fulsome, honoring praise
        [of the crowd].
22 Even if you pound such a fool of a man to pieces with a pestle in
        the mortar
    right along with the pulverized kernels of corn,
    his blubbering, closed-to-God stupidity will not at all
        be separated out.

23 **Get to know them thoroughly—of course(!);—study the**
        actual condition of your sheep and goats intently;
        put your heart into tending the herds!
24 [It's true:] "Treasure never lasts forever"—
    even a king's crown doesn't make it through many generations!

25 Hay has to be cut, tender spring grass get shorn,
    and sweet mountain pasture raked into the garner;
26 lambs are there…for your clothing,
    and a goodly number of rams makes the price of a piece
        of open field;
27 given enough milk from the goats, you have daily bread,
    food for the household, and a livelihood for your maidservants:
18 **Whoever keeps on watchfully caring for a fig tree will eat its**
        fruits, and
    Whoever respectfully keeps track of things for one's lord
        will receive honor and glory.

(Proverbs 27:14–17, 19–27, 18)

Some people who witness make a nuisance of themselves. They come on like a cold shower, when the person who receives the attention was expecting simply a warm, spring rain. And some people, man or woman, persist in making their point long after it has been made. It happens in the family setting, between those who are married, on the job with your boss, and sometimes during a Sunday sermon. An old Arabian saying calls it "killing a dead horse."

Such abrasive, obstinate folk tend to justify their one-track selves, points out Proverbs 27. "Iron gets sharpened by scraping with other flinty iron." Stand up and be counted like a man! You can't cut dead wood! If you can't take the heat, get out of the kitchen! If you understand what's up, why don't you do it?

No, says the Bible. To love your neighbor means to mirror his or her face with yours so that you can be joined! Until you have a heart-to-heart openness and sensitivity for your neighbor's need, any witness, point, or help you want to give, in Christ's name too, will only look like a tough-minded establishing of your own self. It may take iron to sharpen iron, but a child's face in school and your husband's hurt ambition and a lonely woman's hand is not a piece of iron.

The same holds true for the human relation to plants and animals in God's world, says Proverbs 27. Like the grave keeps on swallowing what God made good, just so covetous human desiring of forests and seas, food and minerals and space, never tires of their destructions. Curiosity killed the cat. Well, human greed vaporizes a man and a woman into a hurried, evil snort *and* rapes the world. This is so no matter how much the blubbering sales pitch and seductive color advertisements get exposed for their stupidity.

The pride to reach the moon first (so everything got shipped air-mail and pay was constant overtime) rather than feed the poor, even in America, was a Babel foolishness that is boomeranging on more than the Hearst family.[1] And the corner supermarket for us supermen and wonder women who want convenience, has largely killed in suburban and metropolitan chain-stored humans the knowledge of produce fresh like manna from the Lord's bountiful hand. Instead, we come armed with the snowmobile-thrill mentality that treats field and stream and all wild life as if it too were iron.

---

1 Patty Hearst, heiress of the extremely wealthy Hearst publisher family, was kidnapped in 1974 in Berkeley by "the Symbionese Liberation Army" radicals, who Robinhood-like forced the Hearsts to make food available to the poor. Patty Hearst took part in a San Francisco bank robbery by the SLA, was caught in 1975, and served 2 years of a prison sentence before her sentence was commuted by President Jimmy Carter in 1979.

Not sharpening iron, but sharing weakness

Proverbs 27, however, is not a brief for the Rousseauean world of friendly brotherhood, idyllic fishing trips to Northern Canada, and a generally relaxed, connoisseur attitude toward fellow humans and homeland. God's Word has *blessing to* give! not just exit signs for our secularized life.

Put your heart into tending the sheep and goats—thank God for such biblical revelation! "Treasure never lasts forever"; so don't push to stack up possessions in a big new barn, or bank vault (and Solomon adds the ironic commentary—even a king's crown doesn't last through too many generations). But mountain pasture, the lamb and fig tree, are there for your respectful use and to enjoy forever, says Proverbs 27. Give yourself wholeheartedly to the task at hand of milking goats, polishing woodwork, setting the children's consciousness to praise the Lord, analyzing Kant, selling real estate, protecting the helpless from violence.

> "I'm telling you, the one good thing I saw, a wonderful good! is eating, drinking, finding joy inside all the miserably hard work a man sweats at daily under the sun for the so few days of life God gives him. It's a wonderful good! allotted him—I mean this: whatever money or possession God has given him, everyone who is enabled—this is *God's* giving!—enabled to eat from it, enabled to freely, fully, actively receive what God has specially portioned out for them, who is enabled to be genuinely happy in our sin-cursed laboring—that is a wonderful good! because then a man or a woman does not cumber oneself so much thinking about the meager span of one's lifetime: God keeps him or her preoccupied with a heart full of gladness!" (Ecclesiastes 5:18–20)

To work with integrity at cultivating what the LORD has created is a livelihood! a living, lively man and womanhooded calling of obedience, which the LORD shall establish by God's Word, and use to proclaim salvation. That is the promise of Proverbs 27: whoever faces one's neighbor in love, and puts one's heart into tending the sheep and goats for our Lord, will receive honor and glory, power and dominion, forever and ever, when the Son of God returns.

The Newer Testament Amen to Proverbs 27 resounds in many places—James 3, Luke 12, Matthew 25. But there are especially two things that must be said:

(1) Nobody may preach the good news of Proverbs 27 about work if you do not lift a finger to make the dehumanizing jobs one's hearers suffer under today into tasks the Lord could fill with shalom, albeit in the presence of enemies. Otherwise it will be the Pharisaic preaching that binds guilt on people's shoulders, and treats believers as if they be heavenly souls with iron bodies.

And nobody may buy and sell houses or teach philosophy mindlessly following the speculators' price of gold and land and secular university techniques; for then that person has denied the Lord's claim on God's modern-day pasture and goatherd and become a foolish, faithless steward, good for nothing!

(2) Indeed, our face must mirror the face of our neighbor, and not vice versa, if we wish to show Christian love. Paul said he found peace in restraining the exercise of his Christianly disciplined freedom in order to bring Life to those who were legalists (1 Corinthians 9:12–23). (To "become all things to all men" does not mean "when in Rome, do as the Romans do"!] Proverbs 27 asks even more from those who have found themselves as creatures in Christ: get past your own preoccupations and unimaginative, uncritical, selfish position of security, if you would indeed love those for whom Christ died.

Do not pray for the sick in church, but prepare their meals. Do not talk to the lonely, but play games with them. Do not take a collection for the poor without fasting in prayer so you will know how to present the gift to them with a broken spirit. Do not talk about love to those who lack comeliness unless you are prepared to enjoy their presence. Do not presume to teach the ignorant if you are not truly ready yourself to learn from them. Do not try to comfort the dying unless you are ready to be absent from earth with the Lord yourself. Do not try to walk the first mile with somebody unless the first mile has second mile character, face to face....

I know, even we Christians tend to shut out of our seeing and hearing whatever of God's Word would really change our own particular lifestyle and sloughed off habits. But whoever hears Proverbs 27 and continues to treat our neighbor like iron or dirt and to use the world at large as a disposable diaper, grieves the Holy Spirit.

[*Vanguard*, March–April 1974, 24–25]

10. The Topsy-Turvy World of Faith, or God's Word for Those "In Authority"

Proverbs 28–29, which concludes the section Hezekiah's wise men and women counselors were led by the Lord to copy over from Solomon's "artful comparisons" (25:1), appropriately emphasizes **ruling people**. Secretary of State Shebna, in Hezekiah's reform administration, naturally wanted whatever Word of the LORD he could get from those archives to help him train the princes of Judah to run a borough of Jerusalem, or deal with envoys of Assyria, Egypt, and neighboring strong-arm kings. So we should consider Proverbs 25–29, and especially the last two chapters—remember, John did not record everything Jesus did, but was led to write down what would convict us that Jesus is the Messiah and that we have life in the name of Christ (John 21:25, 20:30–31)—as telling us certain selected wisdom God gave Solomon about governing, which the counselors of King Hezekiah edited under the leading of the Spirit around 700 BC, so that we who have authority today may bear witness to the Truth rather than follow the Lie.

When you read the first section of Proverbs 28 translated here, imagine yourself being spoken to as your country's ambassador to some South American nation, or as a newly-elected legislator in Washington D.C., or as a member of the Metro Council in Toronto. As I pointed out in treating Proverbs 25:2–10, this Scripture holds for anybody with authority over somebody else. But we have such a sloughed-off idea of the office of governing, we seldom realize the terrible ruling responsibility proper to being parents, secretaries, salesmen, or even students wanting a share of academic administrative power. To make laws, execute justice, and set the limits for your neighbor's actions—of whatever sort—is never a picnic. In fact, wielding authority is a matter of heaven or hell (cf. 2 Samuel 23:1–7). To help sharpen us up to that reality in the setting of Proverbs 28:1–14, it would be good to hear it as a civil servant, store manager, mortgage loan officer in a bank, someone "in authority...."

1   **Wrongdoers run away, even if there's no chasing going on:**
       those who do what is right stand their ground unafraid, like
       a young lion.
2   If a country is swamped by lawless revolt,
       it will suffer through many too many leaders:
       but under a person who has deeply knowing discerning insight,
       what is lawfully right can hold on for a long, long time;
3   [however,] a churlish strongman who cruelly burdens
       the poor and defenseless
       is like a raining downpour that washouts the land
       so there is no food possible.
4   **Those who leave keeping-the-Law behind, start appreciating**
       some wrongdoing;

but those who are concerned to obey Law-wisdom
take up hand-to-hand combat with those who undermine it.

5   Wicked people simply cannot intuit the right decision
        on what should be done:
     but those who are busy finding the Lord God
     come to understand all kinds of things!

6   A penniless fellow who walks along in his or her integrity
        is better off
        than someone trying crookedly to straddle two ways, even if
        he or she be rich.

7   Whoever keeps the Law-order faithfully will be a child
        with intuitive wisdom:
        but whoever fools around with those who think life is a joke
        shall shame their father and mother.

8   Whoever keeps adding to his belongings by exacting high interest
        and competing with usurious greed
        is really getting it all together for...someone [Yahweh!]
        who shall show mercy to those who are down and out!

9   A person closes their ear to hearing Law-wisdom:
        their prayer—yes, their prayer!—is a dirty, perverted,
        stinking masturbation!

10   Whoever misleads those doing things right
        into a way of evil disaster
        will fall self into the same trap:
        it is the blameless who inherit what's good!

11   A well-to-do man or woman think to themselves they
        are pretty wise,
        but an unimportant fellow who understands what's up sees
        through them.

12   When those who live justly are able to rejoice, the
        festivities are truly great:
     but when wrongdoers win success, a person had better be
     hard to find.

13   Know for sure—
        it will never turn out well for the person
        who intently tries to cover up one's underhanded double-
        dealings:
        only the one who confesses and stops one's guilt-ridden,
        double-crossing deeds
        will receive merciful compassion.

14   Yes, it will go well with the man or woman who is continually
        open in awe [before the Lord]:
     but anyone who stubbornly hardens their heart will slip
     into utter, final misery.

                                              (Proverbs 28:1–14)

The point to this tightly constructed, almost sonnet-shaped passage
is this: wrongdoers are always like chaff that the wind blows to bits, un-

able to decide things so they go right; while those who seek out the Lord are able to stand their ground and become wise about all kinds of things, how to see through what is evil, and how to order things so there be peace…in the streets. Whoever tries to brazen out double-dealing will get broken by the Lord: whoever stops underhanded finagling or even heartless exacting of one's due (cf. Matthew 18:21–35), that person shall receive mercy from the Lord.

Now this doesn't give you a policy for urban development, or supply ordinances for army headquarters, or guidelines for employee bonuses. But Proverbs 28:1–14 does not just describe the Christians' insurance policy benefits that you cash in on at death. God says here: men and women who do not struggle to obey the Law-wisdom of the Lord are accursed, and themselves a living curse to the people they are actually ruling; while those who have insight into the Law of the Lord for governing and business, teaching and success, bring visible, tangible blessing to all those under such leading.

God's Law-wisdom (*torah*)

And what is this "Law-wisdom" that *Proverbs* is constantly telling us about?

It is not identical to the tables of stone in the ark, the "Ten Words" of Grace and light for the walk of God's people (Deuteronomy 10 :1–5). "Law-wisdom" is also not identical with the autographs of Moses, *biblia,* "the Bible," all the holy writings about sacrificial purifications, prescriptions for cities of refuge, remarriage and lawsuits found in the Pentateuch (cf. Deuteronomy 31:24–27 and 2 Kings 22:8). "Law-wisdom" in our Proverbs passage refers particularly to the ordinances of the LORD God Almighty who established by God's Word the heavens and the earth (cf. Genesis 1, Psalm 33:6–9, Hebrews 11:3, 2 Peter 3:1–7). "Law-wisdom" designates here particularly, for example, the bonds God set for the heavens; night and day, seedtime and harvest (cf. Psalm 19:2–7, Psalm 148:5–6, Jeremiah 33:19–26); the patterns of hunger and sexual drives in animal life (referred to in Deuteronomy 25:4, Proverbs 12:10, 1 Timothy 5:18); God' s Let-there-be-justice in dealings among men and women (referred to, e.g., in Exodus 23:4–9, 2 Chronicles 19:4–10, Isaiah 1:10–20); Let-there-be-economical-service of resources for neighbors' needs (referred to, e.g., in Exodus 23:10–12, Deuteronomy 15:1–11, Amos 2:6–8, 3:9–4:13, Isaiah 28:23–29, James 5:1–6); Let-there-be-bonds-of-troth to end man and woman' s solitariness in the feast of fellowship (cf. Genesis 2:18–25, Song of Songs 4:8–5:1, 7:11–8:14, Proverbs 5:15–21); Let-there-be-communal-public-praise-of-Yahweh so there comes a liturgy of orderly tears and laughter dear to the Lord, building up the saints and attracting unbelievers to worship (exemplified in Psalms 66, 107, 118; notice how David's poem was claimed for cultic use, Psalm 51:18–19; cf. 1 Corinthians 14:37–40).

The creational ordinances of God are particularly what "Law-Wisdom" means here in Proverbs 28.

For example, both revolution and tyranny are evils, it says, because they violate the law God laid down to order the body politic; God did not create us for anarchy or perpetual civic immaturity (28:2–3). God said Let-there-be equity and shared responsibility under statutes of justice that hold for rich and poor alike. To start "appreciating" the purging reform in revolution and the "law-and-order" of an enlightened despotism is playing with fire, and courting a permanently breaking-down society rather than a country where people may live unafraid (28:4, 1).

And no economist who ignores the fact that Yahweh set ordinances for fair value, sparing use of resources, tithe and jubilee, for example, it says, can be trusted to invest your money—or direct the world economy (25:5), because such men and women simply *do not know* that a person who makes a fast buck and lives well-off is less happy than an honest workman or woman bringing their family bread and soup. Nor do such men and women know that those who careen through the superstar circuit, who get GMC corporate vice-presidents' salaries, who make "killings" on the stock market or real estate deals at the expense of others, who try to straddle both raping the earth and feeding the starving, are bound to fall shamefully to pieces (28:6–8). And any such wheeler-dealers who try to cover their guilt with large donations to churches are only gratifying themselves in public (28:9).[1] God's Word for those with economic power and authority is not laissez faire, encouraging survival of the fittest competitors, but rather it is this: Let-there-be-thrift on earth among men and women who are pleasing to God so there will be jubilee possible for all!

Self-made men are a disaster in the eyes of those who are wise, because self-made men and women trust in their own strength, and shall neither inherit the earth nor do otherwise than suck the inexperienced down into the same rat trap (28:10–11).

Where to find God's Law-Wisdom

But how, you may ask, and where do I find this law-wisdom *Proverbs* admonishes us to obey as the Word of God, on pain of ruining those in our charge or of enriching their lives as citizens, employees, clients, students, and the like? Where are we to seek the ordinances of God so they may be found? Where does God speak about political, economic, and pedagogical life so we may do it, and bring healing to the helpless, often betrayed, governed peoples of the world?

---

1 If my literal translation of this verse offends any, then they will know how offended God is when the middle-class ignore the poor of the earth, and what God sometimes thinks today of the motto on American dollar bills; cf. 1 John 3:17 and Luke 18:18–30.

And the answer is in Deuteronomy 30, Job 28, James 3:13–4:10… many passages as well as in Proverbs 28–29: the Bible, which is *God's final authoritative Word for directing our total life* (cf. 2 Timothy 3:16–17), pointing us to Jesus Christ; *the Word of God incarnate* who with the Father and the Holy Spirit is the very artificer, ruler, and saving finisher of creation (cf. Colossians 1:15–23, Proverbs 8:22–36). The Bible says that the ways of the Lord are booked in Scripture (cf. e.g., Deuteronomy 30:10) and laid down in the very warp and woof of our creatureliness (cf. e.g., Job 38–39). God's statutes for his creatures are not faraway somewhere, mystically hidden in heaven, but as close at hand as the books of Moses and the letters of Paul, as *visible* as the limited purifying qualities of the oceans, the life-bringing photosynthesis of plants, and the exercise of one's heartbeat (cf. all the Let-there-be ordinances referred to by Scripture cited above; also cf. Deuteronomy 30:11–14, Psalm 119, Romans 1:18–32). Also, **neither Holy Scripture nor the ordinances of God's creation for creatures can be rightly understood unless we be born again, baptized with the Holy Spirit, that is, live in awe before the LORD God** (cf. 1 Corinthians 2:6–16)!

This means (1) God's commandments and ordering for creaturely life is not found only in the Bible. **The Bible is special** because it alone leads us to be convicted of our sin, to repent and be re-directed in Jesus Christ as adopted children of God. In that written Word of God, given us in history by the Holy Spirit to re-direct our lives, are many concrete injunctions the LORD made to Israel, which hold for us who are believing sons and daughters of Abraham today too. And if we cannot read Leviticus **christianly**, for example, so it literally speaks to our habits of eating and drinking and making merry in AD 2019, why then we have dispensationally broken the seamless fabric of Holy Scripture and gnostically disposed of large portions of the "infallible" Older Testament?

But people who think God has spoken to us **only** in the Bible make the biblicistic mistake of the Pharisees, which both Christ and the apostle Paul tried to correct: you search the Scriptures as if **they** will give you eternal life, but then you miss the person who alone is the Way, the Truth, and the Life (cf. John 5:36–47, especially 39–40); you read the Scriptures with a horse-blinder veil over your eyes, and add precept upon precept that constricts newly covenanted lives from praising God in the freedom of the Spirit—shame upon you blind leaders of the blind (2 Corinthians 3:12–18, Luke 11:37–52)! [And many an evangelical communion, I think, parallels orthodox Jewry this way today, substituting for the Talmud an unwritten, but as stringent, code of taboos, mores for dress, liturgy and what not, inhibiting the freedom we have in Christ to serve God daily.] Instead, **once we men and women know Christ maturely as Savior, we may in saintly communion discover the speaking to us in creation at large too.**

This all means (2) **God's ordinances for creaturely life cannot be found and understood as if they be formulae or data won by mere observation. Only** the **righteous** come to see the ways our Covenanting LORD would have us as God's creatures respond to God. Only those who are **wise in Christ**, outfitted with the fruits of the Holy Spirit, whose consciousness breathes out an intimacy with Holy Scripture: only those who trust God, are continually open in awe before the LORD, that is, **walk in wisdom,** shall gain insight into the LORD God's will for political, economic, pedagogical shalom on earth (cf. Job 28:28, Proverbs 28:14, 25–26, and again, 1 Corinthians 2:6–16). And that prerequisite Wisdom is not cheap. In fact, it is not for sale at all. You cannot become wise with a life subscription to the *Christian Courier,* or even by being admitted to the Toronto Institute for Christian Studies. That was the evil expectation of Simon, the converted magician of Samaria (Acts 8:9–24). Wisdom is wholly a gift of God. To those who are repentant, faithful, and diligent in **working out their salvation** with fear and trembling (cf. Philippians 2:12–16).

Practical out-working is complex and crucial

Quite practically: you are not working out your political obedience to the Lord with awe and trembling if you walk into the UN with a New Testament in your vest pocket, but give a thoroughly secular speech. Not even if you sprinkle it with Bible quotes or refer to God a few times (as most U.S. presidential inaugurals do in the last sentence). And you mislead yourself if you think, "I don't Watergate; the system may be bad, but I'm OK, at least I'm doing my best, and that's all God requires of us Christians who are in government...."

No! God requires of you this day to speak out with the mind of Christ, let's say, on offshore fishing rights—where is your statement for the press? And the point of Proverbs 28:1–14 is this: the christian mind on political shalom for fishing rights is not a one-man show, and you don't find the christian answer **in the books of the Bible.** You need a team of Holy Spirited men and women, imbued with Biblical sense, doing historical research on the idea of territorial waters (the three-mile limit arose because that's how far a cannonball could be shot in Hugo Grotius' day), spending time investigating what redemptive action can be taken by political economies locked geographically into basically one commercial product, like Iceland or Chile, and what ordinances of God are violated when strong naval powers and fleets of industrialized trawlers tyrannize local fishermen who are technologically less outfitted, gorging up fish from the sea.... And unless you can speak law-enacting wisdom on the 200-mile offshore fishing-rights limits, the blood of the defenseless poor Chileans, Icelander, and countless others will be required by the Lord from your hand, if you are politically enacted "in authority" near that problem.

Or, take teaching, for example: Wicked people cannot intuit that to treat children like cookie jars needing to be stuffed full with facts so they can get good scholastic aptitude and social cognitive skills test scores is evil, treating children like cookie jars. Also that leaving children to their own "creative" selves in the classroom, as if memorizing fact knowledge and disciplined reading came by charismatic osmosis, is a tandem evil. I dare say that joy in learning is the christian norm for teaching, and teachers had better scramble communally to test and obey whatever God's law be for your profession. Again, you don't direct your search for pedagogical laws into the books of the Bible, turning texts like Proverbs 23:13–14 into backing up corporeal punishment, as if that takes care of christian education. But what God requires is a saintly communion of gifted teachers qualified like the first deacons (cf. Acts 6:3), utterly at home in the Scriptures, working fulltime at probing the creational ordinances of God holding for discovering things, making distinctions, remembering and implementing knowledge wisely, and getting such understanding normatively embodied in specific curricula. Any adult who makes school an authoritarian hell, or a permissive one, a veritable jail term or a wasteful pass-the-time-of-day trip for the young, has pedagogical blood on their hands, that no amount of gratuitous piety and prayer, says Proverbs 28:1–14, can clean away.

If there is one thing this passage makes clear, it is that the prayers we are called upon by the apostle Paul to make for those "in authority," may never be perfunctory (cf. 1 Timothy 2:1–4): too many lives hang on the obedient exercise of such ruling power (cf. also James 3:1).

The hard Biblical truth is good news

One more thing I have to make clear, briefly. Proverbs 28:1–14 tells us how things **are**. This passage, like all Scripture, has the force of **the truth**: it is **good news**…for those who receive it in faith. That's it.

No one may say, "I don't think Proverbs 28:10 is really logical, that persons who are clever enough to lead others into a trap get caught in it themselves." Or, "let's wait and see whether Proverbs 28:13–14 describes what is really so; if Nixon pulls himself together and enjoys his pension,[2] then either he was not guilty or we have to futurize these verses, eschatologically, or make them a kind of hovering, Kantian categorical imperative…."

No! these are ways men and women break the power of God's Word brought to book. Proverbs 28:1–14 does not need propositional tightening or empirical verification! GOD SAYS—and it is a staggering blessing

---

2   As it turned out, Nixon resigned the office of USA president in August 1974 in order to avoid a probable impeachment by the US Congress because of his implication in "the Watergate scandal."

of God's Grace that the Lord talks to us and directs us as specially here as God did to Adam and Eve in the garden!—**wrongdoers are hapless bunglers** and **my children are flourishing here and now as well as in their inheritance.** If you don't *think* so nor *see it* that way ("Unbelievers look pretty knowledgeable to me," or "The godless are doing well, if you ask me"), then you do not know the topsy-turvy world faith inhabits, the *real world* of God's comforting Rule (cf. Psalm 1 and Matthew 5).

To be men and women "in authority" in 2019 AD, as we *all are* somehow, is too much for us to bear, unless we hear the Good News of Proverbs 28: 1–14. Hearing and believing, our urgent publican plea must be: "Lord, give us eyes to see things around us with the look of biblical faith; fill us with your Spirit so we get enough courage and wisdom to band together as your children, busy ferreting out and keeping your Law-wisdom, so we will turn our priorities topsy-turvy and enjoy your mercies rather than the empty gains of a secularized cultural world."

Note:
I am not propounding a doctrine of "natural law"—a concept that has not been integrally reformed by an awareness of the Newer Testament reality of the Holy Spirit's presence among believing men and women since Christ returned to heaven, leading them alone into fruitful knowledge of all kinds of things (cf. John 14:25–26). And Proverbs 28:12 cuts through most of the double talk surrounding "general revelation."

For example, when the USA landed the first man on the moon, some would say, "Chalk one up for common grace." Instead, I refused to walk across the street in Worth, Illinois, to watch it on TV (we ourselves did not have a TV), but purposely hid myself that night in my Chicago study, redeeming the time—"when wrongdoers win success, a man had better be hard to find." (I realize this was probably an anti-historical act on my part, influenced by the protest movements of the 1960s; still, to this day Proverbs 28:12 gives me comfort on that score.)

[*VANGUARD*, January–February 1975, 12–14, 31]

11. How God's Word of *Proverbs* Communicates

¹⁵ A godless ruler stands over one's folk
  like a lion growling or a bear lunging at prey—poor folk—
¹⁶ and the more meager a leader's Understanding,
  the more violent is one oppressed.
  Only if you thoroughly hate cutthroat success
  will your days prove to be good ones.
¹⁷ Don't try to hold back the person who is running scared
    straight into a dead end,
  driven on roughshod by the blood on his or her hands:
¹⁸ he or she who walks around without guile shall experience
    true freedom,
  but those busy finagling crooked ways shall all of a
    sudden… collapse!

¹⁹ Whoever works at one's little plot of ground will have more
    than enough daily bread;
  but whoever chases what's hot air shall get filled up with
    emptiness!
²⁰ A man or woman who is truly faithful seems to teem
    with blessings;
  but a man or woman in a hurry to get rich never remains…
    unpunished.
²¹ (It's simply not good to play favorites among people;
    that way even a strong person can get tripped up over a
    mouthful of bread.)
²² Anybody who is intently out to get possessions has an evil eye,
  and it never occurs to him or her in their guts
  that total emptiness is what shall overtake them.
²³ (If you reprove a man or woman fairly, you'll find they respect
    you later on
  much more than if you had lathered them with a
    swiveling tongue.)
²⁴ Anybody who withholds from one's father and mother their due
  and says, "It's not really a crime"—
  that fellow is a co-worker with the Man of Destruction!

²⁵ **The person who always wants more, constantly stirs up only
    contention:**
  **the one who rests trustingly on Yahweh, however, shall wax
    quietly refreshed.**
²⁶ **Whoever rests easy in one's own heart, of course, is a
    downright fool!**
  You have to walk in Wisdom if you would be saved:
²⁷ **whoever gives to the destitute shall never, never suffer lack;**
  **whoever closes one's eyes to such need will be richly…
    cursed!**

²⁸ Remember:
>   when the godless wrongdoers win success,
>   a man or woman does well to get out of sight;
>   but when such VIP's go to pieces,
>   then shall those who live justly grow strong!
>   (Proverbs 28:15–28)

The catch to reading *Proverbs*, as a believer, is to realize it is not a book of atomic aphorisms. *Proverbs* is much more like Christ's parables, where it takes four or five verses to cumulate to a single point. And frequently one multiple-verse point is set next to another multiple-verse point as variation on a theme or by contrast leading on to a still more central, unifying point that hits the target bullseye: our listening hearts.

We have been trained by so many translations to chew the Bible into odds and ends of verses (the Bible has been broken up into verses for only the past few hundred years) that it's hard for us to realize how connectedly it should be read. The mass media today also hinder Bible reading, because they gear us for instant communication.

> It's the headlines you want, man! the TV news clip of a dramatic incident —one picture is worth a thousand words—why wait ten sentences for the enriched point if you can get it out in ten words or less?—telegraphic prose —speed!—instant communication—get it while it's hot!—besides, people are busy, so make it snappy.

Most of us are suckers for the razzle-dazzle, and do not notice how it cheapens meaning. So, "Jesus Saves" becomes a bumper sticker slogan like "Things Go Better with Coke," and we think that's Gospel. Meanwhile, the Bible, especially the Older Testament, becomes a closed book. Or a paraphrase.

You will never understand the Bible if you read it fast. And you will certainly never understand *Proverbs* if you take it as a collection of discrete propositions, which allows you the liberty to pick here and there for what strikes your fancy, fits your personality, or serves as infallible backup for this or that argument you want to make. Proverbs 28 is simply not written that way, and should not be read as an almanac on "Successful Christian Living."

A *Proverbs* "poetic paragraph"

A man or woman who has power and is not constrained by the love of Christ to seek the common weal of those whom they are to serve are predators. And every victim of such a godless leader's rape only feeds the blindness for more extortion, more blood, more unjust gain, at the expense of one's defenseless subjects. Don't get caught in that web of backroom deals, compromised success, and everlasting conniving. It is a hell-bent, brutalizing stupidity! (28:15–18).

If you want to amass wealth, if you are obsessed by the idea to enlarge your little nest egg to outlast inflation, it will warp your life. If you speculate how to get ahead, scramble to know the right people, smooth talk your way into positions of power, poor you! sold yourself to the devil! For example, you will live as if money is thicker than blood, the blood in your veins from your parents; and you will live in constant poverty— always needing more than you have! Ironic. It is those you can count on to be faithful in doing little tasks, who are content with less, that have an aura of having more than enough, as if they are…rich! (28:19–24).

Those who struggle to get ahead are anti-christs, and ferment everlasting trouble. Those who drop out and suck a pacifier are simply fools! You have to **walk in Wisdom if you would be saved**; holding on close to only the LORD for security, quietly refreshed by the LORD's living Holy Spirit, you give away all that you have to the misled, waylaid poor of the world, who have been abandoned by the godless who ruled them to ruin (28:25–27).

Remember: bide your time and truly wait upon the Lord as you build your shadow culture. God has never wanted headlines. In God's time Christ will return to extirpate godless rule and culminate the talents his people, his poor people, have traded in the marketplace (28:28).

You see what a tightly meshed, unit structure Proverbs 28:15–28 shows. The section begins with a graphic image of wicked leaders, who in their betrayal of office are like beasts, like swine before whom you should not cast pearls (vv.15–18). Then the same theme of the godless who, because they are godless, necessarily play God and botch it, rampant with destructive power: that theme is developed in loco greed, in contrast to the man or woman who is like a tree planted by running waters, which bears its fruit on time and whose leaves do not fade (vv.19–24). *Sotto voce*, as it were, the inspired writer comments very experientially on the seduction of just a little duplicity (vv.21,23). And finally comes the formulated nub of the whole passage toward which verses 15–18 and 19–24 were aimed: those who scramble for more, who are religiously self-reliant and selfishly closed in their covetousness are damned! and a blight upon their neighbors: those who rely on the LORD and walk in God's ordinances *are* blessed, and shall inherit the earth (vv.25–27). After that epitome, 28:28 echoes 28:12 and anticipates 29:2 and 29:16, tying this section in with other sections, reinforcing the crucial thrust of 25:21–22 and 29:25–27, which govern this whole corpus of five chapters copied over by Hezekiah's wise counselors (25:1), and articulates the apocalyptic dimension with which Scripture is always pregnant.

Not atomized Delphic oracles

This means that the old standard *International Critical Commentary* on *Proverbs* is false when it says again and again, "The words yield no sense. The sentence ... was inserted here by mistake" (Toy on 28:17, p. 502), etc. And *The Living Bible,* which treats *Proverbs* atomistically, begs to be misunderstood when it says, "Hard work brings prosperity; playing around brings poverty" for 28:19—nothing could be more superficial and further from the truth if in its splendid verse-isolation it is read to mean, "God helps those who help themselves." No! That Protestant work ethic that absorbs God's blessing into man's effort and promotes partnerships like Seerveld God, Inc. (rather than Seerveld, "a field for the Lord to work in"), encourages, I am afraid, the hyperactive oppression that *Proverbs*, rightly read, denounces. **Faithful work is an unselfish response to the Lord's calling, and is not pulling yourself up by some sanctified bootstraps....**

But my thesis and argument—what I am *demonstrating*—is that Proverbs 28:15–28 is of a piece. And you violate God's Word, manipulate it! if you read it like an anthology of atomistic propositions. That's the way the sects always mutilate Scripture (and the way clerics, in a pinch, use the Bible as a grab bag of verses to bolster a hurried, pastoral homily). What God says in *Proverbs* will be missed if the book is construed as bits and pieces. Such an atomistic prejudgment conceives the *Proverbs* text to be structurally context-less, like a string of Delphic oracles, which you interpret to suit the occasion. What makes things so confusing is that the hermeneutic of atomic verse units commits one compositionally to an essentially arbitrary reading. While a given exegete or wise parent working with *Proverbs* atomistically will often import a cohering biblical context by virtue of having a living Christian faith, the hermeneutic method they assume nevertheless promotes a whimsical exegesis. What's to stop you from letting your sanctified imagination roam if you are dealing with oracles dropped out of the blue?

But the fact is that Proverbs 28:15–28 is *not* a collection of Delphic oracles. It is an artistically edited whole of an interlocking structure that weaves together richly a single, powerful message that is unambiguous. And Proverbs 28:15–28 fits snug into chapter 28 and in the unit of Proverbs 28–29, which connects closely with chapters 25–27, all of which hark back to the tremendous climax of Proverbs 8:22–36, bookended by Proverbs 1:20–33 and chapter 9, cued by the book's prologue, 1:2–7. And Proverbs 28:15–28 calls to mind *literally too* the context of Psalms 1 and 2, portions of Amos and Micah, Matthew 5–7, James 4:1–5:11, 1 John 3:11–18 (and so one could go on). God's Proverb Word communicates not aphoristic-atomistically, but connectedly, in a highly artistically fashioned, Wisdom-literary way. Once one understands that about God's Word of *Proverbs*, there is much less room to read it arbitrarily. On the other hand, so long as you pick up and use *Proverbs* like a telephone book, you are most likely to get a wrong number. I know, one can read Proverbs 28:15–28 in its integral wholeness and still not hear it. We are so hard of hearing because if we heard and obeyed the truth of Proverbs 28:15–28—You have to walk in wisdom to be saved—why it would mean we'd have to change, quite concretely and radically, our habit of life as citizens, customers, sales persons, administrators, teachers, parents, you name it, and that's almost like Jesus asking that fellow to give up all his goods to the poor, and follow him. You don't really mean that, do you, God?

God does. Have mercy on us, Lord!

But my point this time is that we should learn to read *Proverbs* as it is written. Maybe then it will be harder for us to wiggle out of responding with our life to the total impact of God's living *Proverbs* book, which should be cutting us to the quick to repent, reform, and to hope.

[*Vanguard*, May–June 1975, 10–11]

12. Give the Helpless Justice or be Damned

The Holy Spirit used Hezekiah's wise men and women to copy down wisdom God had given Solomon and his counselors that would be especially helpful for "those in authority" (cf. Proverbs 25:1). To read Proverbs 25–29 correctly, one has to realize that Solomon was not a romantic poet in a nineteenth century garret who, lonely and consumptive, penned his random, inspired thoughts for posterity. God's servant Solomon was also no Benjamin Franklin whose *Poor Richard's Almanac* epitomized the Enlightenment spirit of the American colonies, gathering up their loins for INDEPENDENCE. *Proverbs* is not a daily devotional on "How to get ahead with God—brief thoughts for each day of the year."

What we call Proverbs 28–29 is one whole piece, one cohering piece embedded in history that calls and directs us to godly rule and wise governing in exercising the authority each of us has. And I have been arguing in previous paragraphs that one must give more than lip service to that cohering context, if you want to understand *Proverbs* as it is written and related to the whole, true Bible story of the Covenanting LORD revealed in Jesus Christ.

One should stop trying to squeeze an oracular sermon (or "moral") out of each single verse and start hearing the interplay and reinforcement one passage gives to another, how 28:12, for example, resonates in 28:28 and echoes in 29:2, tying those paragraphs together. If one misses the connections and contrasts and development in the piece as a whole because of an atomistic prejudice, one may unwittingly be converting the living Word of God into a footnote, prooftext apparatus for one's pet doctrines. And that would be devilishly evil (cf. how the devil quotes Scripture in Matthew 4:1–11), for then one presumes to stand above Scripture, parsing it out like vitamins, rather than let the well-knit, God-breathed text cascade down over your head with a sure, correcting, comforting, illuminating mercy.

Notice how the section 29:1–14 moves from a renewed warning about stiff-necked unrepentance (cf. 28:9, 14) on to the passionate call of both chapters: instead of an aggressive show of strength, O man or woman in authority, give just recompense to those who cannot help themselves (cf. 28:26–27).

1 **Anybody who receives repeated correction and**
   simply becomes more stiff-necked,
   will suddenly have his neck snapped—and there's no
   cure for that.

2 When those you can count on to deal justly grow in strength,
   the people as a whole become glad:
   but when crooked men or women come into positions of ruling,
   the folk start to breathe anxiously.

3 **Whoever really loves to become wise will gladden the heart of**
   one's father and mother:

**but whoever likes to hang around with loose women or men
squanders whatever inherited talents he or she owns.**

4 A king can set the country on its feet
by seeing to it that rights are dealt with justly,
but a ruler who tries to exact the most one can get (out of
people) will topple the land into ruin.

5 A fellow who lathers his or her neighbor with a smooth-talking
tongue
is really spreading fishnet in front of the neighbor's feet
to trip him or her up.

6 A wicked man or woman always gets trapped by their
daring misdeeds;
however, a person who deals justly day in day out
is able to jubilate and be glad.

7 **The person who keeps on doing what is just comes to know
firsthand the struggles for vindication that those who are
helplessly down and out suffer, but a godless, shifty man or
woman doesn't ever bother their head about or even know
how to recognize such matters.**

8 Loudmouths who like to sound off can keep a community
continuously agitated:
it takes wise men and women to calm down the
enflamed feelings.

9 But if a wise person enters into dispute with a stupidly
closed person,
the blockhead just gets all the
more excited, continues to make a fool of oneself—
but there will be absolutely no rest for anybody.

10 Men and women who deep down feel guilty about the heads of
others they have hunted, outrightly hate the peaceable person:
but those who are straightforward and upright look out for
such a wholesome one.

11 Anybody who just lets oneself go, blasts out his or her temper
all the way, is a fool:
only the wise man or wise woman is able, finally, to still
such troubled passion....

12 If a ruler pays attention to misleading words, [you can
count on it:]
every one of his or her assistants is a conniving opportunist.

13 **[It's true:] the broken-down poor fellow and the person who
tyrannizes others have something in common:
the LORD God Yahweh gives light to both of their eyes;**

14 **but only the kingly ruler who truly, steadfastly
dispenses justice
for the defenseless ones who don't seem to count—
only that ruler's seat of authority shall remain established
forever and ever.**

(Proverbs 29:1–14)

Historical setting

The kind of back-and-forth conversational opening of this section could serve practically as an inspired commentary (especially 29:3) on how the LORD's anointed one, King Solomon, developed from the young statesman desiring wisdom (1 Kings 3:4–15 and 8:1–66) to the wheeler dealer of political power plays and illicit alliances (1 Kings 11:1–13).

More poignant still is the fact that these sayings were booked just after the ten tribes of Israel had had their stiff necks snapped by Shalmaneser and been carted off captive into northern Assyria (29:1, cf. 2 Kings 17:3–23, especially v.14). So it was appropriate indeed for the wise men and women of Judah to record for God's remaining people the persistent truth that you were glad as a nation or became a laughingstock in the world, depending upon whether you had an Ahaz or Hezekiah as ruler (29:2, cf. Proverbs 14:34). It was most fitting too (no matter whether it was Solomon himself or Hezekiah's editing wisemen in the grip of the Holy Spirit) for God to reveal again at this point in history what Solomon, son of David, certainly came to know by the miserable end of his days: inherited blessings can be dissipated within a lifetime (29:3). And although Yahweh is faithful generation after generation, the covenanted son or daughter may break down what the believing father and mother built up. Young God-fearing Solomon had set the country on its feet with his stunning judgments (1 Kings 3:16–28), but his son Rehoboam listened to flattering advisers (1 Kings 12:1 20) and plunged the land into civil war (cf. Proverbs 29:4–5). Young Hezekiah immediately did what was right in the sight of the LORD when he became king, following David, and reformed the temple liturgy (cf. 2 Chronicles 29, especially vv.25–30), but Hezekiah's son Manasseh copied the ways of the heathen roundabout and ruined Judah (2 Kings 21:1–16)....

So 29:6 does not just drop out of the blue and make an abstract point, like a latter-day tract; but Proverbs 29:1–6 is freighted with the LORD God's agonizing over God's pigheaded people, especially the historical leaders, who have been rising and falling because they never seem to learn that sin is a dead-end trap, and that only a trustworthy deed of protective mercy shall endure forever and bring joy (cf. Proverbs 28:1).

Restore what is right for the defenseless

With that introductory background the main point of the section is broached (29:7): whoever *does* justice concerns oneself experientially with those who cannot protect themselves; the person who is guilty of wrongdoing never even thinks about the helpless who are done in by unjust people.

Then follows parenthetically, as it were, God's wisdom on revolutionaries, public controversies, temperamental fools—all those who *talk* a good game of justice. If such deceitful agitators begin to affect the ruling powers, you have chaos on your hands (29:8–12), and "those in authority" themselves become prey to such loudmouths. While the weak people continue to suffer, unattended.

That's right, says the concluding couplet (29:13–14): Yahweh is the LORD over tyrants, victimized persons, LORD over both pious blabbermouths and peaceable folk. But only those exercising authority—in politics, the church, home, in the media or in schools—an authority that brings the fullness of an obedient life (justice) to those who are unable to fend for themselves: only that rule shall last with blessing beyond the moment.

This wisdom is for God-fearing leaders

Proverbs 29:1–14 becomes very sobering once you realize it is not the riot act read to unbelievers, but is God's Word specially aimed at the leaders of God's own people! God's Spirit had Proverbs 25–29 copied down about the same time Isaiah 1–12 is being written, where the Covenanting LORD God says: I've had enough of your worship services, you pious frauds! give me concrete justice for the outcasts of society! How else could your scarlet sins be turned to the purity of white? (Isaiah 1:10–20) I'm going to cut off the most respected, oldest leaders you have, and your preachingest prophets, like the head and tail of a beast, because they beguile my people; the dirty chrome-plated hypocrites mislead my people away from giving support to the helpless (Isaiah 9:8–10:4).

If you hear Proverbs 29:1–14 and belong to the political or ecclesiastical, academic or journalistic establishment, you know how fearful a thing it is to have, take, or wield authority in your sphere, which affects all of life.

It's easy to dispense bread and circuses to the populace, and pay state visits to foreign capitals, but what counts in God's eyes is whether old people can pay their heating bills. It's one thing to devise inspirational meetings at the drop of a bended knee, but does the orthodox evangelical church know the charity of a christian legal aid society for indigents?[1] Do God-fearing persons in academic office know how to speak the classroom word of quiet wisdom rather than just researched blather "solving" the world's problems theoretically, in neat outline form? And how tempting it is, especially in church-related papers, to assassinate one's neighbor in words (no telltale blood), instead of wielding a healing justice that is deathly afraid of false witness.

Jean Calvin's biblical dictum that civil authority is the most sacred calling in the whole life of mortals *(Institutes of the Christian Religion,*

---

1   While Joel and Jeannie Huyser served as Christian Reformed Church missionaries in Nicaragua (1996–2013), he co-founded the Nehemiah Center in 1999, which organized "Houses of Justice" in various local communities, providing the poor with legal and related help.

4.20.4) deserves extension, in the light of Proverbs 29, to all magistrate type authority and judgment affecting daily life. Proverbs 29:1–14 should cut to the quick everyone who has leadership authority among God's people, so he or she find out *who are the helpless* in his or her area of service? The falsely imprisoned or cruelly expropriated poor, the fatherless child and confessional misfits, the brilliant student without a redemptive direction, the falsely maligned in anonymous newsprint: the helpless, those without recourse, who cannot stand up for themselves in the public arena, deserve merciful justice, says the Lord, at the hands of those who confess Jesus Christ.

The professional pharisees among us, and the face-saving lie in every one of our hearts, find it difficult to kneel under this Word of God. But then 29:1, written at the beginning of the seventh century BC, takes on the devastating dimension of Hebrews 5:11–6:8 (especially 6:4–6) written for convicting us to repentance in the first centuries AD Christ himself, in exasperation at the hairsplitting, freedomless, self-righteous leaders of God's people who could never be caught *outwardly* with their phylacteries down, told them, STOP JUDGING LEST YOU BE! (Matthew 7:1–5 and 23:13–33).

Evenhandedness is what you expect from secular people. Should the leaders of God's people not do more in the way of obedience to the call for justice? Only if our mouth is shut and our rehabilitation of brokenness is truly redemptive—praising God, building saintly communion, attracting disbelievers to our God-service—in the church and school, body politic, books and pamphleteering, only then will our work be righteous and blessed by the Lord.

God does not help those who help themselves. God punishes those who withhold a merciful justice from those outside the establishment. And God self will protect the helpless left in the lurch by leaders of God's people who act themselves like cynical dogs to the call for repentance and for doing justice (cf. Matthew 7:6–12).

[*VANGUARD*, January–February 1976, 4–5, 22]

13. The Evil of Authoritarianism:
An Exploration in Proverbs 29

To understand the book of *Proverbs* you have to remember that Solomon debated with the wisemen and wise women of Egypt (1 Kings 4:29–31). Debates in those days were somewhat like tall-storytelling contests or, can you top this riddle? A wiseman would formulate a nugget of wisdom that stretched your imagination and made a telling point, like Agur's "There are three things, really, that never stop craving—four, you could think of, that never say 'Enough.'" Pause. And then follows Agur's answer (Proverbs 30:16):

> the Grave,
> a woman's womb unable to bear a child,
> the Earth, that never stops wanting water, and
> Fire, which never says, "Enough."

Then the next wise person would try out his or her comparison. "There are three things, really, that are miraculous, too wonderful for me to grasp—four, you could think of, that I simply do not understand." See Proverbs 30:18–19 for the pay off, and for its meaning (cf. below pp. 143–144). And the wiseman or woman who showed the keenest knowledge and sharpest insight won the contest. Solomon in his day was the sharpest, most subtle, deepest-going wiseman under the sun.

Expect "Yes, but" comparisons in *Proverbs'* paragraphs

That's the temper of Proverbs 29—back and forth repartee—which the (debating) wise men and women at the court of King Hezekiah copied over from the Solomonic archives, under the leading of the Holy Spirit (Proverbs 25:1). But Scripture is not just a collection of interesting proverbs that are kosher because Solomon said them. Scripture uses the "Yes, but" method of the wise (cf. below pp. 161–165 Stek festschrift), like David's poetic method in certain psalms, to tell us **who God is** and what is **the Lord's way of doing things**.

Now debate is a tricky thing. The truth of the matter often lies somewhere in between both of the sides taken. Like Job's cursing the day he was born (Job 3), and friend Eliphaz replying, well, you deserve it, you sinner (Job 4–5). Neither is quite right. All three chapters are authoritatively God-breathed, but you have to read the whole book and hear God's summing up voice (Job 38–41) before you know what the score is. You are not finished when you say Eliphaz's speech is infallibly inspired, because *the Gospel* is that chapters 4 and 5 are *not* the way of the LORD (Job 42:7–9)! And you don't have to believe people who talk like Job 4–5, even if they sit next to you in church.

This wise person's back-and-forth way of getting at or getting out the truth sometimes confuses people. To this day Ecclesiastes 3:1–8 is read by many as if it means there is a time and a place for everything. And that is revealed as *partly* true. Because in context the point is: there *seems* to be a time and a place for everything, it's all relative and unstable and never ending, what do you get out of it all, this hectic cosmic life (Ecclesiastes 3:9)? Nothing?! Hot air and chasing the wind? And the Good News comes in the next verses, Ecclesiastes 3:10–15, which stop the believing reader from taking Ecclesiastes 3:1–8 in an unqualified, straightforward, indicative, factual manner.[1]

Another way Solomon's wiseman method was taken amiss is this way: imagine people who had attended a debate of "artful comparisons." They went home dazzled, remembering the most striking ones. Or, lesser wisemen or women, as teachers of the folk, would wrap up their point by using an "artful comparison," riddle, or parable-like story, which they had learned from a master wise counselor. Some who picked up proverbs began to use them as slogans, or to parade their newly acquired knowledge, to sound Solomonic, or to end the argument with their neighbor by quoting kosher insight (like people who shut off discussion on something by saying, "Well, it was Providence"). Then the "artful comparison" no longer is wise, but pseudo-wise—just as you have pseudo-prophets. This kind of terribly conservative canonizing of proverbial slogans, encrusted and fossilized pseudo-wisdom, is what Jesus had to contend with when he debated the pharisaical scribes (= school-bound wisemen).

I have been arguing in these pages that the book of *Proverbs* is not atomistic but hangs together in paragraphs and much larger units. If you still read *Proverbs* atomistically, verse upon verse like jot upon tittle, I think you miss the Word of the LORD because of a misleading (perhaps positivistic) hermeneutic. I have been offering an alternative. To hear the difference, please first read, in your favorite translation, Proverbs 29:15–24, and see what you get out of it. Then read the following translation aloud, to which I have put headings (comments, commentary), to help you hear the unified, Job-and-his-friends-debate-like progression of the section, as I understand it. To highlight my point in reading the translation here, a man's voice could take the odd-numbered verses and a woman's voice the even numbered verses.

Hardliner (stock quote)

15 **"Correction with a stick makes a fellow wise up:**
leave a young boy to himself, and he will shame his mother,"

Corrective comment (countering)

16 **When brutal people ride high, wholesale apostasy happens!**
Those who do what is right will see them all cave in.

---

1   See my *Take Hold of God and Pull*, 31–35.

Hardliner (a quote response with a "personal experience")

¹⁷ **"Straighten your boy out, and he'll do everything you want"**
   —he'll even treat you to titbits of utter repose!

Corrective comment (sorrowing)

¹⁸ **But without a vision (of their own), a folk will hang**
      loose like disheveled hair!
   However, whoever keeps the LORD's order will be blessed.

Hardliner (starting to argue rather than quote old sayings)

¹⁹ **You can't shape up a worker with words!**
   Even if he understands, he doesn't have to respond.

Corrective comment (arguing back)

²⁰ **Have you ever really looked at a man in a hurry with his words?**
   Why you can count on a fool more than you can count
      on a hot-headed talker!

Hardliner (shouting)

²¹ **But if you coddle and pamper a worker from his youth on,**
   all you get finally is pure obstinacy!

Corrective comment (bringing critique close to home)

²² **Indeed, a testy, angry man kindles quarrelsomeness all around.**
   Whoever is mastered by uncontrollable rage commits
      untold destructive evil!

Hardliner (gets the point somewhat, remembers an appropriate saying, calming down, a little pompously)

²³ **"The presumption of man will humiliate him,**
   but he who hath a humble spirit shall attain glory."

Corrective comment (still correcting such full-blown, unthinking, abstract quoting, ironically, somewhat exasperated)

²⁴ **Whoever deals with an inveterate deceiver**
   is unable to stand it with oneself after a while:
   she has to listen to the cursed stuff, but just cannot
      straighten it out.

(Proverbs 29:15–24)

Then follows immediately a coda, as it were (29:25–27), which sums up the thrust of the whole five chapters, Proverbs 25–29 (cf. next article #14). But let me explain a few things about the translated section right here: how do you know it is debate-like?

The first verse says, "A stick and correction give wisdom…" (29:15). Isn't that true? Doesn't the Bible ask us to spank our kids, use the ruler or strap on grade school students, keep your workers in line, and punish criminals? Are you one of those liberal mollycoddlers that wants to take the hell out of our Bible? Do you perceive my meaning?

Proverbs 29:15a is only half-true taken all by itself, and it is *false* if mouthed by somebody taking a hard line as Job's friends did. You can't scare anybody into heaven, and you can't beat a kid into wisdom. **Only the Lord gives wisdom**, says Proverbs 2:6. And my suspicion that "A stick...gives wisdom" (29:15) needs correction is strengthened by the expression, "Straighten out your boy, and he'll make it easy *for you;* he'll bring repose, sweets, and relaxation to the very heart *of you*" (29:17). For it's a wrong focus to force children into line so they are good to *us,* don't cause *us* trouble, don't embarrass *us*! Children (and grownups, like parents too) are to be disciplined only so that they will serve *the Lord,* with gladness—right?! And it is very significant that the half Bible text most used to support Christian day schools, "bring them up in the nurture and admonition of the Lord," mentions in the first half of that Bible verse in the context of Paul's exegesis of the fifth commandment (Ephesians 6:1–4):

> **Fathers, don't** you **drive** your **kids to** rebellious **anger,**
> **but** get them to grow up and flower **in the discipline and mindset**
> **of** THE LORD.

Proverbs 29:19a doesn't sound quite right in isolation either—"a servant cannot be educated by words"—because *Proverbs* is full of the fact confessed that God's Word *does* things, and human speech too, either *heals* if it is wise, or *actually kills* if it is idle (cf. above on Proverbs 25:11–15, 23–28). It's so, fools are beyond reach, but that is not the norm; and 29:20 immediately challenges 29:19, saying that words spoken in frustrated anger are worse than foolish, and naturally do not affect the righteousness of God (cf. James 1:17–27, especially v:20). "But!" sputters the black-and-white-thinking, hard-lining antagonist, "If you don't use force, you get spoiled brats, recalcitrant workers, and just stubborn disobedience (29:21)! Don't you see!"

I see, says the Word of God in Proverbs 29:15–24, that angry men with power and authority commit untold destructive evil in the world (29:22). Violent action is simply sin, and destroys the center of those who are violated, so that while you may shape up the child, student, worker, or believer on the outside, inside a deep-seated, disloyal desertion sets in (29:16). If a person, a student body, a work staff, or a people of God do not have their own integrating vision of the LORD's order for their life building up within them, no amount of yelling or rules, punch clocks or pulpit pronouncements shall stop them from disintegrating, each going one's own unstructured way, like sheep and children and handicapped people scattered on a thousand hills (29:18).

At this point in the argument, 29:23 strikes me like this: suppose an opulent, paunchy fellow in an expensive limousine or one of those famous sports idols with a seven-figure income, in a lowly Ferrari, glides into your driveway, power rolls down his air-conditioned window, taps the ashes off his Cuban cigar on the shiny side, looks you straight in the eye, and says, "My only comfort is that I, with body and soul, both in life and death, am not my own, but belong to my faithful Savior Jesus Christ"—what would you think, as you surveyed the scene?

I'd think Proverbs 29:24, and wince. He gave the right answer, all right, but who cares if it is only pseudo-wisdom, blocking a self-examining repentance, warding off the Word of the LORD by generalizing it into an abstraction...or applying it only to your neighbor. 29:23 was a commonplace, all right, quoted by everybody. Eliphaz quotes 29:23 to finish off his judgment upon Job (Job 22:29)! (Notice the context, for example, in which Matthew reports Christ quotes 29:23—ironically? touché on something the scribes would never have thought of applying the saying [read Matthew 23:1–12].) So what does it mean? If you interpret it atomistically, it is a formula of orthodox warning and reward. If you read 29:23 in the context of 29:15–24, then you see revealed the spiritual, anti-christ blindness and cover-up of a hard-lining, self-righteous authoritarianism, whether it show up in the home, school, at work, or in the church.

Just a couple of things yet.

(1) Godly authority becomes demonic authoritarianism whenever those persons who wield the power or direct the course assume the prerogatives of God, a merciless god with no penultimate loopholes, who reaps what is sowed, period (like the God of Job's friends). Parents who stifle a disobedient child's response through fear are authoritarian, and do not save him or her, but curse the young one with an everlasting resentment (29:16). Teachers who break the spirit and mind of a student by covert threat, coercing deportment and thought into a single, accepted track created in their own image, are authoritarian, and do not lead the boy or girl into knowledge, but wilder them for years and years (29:18). Church leaders who are so touchy and self-serving smother every breath of congregated believers who sigh for renewal in liturgical response, doctrinal emphases, church life priorities: they are authoritarian, and do not shepherd God's children but gravely kill them with immaturity (cf. Matthew 23). And anyone, including Christ-believers, who judge their neighbor not to heal things straight, very concretely, but to show who is right, quite abstractly! "are accursed, a blight upon Christ's body" (cf. Matthew 7:1–5; cf. also above on Proverbs 25:2–10).

(2) I believe the Bible is authoritatively inspired by God, and happily "believe without a doubt all things contained in them" (*Belgic Confession* [1561–1566], article 5). I also believe that many *uninspired* ministers, teachers, and parents have not known how to break the Word of LIFE to men and women, but have just broken people into bits with the

Bible. And I cry in my study for those I know who are dead to God and closed to the joy of creaturely life within the Lord's ordinances because of the ways they were misread the Bible. I know, we do not need scapegoats. We need a reformation away from a pharisaic hermeneutic.

But I sense what a fearsome thing it must be for any middle-aged churchgoer, especially a pastor, to face the possibility that you, *as a believer,* might be reading the Bible, *Proverbs,* in a wrong way! How do you know—who can you trust to open up the Scriptures in spirit and in truth?! Yet it is desperately important that we not be like the proof-texting Pharisees Jesus referred to in John 5:39, who can win Bible quizzes, but lack knowing the Lord in God's full-orbed, judging mercy for daily life, pedagogical life, laboring life, liturgical LIFE. The Scriptures are not an insurance manual with hard-lining regulations on what to do if fire, theft, and murder occur. The Bible is our Father in heaven talking to us in a special way that enlightens the eyes of our heart so that in Christ we begin to receive the wisdom needed for searching out and keeping God's creational ordinances.

Note: As I become more and more sure of what I am doing, I see how exposition of *Proverbs,* in both conservative and liberal theological circles, is going to have to be radically reformed. Since the matter is so serious, if any of you regular believers feel ill at ease with what I am discovering, if it does not ring true, discuss your misgivings with others and write me a note.

[*VANGUARD*, September–October 1975, 8–9, 24–25]

14. Entrapment and Abominations

²⁵ To be scared stiff of humankind (אדם) is to set
   yourself up for entrapment,
   but whoever trusts (בוטח) in the Lord God shall be
   kept protected.
²⁶ Many people try to curry favor before the face of a ruler
   (with power),
   but from the Lord God a man or a woman receive a restorative
   just judgment (משפט).
²⁷ A person who is false (עול, utterly willfully intrinsically deceitful)
   is an abomination (תועבת)
   to trustworthy fellows who have integrity(צדיקים);
   and an ingenuous person who simply walks a forthright
   Way-of-life (ישר־דרך) is an abomination (תועבת) to a (vicious)
   guilt-hardened evil-doer (רשׁע).

(Proverbs 29:25–27)

To live in fear of what humans with power can do to you and your
loved ones instead of expecting, against odds, that Almighty God will
finally come through for you in danger, is to make yourself extremely,
unnecessarily vulnerable to harm—"entrapment"! Entrapment is the last
thing you want to do to yourself. It makes no sense, when you set out to
experience good results from your honest effort, to arrange for your own
checkmate. That's making a fool of yourself!

But that is what happens, says *Proverbs*, whenever you, as a child
of God, let the twisted human cultural setting you inhabit set the parameters for your existence and activity. To follow the "madding" crowd
today usurps your own initiative. To be "politically correct" emasculates
your frank speech. To take the alluring bait of self-indulgent happiness
promised by human TV and media advertisements risks losing more than
time and money: you throw up for grabs the solid restorative shalom
given by God the Lord.

Proverbs is telling us the truth about the trickery of sin. **Sin is its
own punishment.** The Creator God ordered the world of creatures to
live and beget life, but sin destroys creatures and kills life, albeit inadver-
tently. When you plot and pull off a robbery, you convert your neighbor's
goods into contraband that must be surreptitiously disposed of, and you
yourself become a hunted thief. When you betray a friend's confidence
by telling a secret to an outsider, you destroy a bond of trust and become
a Judas-kiss enemy to your former friend. When you covet and sexually
unite with a woman or man who does not belong to you, you desecrate
the heart of human bodily union, and cannot help but produce bitterness, regret, and an unsatisfying addictive desire ("To Carthage then I

—109—

came ... burning, burning, burning, burning").[1] The sinner traps oneself.

To flatter an important person cuts yourself down to be an obsequious nobody. To gossip about anybody is to falsely pretend you have godlike discernment, but show yourself to be a sallow grudge. To do any kind of evil, even if it not be illegal, like miserly worshiping possessions and money, always kicks in the Midas-touch: you yourself become a heartless gold nugget of a person who treats other people like small change.

What is so insidious about wrong-doing is that such human action is parasitic on something good, and we men and women are masters of self-deception, and tend to assess any waste or breakage or destruction we bring about as simply a mistake. We did not intend and are not responsible for the war our hardline intransigence begat; our permissive kindness is not the culprit for that youth's wayward lostness; our earnest attempt to **get** ahead did not entail our neighbors' losing the vision of **giving** to the incompetent and poor.

But *Proverbs* takes excuses for neglectful, shoddy, or faithless behavior as seriously as Christ did the servant who hid his inherited talent in a hole in the ground (Matthew 25:14–30). Those who cringe before dominant alpha males, or who are seduced by the sweetness of power and pleasure (29:25–26), will never make good leaders. God wants resolute, imaginative, merciful, wise, and resourceful men and women as the Lord's ruling ambassadors in God's troubled world, who are enabled, believe it or not, to cough up doing good even to one's enemies while waiting for the LORD to straighten out what has gone crooked (25:21–22). And *Proverbs* uses the strongest language possible to paint a vivid picture of how the **tzaddiqim** (the trustworthy fellows with wise stability) and the **rasha'im** (the willfully deceptive vicious evil doers) appear to one another and to God: "trusting naive children" and "abominations" (29:27).

The best interpretation today of the biblical matter of "abomination" might be "an experienced atrocity." I say "experienced" atrocity, because the outrageous savagery documented by daring reporters on TV screens and newspaper photographs has been distanced for us from the pained reality by the media-technical reproduction and the frequency of their happening. You would need to be actually present, and next in line, for the cruel killing and evisceration of a pregnant woman, or be witnessing firsthand the monstrous horror of your children's eyes being gouged out, to grasp the visceral revulsion meant by the biblical designation of "abomination." The monstrous horror of unimaginable, sacrilegious perversion taking place before your very face and felt with helpless nearness, is what *Proverbs* means by **abomination.**

Although at first it seems counter-intuitive to us, **God does love sinners.** God may have gut spasms watching the debauchery of "big

---

1   T.S. Eliot's reference to book 3 of Augustine's *Confessiones,* in "The Waste Land" (1922).

city night life" today, as in the days of Noah (Genesis 6:5–6), but the
LORD vociferously denies God wants the death of the wicked: God wants
evil doers to be turned around in their tracks so they can live (Ezekiel
18:19–24)! However, **the LORD God does not love hypocrites** (nor did
Jesus, cf. Matthew 23). It is the deceit, the pretense to be pious, holy, and
good that rankles the Lord. The **false** person, who is a stubborn heart-
hardened fake, who feigns to be God-obedient but is really a follower of
the Father of lies (John 8:44), borders on committing the unforgivable
sin against the Holy Spirit (Matthew 12:31–32), because you do evil as if
it be good, with a straight face, and so **mislead** the inexperienced generation who are seeking wisdom, wellbeing, safety, and joy.

We hypocrites are an abomination to the LORD, and deserve the
curse of God Almighty—"Go to hell!" (Proverbs 3:32–33). The respectable dissemblers with political or economic authority in society, who can
by quiet fiat or by persuasive counsel ruin the livelihood of many men,
women, and children, dumb animals, plants, earth, and water, are, and
should be, according to God's proverbs, abhorrent and disgusting to the
pure in heart (29:27).

And it is no surprise when *Proverbs* reveals that those who disarm-
ingly speak "Yes" and "No" instead of using tricky words (25:11–12,
James 5:12), who are disciplined, diligent workers instead of lazy procras-
tinators (24:30–34, Romans 12:11), who serve their neighbor with so-
licitous care rather than disdain (29:7–8, Romans 12:13), and are simply
God-fearing resourceful men and women: they are a veritable abomination! to the hypocritical wicked connivers for esteem (29:27). The innocent are hated by the guilty, because there is a serenity that pervades
those who do what is right that exasperates those who are underhanded
and covetous but don't want to show up bad.

The *tzaddiqim* are not Mark Twain's "innocents abroad," *ingénue*
prey for shysters, country rubes, simpletons who are easily taken in by
clever operators. The ingenuous, open-hearted persons acclaimed by
Proverbs and detested by vicious manipulators are those whom Jesus
Christ called to be his disciples.

> Look, I am sending you out as sheep into a pack of wolves.
> So you all become worldly-wise as snakes and (remain) innocent as
>   doves.   (Matthew 10:16)

The "right-doing person" enjoined by *Proverbs* is "single-hearted,"
not "simple-minded." You simply do without questioning what God's
guiding Word and the Wise tell you to do. So you become seasoned by
hardship, buffeted by opposition, even as wary as a snake, but **remain** as
guileless and unjudgmental as a dove.

No wonder a *tzaddiq* is a detestable abomination to a hypocritical
crooked person, because the ingenuous trustworthy fellow sees through

the fake facade, and is not intrigued by the sophisticated evil. It is a great blessing to be intimately aware of the steps to lustful entrapment (Proverbs 7:6–23), but still instinctively blush at an invitation to sexual evil. It infuriates a guilt-ridden wicked tempter wanting company in the misery, when the targeted victim is not attracted to the scheme to defraud the unsuspecting, but whose eyes tear up at the mean-spirited stupidity of the treachery. A kind of sanctified ignorance can be a wall of innocence protecting one from seduction. There really is no concourse between the naively wise and clever fools (cf. 2 Corinthians 6:13–18!).

Despite the conflictual gulf between good and evil that those in authority—parental, political, commercial, educational, whatever authority —are called to bridge by ruling matters that provides hope with mercy, the gospel message, especially in these five chapters of *Proverbs,* is: to trust and follow the Way of the ever-faithful LORD God is to be protected from unravelling disarray, despite incidental failures. And our human task to heal brokenness and restore justified wholeness for the poor in God's world, is an on-going ministry fraught with weakness, world without end! to be extended even to wicked enemies, because God self insures the final eschaton of shalom (25:22). So, do not vainly chase the entrapping idol of successfully bringing in the millennium yourselves, but only remain faithful, praying ministering servants of the Lord. Of such humble, glocally wise rulers is composed the coming Kingdom of God.

(written January 2017 AD)

15. A Wisdom Hymn and Agur's Parable on Getting Understanding: Proverbs 3 and 30

God didn't use many Arabs to get the Bible written, but Proverbs 30 is probably one place God did so. It records "Words of the Arabian Agur Jacobson" (30:1a), a descendant in the line of Ishmael.[1] If chapters 30–31 were appended to the book of *Proverbs* around the time that chapters 25–29 were Holy Spirit edited into it (cf. 25:1), God may have found Agur to use among the (proselyted) Arabian soldiers Hezekiah had in his army defending Jerusalem against the Assyrians.[2]

To understand the point of Agur's parable (Proverbs 30:1–6), we do well to read first the antiphonal hymn on Wisdom and Understanding found in Proverbs 3. In the large first section of *Proverbs*, chapters 1–9, God has Solomon sometimes compose and juxtapose to the "My son" paragraphs of instruction, more poetic strophes, to heighten the main point about Wisdom. Just as Job 28 "interrupts" and poetically emphasizes the "argument" in that biblical book. Proverbs 3:13–20 is such a hymn.

¹³ **O good! for the man or woman who has discovered Wisdom!**
Blessed indeed is everyone who is able to get a certain
special Understanding out into service!

¹⁴ The advantage of apt insight is greater than solid money.
The fruit of God-fearing discernment beats the yield on good
old gold!

¹⁵ That's right: Wisdom is more rare than dark pearls!
The sum total of your most treasured things does not equal the
worth of Understanding what's up.

¹⁶ Wisdom holds in the right hand, as it were, a life whose days
last long,
and in the left hand, riches and honor you can hardly imagine!

¹⁷ The ways Understanding goes to work are kindly, joyful ways;
even the littlest footpath of Understanding walked on
means shalom!

¹⁸ **Wisdom is a Tree of Life for whoever takes hold of it**
for support!
Whoever holds on to Understanding continues to be
blessed!

¹⁹ **Do you realize—**
the LORD God Yahweh set up the earth in its ordinances

---

1 Some scholars translate the Hebrew word *hammassa* to mean "the oracle," but I take it as a reference to the place-name in Genesis 25:12–18 and 1 Chronicles 1:29–31, the North-Arabian tribe of Massa.

2 Cf. the prism of Sennacherib, on the siege of Jerusalem, *The Ancient Near East: An anthology of texts and pictures*, ed. J.B. Pritchard (Princeton NJ: Princeton University Press, 1958), 200.

with the help of Wisdom!
the LORD God used Understanding to get the heavens
firmly established!

20 It took the LORD God's know-how to have the original
flood of waters break down [into oceans, rivers, springs,]
and to set things up so that clouds can trickle a dewdrop rain....
(Proverbs 3:13–20)

To use a Newer Testament idiom: if there is one thing utterly certain from *Proverbs*, it is that Wisdom and Understanding is the pearl of great price for which one should sell everything one has, and even lay down one's life (cf. Proverbs 8:10–11, Matthew 13:45–46). When young king Solomon withstood the temptation to ask for long life, riches, and honor, and prayed for the gift of "a listening heart so that I may lead your people," God gave him the Spirit of Understanding and sent him back to Jerusalem a wise man. And the LORD God gave him shalom to boot (1 Kings 3:3–14).

It is very important for understanding *Proverbs* to realize that Wisdom is not something vague and abstract just because it deserves a capital letter. Wisdom in the Bible is not some remote, abstruse Idea for which you philosophically yearn, and study years and years to fathom. Wisdom and Understanding in the Bible are also not some final Revelation that you receive in a sky-rending, fiery baptism, and then walk around like a shining-light guru touching things with Enlightenment. Wisdom in Holy Scripture has nothing to do with looking astute while smoking a pipe, being very learned, or acting like a charismatic visionary.

Quite bluntly, **the key to a christian understanding of *Proverbs* on Wisdom is to realize the Bible is telling us about the Holy Spirit**. When you read Wisdom in Proverbs 1:20–33; 3:13–20, and chapter 8, think Spirit of the living God, who brooded over the face of the waters in the beginning and played happily with humankind, and is the source of Life, blessing, and a holy, fruit-bearing walk among men and women. That's why you can't hunt Wisdom down with a gun, mine it like gold, or buy it with dollars (remember Job 28). The Holy Spirit is not for sale on the stock market, and cannot be awarded along with a university or seminary degree. You could even sit in church for a whole lifetime without seeking and being found by Wisdom, without being caught by the Hound of Heaven and filled with the Spirit of Understanding, discovering Wisdom.

Yet Wisdom, says *Proverbs*, is what counts. So how do you get Understanding?

Listen to the parable told by Arabian Agur Jacobson:

Parable setting:

1   The robust fellow is saying, "I'm tired out, God!
     O God! I'm tired out! I give it up!
2   Okay, so I'm too stupid to count as a human being!
     So I don't have a human intelligence—so what!
3   That's right! I never learned WISDOM
     so that I got firsthand inside dope on the Most Holy One!"

Rhetorical questions to the upset fellow:

4   Do you expect somebody to climb up and down the heavens
         [like a yoyo]?
     What man has balled the wind together in his cupped hands?
     Who can hold the rains wrapped up in the shawl [of a cloud]?
     Who do you think set up and keeps established the very last
         limits of the whole earth?!
     Could you name the man? What's his son's name!
     Spit it out, if you can.

Simple directive:

5   All utterance of God is refined from every impurity.
     **God is like a protective shield for those who run to take
     shelter with the LORD.**
6   Don't belabor God's words lest the LORD catch you, and you be
     found out as an adulterator!

                                                 (Proverbs 30:1–6)

Some people try to track down the Holy One and mine the final
Secret of the universe without realizing their profane habit of searching.
People who try to figure out God on the basis of "I'm O.K., God's O.K.;
so what's the big deal?" will never find God. The redeeming Creator God
is too overpowering to be pinned down even by baptized little Fausts. No
man can plumb God and corner Wisdom, says Agur.

But I'm afraid centuries of educated Christians have fallen into
the temptation to do just that, as part of their "growing in Grace" or
apologetic to secular man. Modern orthodox have often colored Yahweh revealed in Jesus Christ like Newton's God, while "liberals" preferred
Kant's Deity of benign equanimity. So when *Proverbs* says God created
the world *by Wisdom,* it is mistaken to mean that the creating God was
super-smart, with a mind like Einstein only raised perfectly to the nth
power—look at the complexity of planetary orbits and galaxies!—and if
we only *think* God's *thoughts* after God, we shall become wise. And those
who polarized against such scholastic natural theologisms said, No, Wisdom is to *act like Jesus,* then you are kosher for the judgment day. And in
our generation, there are Existentialistically bitten children of God who
misread Wisdom an other dead-end way, to be *the experience* of contemplative illumination. There have also always been Pharisees who identify

Wisdom with the sacred writings (e.g., the Torah to the scribes of Jesus' day), and promise absolution if you *case the text.*

No wonder there is such confusion on WISDOM, even when people look in the right places—Scripture, creation, communion of the saints, where Wisdom is audibly and visibly at work! So many well-meaning, loudmouthed leaders have belabored God's words and adulterated Wisdom until their tiresome, obscuring misleadership is unforgivable....

Wisdom and its attendant shalom come to those who give up trying wrongheadedly to put things right themselves, on one's own terms, and are instead moved to trust the Lord revealed in Jesus Christ and witnessed to by *Proverbs.* If one quietly, willingly listens to God speak, and asks to be put on the footpath of obeying the Lord of creation with praise and a healing joy, then God in heaven will outfit you with the beginnings of Wisdom.

The beginning of Wisdom and Understanding is free to those who repent and want to be held by the faithful One (cf. Isaiah 55). Even if you look in the mirror and see a respectable pharisee. Or if you've been told you are an outcast of society. If you repent of being your own boss, if you turnabout from making your own "ordinances," then as surely as rain falls from the shawl of a cloud, say the Hymn of Wisdom and the parable of Agur in Proverbs 3 and 30, so surely are the Grace of God, the love of Jesus Christ, and Wisdom of the Holy Spirit proffered to you. "God is like a protective shield for those who run to take shelter with the LORD."[3]

[*VANGUARD*, March 1976, 4–5]

---

3 A critic of *Vanguard* wrote: "You and Columbus, Seerveld. Think you're discovering India with your *Proverbs* studies. The true church has always preached what you are 'discovering.'" Answering such an older son, I replied: "Then let us kill the fatted calves, make merry and be glad! because the Bible has got to get through to every reader who is not joined to the Reconciliation army of Jesus Christ in the world."

16. Agur and Christ on False Witness, and Sin against the Holy Spirit

> [10] Don't gossip maliciously about a servant to his or her master,
>> lest the servant cut *you* down to size and you be shown up as guilty.
> [11] Some people even cut down their fathers
>> and never wish their mothers well.
> [12] Such people smugly think they are so clean,
>> but haven't really been washed up themselves from their own muck,
> [13] a generation—do you see how overbearing their looks!
>> arched eyebrows and all—
> [14] people whose teeth connive like knives,
>> jawing away like butchers' cleavers
>> to rid the earth of the woebegone,
>> to chew to bits those who can't help themselves, as if they weren't even human!
>
> (Proverbs 30:10–14)

Agur Jacobson does not mince words. His parable that stops short those trying to figure out God (Proverbs 30:2–6) and his poignant prayer for daily bread (30:7–9) give you the sense of a roughhewn fellow who calls a spade a spade. Agur was a passionate wiseman. Acute and direct. Perceptive, graphic, jealous for the Lord, and miserable about the callousness of God's so-called people toward their neighbors. If he was an Arabian soldier in Hezekiah's army, maybe God used the racial prejudice he may have suffered from the more kosher sons of Isaac to intensify the Word being booked.

Don't speak evil of someone who cannot confront you, says Proverbs 30:10, lest the LORD find you guilty of murder! And no verbal murderers inherit the kingdom God (cf. Revelation 22:15).

I mean respectable people, says Agur. You people who wouldn't be caught dead associating with ruffians. You educated, self-sufficient, stuck-up…slobs who think you are so righteous! I hate with a perfect hatred, says Agur and the LORD, the sophisticated ones who never commit faux pas in their snug little cliques, but dispose of their neighbors with a knowing wink over their coffee cups. "At every word a reputation dies."

I see you chicly-dressed people cut down the old-fashioned generation. I watch you meticulously slip knives into the ribs of your professional colleagues. I see you hack away at the unfortunates—real flesh and bloody people like the unemployed, divorced, alcoholics, backsliders, criminals—as just so many misfits for statistics. In fact, you will slander the incompetent and those of different cultures with jealous ethnic slurs and judgments of incorrigibility. And not even shed a tear as you pray for their souls.

All such cultivated oppression, says Agur in Proverbs 30:10–14, is hatred of your neighbor and a false witness that is as serious as hell: adulterating God's very Word (cf. 30:5-6).

Christ raises the ante, you might say, when his special power for bringing healing, freedom, and blessing to people on earth who were stymied by sin and the evil one was ridiculed by the pharisaic leaders as being itself "evil."

> 31 …I tell you, All kinds of sin and discrediting talk will be forgiven people, but discrediting
> 32 the Holy Spirit will not be forgiven. If somebody says a word against the Son of Man, it will be forgiven them, but let someone speak against the Holy Spirit, it will not be forgiven them —neither in this age nor in the age to come.
> 33 "Make a tree good, and its fruit will be good:
> make a tree rotten, and its fruit will be rotten."
> **The tree can be told by its fruit.**
>
> 34 You batch of little snakes!
> How can you speak good things when you are really wicked!
> The mouth spills over with what the heart is over-full.
> 35 "A good person produces good things from one's store of good:
> a wicked man or woman produces wicked things from their store of what's wicked."
> 36 **So I'm telling you: for every unfounded word humans speak they will have to give an account on the Day of judgment. You shall be justified by your words! and you shall be condemned by your words!**
>
> (Matthew 12:31–37)

When it comes to the false witness of pharisaic religious leaders, rabbi Christ can be as sharp-tongued as wiseman Agur. People may be mistaken about my ministry, says Christ, and sin in horrible ways—it can be forgiven. But those who face the working of the Holy Spirit and call it evil, who are confronted by wonderful changes being wrought in people's lives by the power of the Holy Spirit, and are hardened into calling it "devilish," they cannot be forgiven.

Those who cite Mosaic chapter and verse against faithful persons harvesting food on the Sabbath specifically to reach the starving, bind heavy burdens on such farmers' backs, but do not move a finger to help anyone. Those who quibble about jots and tittles of a christian philosophy that the Comforter is able to use to cast out aimless despair from university students, and convert them to a world and task of meaningful praise, are blind guides who mislead God's people. Those who blackball genuinely christian medicine and psychiatry struggling to reclaim the wastage of sexual blockage, raising suspicion that such servants of God condone sin, are themselves whitened sepulchers. And so Christ could go on about the little snakes who are professionals in false witness, backbiting, and innuendo, which ranges from hating your neighbor to denying the Holy Spirit.

Practical good news

The good news of Agur and Christ on false witness and sin against the Holy Spirit is very practical. Just listen to the next idle conversation you hear while the tea is steeping or during a meeting break at an official ecclesiastical assembly, the small talk in your carpool or during lunch at school, the rather thoughtless remarks tossed off in the locker room or at a business lunch. "The mouth spills over with what the heart is over-full." To dispose of your neighbor as a "welfare bum," "queer," "spic," "nigger," "ex-con," "Fundamentalist" or "Commie-liberal" is an act of hate. What cuts down another does not build up. And to knowingly undercut christian endeavors where the Spirit of God is a moving, troubling-force in our secular society is unforgivable.

The Lord calls each one of us to discern the spirit of what we encounter, whether it be earthily holy or spirtualistically false (1 John 4:1–3). The Lord warns us again and again not to think we are muck free and able to set everybody else straight (Psalm 130:3, Matthew 7:1–6). And the Lord takes ordinary conversation so seriously, backroom politicking talk, and the tiresome infighting so common among serious believers, to tell us that every unfounded, undermining word uttered will damn us to hell in the last day.

We must pray hard for one another that we be kept from false witness, that we can learn how to broach repentance to one another in love and imagination, and that we be wise enough to shun the perverse witness that is "unto death" (1 John 5:14–17). God protects God's folk who are oppressed by false witness, but woe to the man or woman by whom such oppression comes.

[*VANGUARD*, June 1976, 6–7, 28]

17. Dumb Animals and Christian Leadership

The trick to judo is to let the other fellow kill himself by his own force and momentum. That always intrigued me. "Those who grab for the sword shall die by the sword." But I've come to see the Buddhist lameness inside judo and what that nonresistance principle means if carried over into other life activities. If Christians carry on culture in judo fashion, they abdicate responsibility for giving formative direction. Then you don't presume to take cultural initiative. You just counterpunch or let the other fellow go to cultural hell, tripping over your saintly body. It is the loveless flaw in pacifism.

Our North American mentality, however, is still largely dominated by the hockey mentality. We are prone to carry over violent contact into human relations, to win goals, of course. We may sublimate the brute force quite sophisticatedly when we carry on business or do politics in hockey fashion, and there are rules (laws) against overt cussedness. But most of us are not above a little Darwinian push and shove when it comes to life in society.

Since the christian community can no longer run away from the secular cultural giants in the land, we need to become biblically wise in how to fight the good fight of faith that brings forth cultural deeds worthy of repentance. It would be sheer unfaithfulness on our part just to practice cultural judo or play games of cultural hockey with each other and our neighbor.

Part of Proverbs 30 is relevant for getting biblical direction and for becoming wise on this matter of *how-to-lead*:

24 Four things there be, insignificant on earth,
   that nevertheless—would you believe it?!—
   are wiser than many a wise man or woman:
25   ants are a people without strength,
      yet they get their food together ahead of time during the
      summer;
26   badgers are a people with no pull,
      yet they set up their houses in clefts of solid rock;
27   there is no general in a horde of locusts,
      but they cover the ground, all of them, in organized bands;
28   you can grab a lizard and hold it caught in your hands,
      but the very same beast crawls around in the palatial halls of a
      king.

29 Three things there be, that have an imposing stance—
   four, you could think of, whose stride commands attention:
30   the lion, mighty hero among animals,
      who never turns tail in the face of a single one;
31   a strutting bantam rooster;
      yes, the (sure-footed) mountain goat;
      and a stonewalling king whose people do not dare stand up to him.

[32] No matter whether you have acted foolhardy in
    pushing yourself forward,
  or whether you've done it in calculated fashion:
  hold your hand to your mouth quick!
[33] That's right!
  Pressure on milk produces butter,
  but pressure on a nose produces blood—
  and pressure applied to angry nostrils (only) makes
    contentiousness flare.

(Proverbs 30:24–33)

These "animal riddles" are in the context of 30:15a—people who never have enough are like bloodsuckers. And all those who crave power and authority and satisfaction that is not due them, pervert the order of God.

Men and women could well learn from certain measly animals, says the Bible here, how to be provident, full of ingenuity, and banded together. Also, though you be as lowly as a lizard, the least of dumb animals, you may still find a place in king's palaces! God is no respecter of animals either, it seems. He always uses the weak things of the world to confound the strong, lest any boast of their own strength (1 Corinthians 1:26–31).

In addition, one could learn to understand that the formidable lion, the scrappy fighter of a cock rooster, and the mountain cliff climber of a goat, show up kingly rulers who keep their subjects cowed by bluff. Not all that is gilded is gold, and not all that is impressive deserves praise. In fact, it may be sham. With or without the Good Housekeeping seal of "for the glory of God."

It is crucial, says Proverbs 30, for understanding deeds on the earth to discern the spirit and the fruits. Whatever is self-reliant *or* pushy is evil: whatever is redemptive *and* born out of a humbled heart of faith, is obedient to the Lord (cf. James 3:13–18).

But who then can be saved, asked Christ's disciples? Who can ever live christianly in an unchristian society? How do we know whether certain cultural acts are approved by God or not? How can Christians ever *lead* unbelievers who are playing cultural hockey (or believers practicing cultural judo) without bullying them into line?

The biblical answer might begin with a few riddles close to Proverbs 30:

When is schooling christian schooling?
  – When the students learn to turn up with intrepid insight in the North American palaces of learning, and forsake acting like lions at sport.

When are parents christian parents?
  – When the home has the security of a cleft in the Rock, and discipline does not bring forth psychic blood.

When does a rich man enter the kingdom of heaven?
– When he works like a happy ant, and holds a hand over his mouth about his generosity.

When is a political pressure group or lobby a christian "pressure group"?
– When it brings forth butter rather than sour milk.

We all know that not everything done in Christ's name is truly obedient (cf. "Lord, Lord…," Matthew 7:15–23). It is also true that in keeping the law there is no reward (Galatians 3:1–14). There is no lasting security in brilliant intelligence, in maintaining troth, or even in doing justice, if it is not anchored in hearts that expect the Lord to come—even the unbelievers do as much and more! (cf. Matthew 5:43–48).

Followers of Jesus Christ are called to go a second mile, or better, to teach and study, to raise children, earn and give away money, and plug for policies that testify winsomely of Christ's lordship in educational deed, family times, monied acts, political imperatives, and so on (cf. Paul's hint and James's counsel to make others *jealous* of our meek, merciful wisdom: Romans 11:11, James 3:13). Unbelievers have the right, you might say, to hear and meet the good news in concrete, righteous deeds that exceed that of stonewalling scribes and pharisees (cf. Matthew 5:20), and that are permeated by a spirit of humbled praise that is mirrored in the lowliest of God's dumb animals. Such deeds of faith will posit *christian* leadership.

Not the least of our mandate to serve the Lord in cultural deed until he come is to not rest with the brokenness of Christ's body, the temptation to form contentious factions, and continue interminable arguments (1 Corinthians 1:10ff. and Hebrews 5:11–6:3)—that is not the way of wisdom that is "chaste" and pleasing to our Lord (James 3:17).

Let everyone who has ears to hear and eyes to see, indeed hear and see what the ant and lizard and the making of butter in creation show to the churches. For without the vision of Proverbs 30, God's people will undo themselves.

[*Vanguard*, March–April 1977, 32–33]

18. Things Mother Taught Me

¹ Words for Lemuel, king of Massa, with which his mother
    set him straight:
² What shall I tell you, my son?
    What are the most important things I should caution you
      about,
    O son from inside my body?
    What counsel can I give you, child consecrated by my vows?
³ Don't ever squander your back-up strength on women;
    don't expose your deep-going ways of life to those who swallow
      kings whole!

⁴ And it's not right, Lemuel, for kings—
    it's not good for kingly rulers to tipple wine,
    nor for leaders with responsibility and authority to grouse,
    "Where's my strong drink?"
⁵ because, who so drinks will shrink back from the full tittles
    of the law,
    and tend to cut corners or adulterate the cause of all those
      caught in need.

⁶ [People say,] "Give strong drink to those about to go under;
    give wine to those tasting bitterness in their guts."
⁷ [That's ironically, tragically true:]
    A down-and-outer drinks and thinks no more about his
      destitution;
    the embittered drown their painful trouble in [a gulp of]
      forgetfulness.

⁸ **But you, [Lemuel,] open your mouth wide...for those
    unable to speak up!**
    **Open your mouth to plead the cause of all the motley
    transients coming and going!**
⁹ **Open your mouth [not to drink! but] to judge with equity!
    Stand up strong for those helplessly pressed down and
    trapped against odds.**

(Proverbs 31:2–9)

Too few people realize God used an Arabian woman to write in the last chapter of *Proverbs*. The Queen Mother of young king Lemuel exercised her office of wise woman (cf. 2 Samuel 14:1–20 and 20:14–22) possibly around the time of Hezekiah.

This paragraph of 31:2–9 is almost a model of what I have been arguing is the general literary cast to God's Word recorded for us in *Proverbs*: rhetorical questions to get interest (v.2), a poignant remonstrance embellished by a vivid image—"Where's my strong drink?" (vv.3–5), the quotation of a maxim (v.6) critically put in its place (v.7), as contrast to the positive point of the paragraph that the LORD makes very explicit (vv.8–9).

There is evidence of sorts that Proverbs 31:2–9, with its title 31:1, was considered very early to be a cohering paragraph, for it appears in the Septuagint translation of the Hebrew Bible as a whole little section just before chapters 25–29. This means that we misread God's Word in 31:6–7 if we take those sentences as a straightforward injunction to go and do likewise, or if we think it is biblical sanction for giving the condemned man a final cigarette, or for making cheap wine available to unemployed heads of households.

Motherly talk

If there's one thing I could tell you, my son or daughter, says the motherly mouthpiece of God, it is this: beware of self-indulgence, and liking to be with "the beautiful people." Wine, women, and dormitory song have ruined more men than kingly Solomon (cf. 1 Kings 11:1–13), and beer, men, and a juke box bar have taken their toll of more women than camp followers. Especially if your calling is to give frightened children, ignorant students, the dispossessed poor, or injured people justice! You can't serve a heady glass of liquor and administer the delicate, complex reality of wrongs and punishment at the same time, any more than you can serve God and Mammon.

I know, my boy, that people say the poor are shiftless, the winos want wine, and the lonely want sex—at least give them what they want before they pass from the scene. But such defeatist "wisdom" is not from heaven (cf. James 3:13–18). You may not treat fear and ignorance, poverty, oppression, and the loneliness of human creatures with mere sedatives! Nor with moral pronouncements over a bottle of wine. Open your mouth to deny *your self*, O man or woman, and become a pair of eyes for the blind, feet for the lame, a mouth for the dumb, parents for orphans, a prosecuting advocate for those who have been molested and robbed (cf. Job 29:14–17). Lose your life in becoming a base of steady right-doing for those who only know how to drift in the world, so that the compassionate faithfulness of the LORD will be made known to them in your saving deeds.

Evasive responses

This godly counsel of Lemuel's mother makes even deeper Christian sense in our day of societal unraveling than it did in 700 BC. But we evade facing its tough message, I think, because just-doing is more complicated than ever, and we Christians think and act in secular patterns more than we would like to admit.

(1) Ever since the myth of Hercules, who stood at the crossroads and had to choose between the high road of difficult work or the lowdown valley of sensual delights, and since Bunyan's Pilgrim set out on the narrow road to Paradise, set off from the ease of Vanity Fair, good Christians have been tempted to pose the problem of sanctified lifestyle in terms of strict ascetic duty versus worldly delights, or an uneasy mix of the two—just

don't go to excess.

(2) Ever since the devil compromised God by quotation (Genesis 3:1–5, Matthew 4:5–7) and Pharisees used prooftexts for sophistic debate (e.g., Matthew 19:1–9), well-meaning heretics, special pleaders, and sects have seriously been able to "prove" practically anything from the Bible that would let them continue thinking and living pretty much as they pleased.

(3) Ever since Marxism practically atheized the millennium, and do-gooding Americanism flipped the Darwinian ethic over into rooting for the underdog, the establishment of justice has become completely divorced from the ground rules of Holy Scripture and, in a word, screwy. As if the poor and the black, the ethnic, and the elected, are by definition holier than thou.

What I mean is that most of us, because of (1), (2), and (3), can read Proverbs 31:2–9 as a brief sermon (v.2) for temperance (vv.3–5), lenience (vv.6–7),[1] and social justice (vv.8–9); we can put down our *Vanguard* with some feeling of righteousness—we're for it all!—and have a glass of wine with our evening meal, if we can afford it. And then we have missed hearing God speak.

The price of forming others wisely

The LORD raised up this Arabian woman for such a time as ours to face us in Proverbs 31:2–9 with the joyful gospel that if disciples of Jesus Christ really would do justice, love mercy, walk humbly with our God (Micah 6:8), and be able to exorcize the demons that stymie us and quell justice among people, then we will indeed go all out in permeating our task with a prayer-and-fasting festivity that bespeaks the Rule of our Lord (cf. Matthew 17:14–21 and Matthew 6:16–18). That is the price and the badge of Christian leadership in our post-christian age (cf. Matthew 19:10–12). Anything less is not worth the Nazarite-like vow of a God-fearing mother (cf. 1 Samuel 1:1–2:10, Proverbs 31:2).

Some children are orphans today in their own homes and need to find their fathers and mothers before the familial blood runs cold. Some politicians debate issues and reach compromises with equanimity, without realizing it all adds up to zero, next to a bona fide law that will free the oppressed to serve their neighbor. Some students knock about at colleges and universities, blindly coming and going with the wind, while profs add kudos to their *curriculum vitae,* in a travesty of trothful education. The times are fierce, and we all live in glass houses. That's why Proverbs 31:2–9 asks not just for hearers, but for doers of the Word.

[*VANGUARD*, June–July 1978, 9–10]

---

1   It became a Jewish custom (based on 31:6–7) to give those condemned to die wine to drink, mixed with something bitter, to dull them before execution. Fashionable women donated the wine. Perhaps Jesus spit it out on the cross (Matthew 27:34) because he knew how Pharisaical the custom was, and how mistaken the exegesis of these sad, ironic verses.

19. The Resourceful Womanly Nature of Wisdom

To close the book of *Proverbs*, following up the guidance given by the Queen Mother of King Lemuel, is the Holy Spirit-led editors' selection of the alphabet acrostic poem celebrating the Resourceful Woman of Wisdom,

As one reads this eulogy of Woman Wisdom, we do well to remember wise women mentioned throughout the Older Testament account of God's Israelite people's history. For example, a "wise woman" of Tekoa was summoned by General Joab to go to King David to make-believe her son who had killed his brother was going to be killed too, leaving her without an heir. When David pardoned the fictional murderous son, the "wise woman" hinted that King David should also pardon his beloved son Absalom who had killed his brother Amnon. And David did it (2 Samuel 14). It was normal for "the wise" to tell stories to help persons in authority come to make juridical decisions, as prophet Nathan had once done for David too, with the story about the poor man's one sheep killed by the rich man, concerning David's premeditated disposal of Bathsheba's Hittite husband Uriah (2 Samuel 11–12).

General Joab himself took the counsel of a "wise woman" of the city of Abel, who confronted him diplomatically not to destroy "a mother (of a city) in Israel" for the sake of a single revolutionary fellow, Sheba Bikrison. The wise woman of the city of Abel, known for its roster of wise women and men counselors, who were professionally trained "peace-making faithful stalwarts in Israel" (2 Samuel 20, vv.18–19), exemplifies how "the wise" served God's people in the old days. *Proverbs* closes now with a tribute to who served as practitioners of Wisdom.

10 Any possibility of finding a resourceful woman (אֵשֶׁת חַיִל)?
    Her worth is far beyond that of red coral
11 Because her husband deep down always feels secure with her
    he knows he will not need battle booty.
12 Completing what is good for him and frustrating what is harmful
    marks the resourceful woman life long.

13 Dunning wool and flax to make linen,
    her bare hands crinkle with pleasure in the work:
14 Every resourceful woman brings home food for the family, from
      far-flung places,
    like merchant ships in full sail.
15 From before dawn she is up to prepare foraged food for her
      household,
    and outline chores for the serving girls.

(9) Jean Siméon Chardin,
La Pourvoyeuse, c. 1739

16 Garden land may catch her watchful eye, and (at the right time)
  she buys it;
   she gets a vineyard planted from the fruit of her toiling hands.
17 Hips and thighs—her loins she girds with
   strength;
   and makes her forearms strong
18 Indeed, she experiences bodily that her
   business transactions are good
   —her lamp does not ever burn out at night.

19 Lightly her fingers reach out to the distaff
   and her open hands hold tight the spindle.
20 More so, her open hand strains to protect
   the defenseless
   and her fingers reach out to extricate those
   hopelessly tangled in poverty.
21 Never does the resourceful woman fear
   the cold of snow for her household,
   since all of them have been clothed
   doubly warm.

22 Ornamental cushions and blankets—she
   weaves them herself!
   her clothing is fine linen and wool dyed
   purple.
23 Public respect greets her husband in the gates
   of the city

(10) Gaston Lachaise,
Standing Woman, 1930

when he goes to sit down with the gray-haired elders who judge
in the land.

24 Quick to manufacture linen underclothes, she even sells them;
the resourceful woman can barter belts and girdles with
the Canaanite traders.

(11) Johannes Vermeer, *De Kantwerkster*, 1669–70

25 Ready strength and rough-hewn splendor constitute her cloths,
so that she stands facing the coming days full of hearty laughter.

26 **She opens her mouth with wisdom** (חכמה)**:**
the law of covenanting love (תורת־חסד) **rolls off her tongue!**

27 The resourceful woman
oversees what goes
on in her household
so insightfully
that no one ever has to
eat the curds of
laziness.

28 "Uniquely blessed is she!"
her standing
children shout in
chorus;
and her husband says,
"Give her a
hallelujah!

(11) Käthe Kollwitz,
Woman with dead child, 1903

²⁹ "Very many young women show gifts of resourcefulness (חיל),
    but you are better than all of them put together!"

³⁰ **Well, it is true: graceful charm can prove disappointing and to**
    be good-looking might just be a mirage,
    but a woman who lives her womanhood plumb
    before the LORD God (אשה יראת־יהוה)—she is worth
    celebrating!

³¹ You all, then, celebrate such a resourceful woman! let her
    enjoy some of the fruit that comes from her hands herself;
    let her deeds hallelu her publicly in the gateways to the city.

[Translation of Proverbs 31:10–31 © 1974,
revised with thanks to Al Wolters, by Calvin Seerveld © 2017]

(13) Henry Moore, *Reclining Figure*, 1929

This poetic paean of praise celebrates the edifying godly Woman Wisdom. But I am afraid the poem is often misread, as if it be a Platonic model of the perfect God-fearing woman one should aspire to be, or worse, the ideal housewife a man should try to marry. Some current Bible readers might tend to say, "What a patriarchal, chauvinistic standard of womanhood, that puts down every actual girl, since nobody could become that impeccable!"

A poem about Wisdom, not about women

However, suppose we approached this biblical text as describing the womanly nature of **Wisdom**, rather than as a poem about an extraordinary woman. Similarly, Psalm 112 is not about a man, but about the manly nature of **tried-and-true Just-doing**.[1]

> As I understand it, feminine and masculine **gender** is a matter related to but distinct from male and female **sexuality**. Men can have womanly gender features of nurturing and stay sexually male, and women can show manly gender characteristics of protecting and stay sexually female.[2]

And if Wisdom with a capital W in *Proverbs* is an Older Testament way of talking about the Holy Spirit (cf. above pages 7–8), then Proverbs 31:10–31 is indeed a vivid revelation of how God's Spirit works out love, joy, peace, patience, kindness, generosity, faithfulness, gentleness, and self-control (Galatians 6:22). So to treat this proverbial poetry even as the personification of an abstract, ill-defined "wisdom" is a mistake. This text is a synoptic recapitulation of the peculiarly womanly way the Holy Spirit works shalom on earth: with unobtrusive firm resourcefulness.

Biblical examples of womanly wisdom

Scripture reports how the midwives Shiphrah and Puah—because they stood in awe of God (Exodus 1:15–22)—parried the Pharaoh's strict command to kill baby boys, by saying that the Hebrew women, unlike the Egyptian women, gave quick birth to babies, before the midwives could get there. So the midwives deflected evil by a "soft" (רך) answer (Proverbs 15:1–4).

When the Moabite refugee woman Ruth was converted to follow the covenantal LORD God of Naomi in Israel (Ruth 1:16–17), Ruth diligently gleaned barley and wheat harvest food for her mother-in-law, but also had the raw courage and venturesome nerve to go alone in the dead of night, prompted by Naomi, to ask the older established Boaz to marry her (Ruth 3:9)! And Boaz, as a kind, law-abiding, Psalm 112 man unabashedly exclaimed to Ruth, "You are indeed a resourceful woman!" (את אשה חיל) (Ruth 3:11).[3]

Beauty Queen Esther showed the deliberative presence of mind in a life-and-death precarious move to convince the autocratic Persian King Ahasuerus of his favorite Haman's perfidy: she took the precious time, heightening the tension and expectation, to prepare a second banquet for the King with Haman before she acted decisively to protect her Jewish people (Esther 5:1–8). Timing and sizing up circumstances are crucial to

---

1 As Proverbs 31:10–31 is about Womanly Wisdom, so Psalm 112 is about Manly Just-doing. So Psalm 112 should not be degendered in English translation to a general plural, as the NRSV and NIV (2011) do.

2 See my "From Suppression of Women to Asymmetrical Mutuality," in *Cultural Problems in Western Society* (Sioux Center: Dordt College Press, 2014), 105–128.

3 My Institute for Christian Studies colleague Nik Ansell pointed out to me that because the book of *Ruth* follows the book of *Proverbs* in the Masoretic Text tradition, we readers are practically invited to take Ruth (and Boaz, גבור חיל, *Ruth* 2:1) as an example of Proverbs 31:10–31.

wise action.

I do not hear Scripture say that only women are wise. Solomon's provocative feint—"Cut the baby in half!"—exemplifies the circuitous step wisdom may employ to uncover the truth of things (1 Kings 3:16–28). And God's Spirit, says Scripture, filled Judean Bezalel and Danite Oholiab men with "the wisdom, skill (know-how) and knowledge" (ובדעת בחכמה ובתבונה), along with the women and men who designed utensils and sewed vestments for the tabernacle worship (Exodus 31:1–10, 35:30–36:1).

But it is striking that the Bible seems to condone the devious way Rebekah arranged for Jacob (his name means "deceiver") to steal Esau's blessing from Isaac (Genesis 27)—because God loved the wimp Jacob? (Malachi 1:2–3, Romans 9:13). And Rahab is blessed with safety (and enters the lineage of David, Matthew 1:5) because she had the backbone and spit to discern that the Jericho police had no right to know she was harboring Joshua's spies (Joshua 2:1–24).[4] Saul's daughter Michal, who loved David, helped him escape with his life by the ruse of covering a dummy with David's clothes sporting a head of goat's hair, and made-believe he was sick, to foil the would-be killers (1 Samuel 19:8–17).

That is, the wisdom, not to say, cunning, exercised especially by the many women figures in the Bible, is not spectacular, but is normally subtle, indirect, quietly persuasive, not calling attention to itself. Dare we call such delicate, piercing judicious, serviceable and nurturing discriminating activity, a particularly womanly trait (cf. Proverbs 14:1)? a wisdom born possibly out of the woman's often subjected station?

The concluding poem of Proverbs 31 about Woman Wisdom highlights that the source of her ready wisdom is the everlasting merciful Guidance (תורה־חסד) of the Lord God (vv.26, 30). The industry of godly Wisdom is both domestically ordinary (vv.13–15, 18–19, 21) and publicly enterprising (vv.16, 24, 27). True Wisdom has a rough-hewn sturdy look that lasts, not an ephemeral pretty appearance (vv.17, 30). Genuine Wisdom brings respect to its associates, who are called to rule in society (vv.11–12, 23). Joyful hearty laughter marks *Proverbs'* Wisdom, even as she tends to the needs of the defenseless and poor (vv.18, 20, 25). Womanly Wisdom always has the hidden resources in reserve to rise to the occasion and find a way to build and explicate God's Will that is not domineering. That's why the poem ends by enjoining all people in the city to celebrate fruit-bearing Woman Wisdom (v.31).

Wisdom as Holy Spirit

---

4 Cf. Dietrich Bonhoeffer, "What is meant by 'Telling the Truth'" in *Ethik* (1949), translated as *Ethics* by Neville Horton Smith (New York: Macmillan Company, 1955), 326–334.

The fact that in patriarchal Israelite society the copious sayings of a community of God-spirited wise men and women begins (Proverbs 1:20–33) and ends (Proverbs 31:10–31) this edited anthology of proverbs with acknowledgement of a womanly Wisdom figure, who apparently brooded with and assisted the LORD God at the very creation of the world (Proverbs 8:22–31; cf. Genesis 1:2) is significant. *Proverbs'* Woman Wisdom is not promoting a superior *sophia* goddess of the Gnostics, but is calling one and all to follow the Word and Spirit of the LORD. "Listen to me," says Wisdom in chapter 1; "I will pour out **my Spirit** upon you!" (Proverbs 1:23).[5] And in chapter 31:27 the text says, "The **law of covenanting love** (= God's gospel Word) rolls off Wisdom's tongue." Like alpha and omega, God's Spirit and Word in tandem govern all the chapters of these collected clusters of proverbs in between chapters 1 and 31, together acting as the "tree of life" (Proverbs 3:16–18).

One can notice too that womanly Wisdom highlights the unpretentious, down-to-earth nature of biblical wisdom and its Holy Spirit-breathed cachet—

> To stand in awe of the LORD God is the grounding path to wisdom: humility surpasses any acclaimed honor. (Proverbs 15:31)

—and is not at all like the Homeric πολυμήχανος heroics (and the ancient Platonic contemplative σοφία) or the Enlightenment practical common sense "proverbs" of Benjamin Franklin's *Poor Richard's Almanac* (1732–57)—

> Early to bed, early to rise,
> makes a Man healthy, wealthy and wise.

Once one realizes that biblically honed wisdom is a gift of the Holy Spirit, and the Holy Spirit works typically in a transformative womanly and motherly way, like a hidden Resource that comes into play obliquely at any occasion in a variety of indirect ways that are both incisive and decisive, which sooner or later bear good fruit, then one has the key of knowledge to the patchwork of the book of *Proverbs*.

Much more could be said, because the biblical *Proverbs* book constantly faces us with the choice between following Woman Wisdom or Woman Foolishness (Proverbs 9). The Newer Testament formulates this opposition as the life-long struggle between πνεῦμα and σάρξ, between Holy Spirit and the Power of Sin in our human hearts and bodily actions (Romans 7:14–8:17). So the point of *Proverbs* is not to memorize proverbs and have them ready to shoot down stupidity or solve moral

---

5   The KJV translation has "my spirit." JB, NIV has "my heart." RSV, NRSV, NIV use "my thoughts" although RSV has "my spirit" in a footnote. I find it strange that Waltke does not want English readers to assume that רוחי (= my Spirit!) might echo God's pouring out God's Spirit upon humans as mentioned in Joel 2:28-29 and Isaiah 44:3 (Waltke, *Proverbs* [Grand Rapids: Eerdmans, 2004], 1:199 n.17).

dilemmas—proverbs can be easily misused by fools that way (Proverbs 26:6–9)—but to become filled with the Holy Spirit! so as to conceive paths that lead to peace-making.

And the Holy Spirit we are to pray for to lead us into the truth, to bear faithful rather than false witness (John 14:25–26, 16:13), to purify and supplement our intercessory prayers (Romans 8:26–27), to allocate us gifts of insight, persistence, generosity, and healing (1 Corinthians 12:4–11), works slowly and surely behind the scenes. Yes, Wisdom occasionally causes an epiphanal stir in public (cf. Proverbs 1:20–21) as at Pentecost (Acts 2:1–4). But normally the Holy Spirit works quietly, flexibly, restoratively. The Holy Spirit begets and germinates wisdom and is not usually ostentatious.

This sturdy, almost reticent way God's Spirit acts is why I translate חיל (chayil) in Proverbs 31 as "**Resourceful** Woman."[6] The Holy Spirit has the wherewithal deep down to outwit the Satan and Power of Sin, whether it show up as a roaring lion or as an angel of light (2 Corinthians 11:12–15, 1 Peter 5:6–9). But the Holy Spirit is not **a hands-on fighter.** God uses angels like Michael to fight evil (2 Kings 19:35, Jude 9). The Holy Spirit is **a Comforter** (Paraclete) (John 14:16–17, 16:7–11), the God who inspires, who strengthens believers to persevere, who guides pilgrims around obstacles and through temptations, who binds up wounds, reconciles, can be grieved, and mysteriously brings shalom out of pain and sorrow (Romans 14:17, Ephesians 4:30, Titus 3:3–7).

Once one realizes the closing Proverbs 31 Hebrew poem is not about an Amazonic Wonder Woman champion, but is about the womanly, motherly working Holy Spirit, the believers' vigorous advocate sent by the Lord God to bring steady, fruitful life to God's adopted children, then one has a sound clue to understanding God's revelation of the nature of redemptive proverbial wisdom.

[written during Lent, 2017 AD, after a conversation with Hye-Jin Im]

---

6 Other translations of Proverbs 31:10 have "a virtuous woman" (KJV), "a good wife" (RSV), "a capable wife" (NRSV), "a perfect wife" (JB), "a wife of noble character" (NIV), "An einem wackern Weibe"/"Eine tüchtige Frau" (Zürcher Bibel of 1531/2007), "ein Weib von Tucht" (M. Buber). KJV keeps the woman unmarried. My colleague Al Wolter's brilliant, exhaustive critical encyclopedia of interpretations of Proverbs 31:10–31, settles for "a valiant woman," situates this biblical acrostic poem in the general genre of "heroic hymn" (cf. Al Wolters, *The Song of the Valiant Woman* [Carlisle: Paternoster Press] 2001, 3–14). But, as I read it, not even Deborah is a "heroic" figure, valiant in killing hand-to-hand combat. Deborah's Spirit-filled leadership gave Barak the will to fight, and she sings about the valor of God's mud! (as at Exodus 14:24–25) and the courage of a non-Israelite Kenite woman Jael (Judges 4:8–9, 5:19–21, 24–27).

20. The Only True Direction to Walk

²⁰ Listen closely to my words, my son and daughter,
    stretch your ear toward what I have to say;
²¹ don't let my words ever slip away out of your attention,
    keep them sounding in the very center of your hearts,
²² because these words mean life itself for those who truly latch on
    to them;
    they bring genuine health to one's total bodily existence.

²³ **Guard your heart with extreme vigilance,**
    for out of the heart springs life itself:

²⁴ You abolish mouthings that mislead,
    have absolutely nothing to do with lips that twist things
    crooked.
²⁵ Give people looks that are straight and—
    your eyes should look into another's eyes without guile.
²⁶ Lay down a path for your feet that is sure;
    make certain all your ways are utterly sound;
²⁷ **don't turn to the right, and don't turn to the left:**
    turn, if you will, your feet (eyes and tongue) away from evil!
    (Proverbs 4:20–27)

A full half of this paragraph in Proverbs (4:20–23) is spent emphasizing that it is a matter of life or death to take what follows to heart. So God must think it's important. And unlike we who think words are just sounds or scribbles in dictionaries, the Bible treats talk with the seriousness of murder (cf. Matthew 12:34–37). What lives in your heart and issues from your mouth shows whether you are dead to God, or one of the Lord's adopted children (Ephesians 4:25–5:14). The emphasis in Proverbs 4:20–27 is not so much on the fact that the idiom of your conversation, the look in your eye, and the way you drive a car, telltale whom you serve. The emphasis rather is that we must get our direction straight.

Cut out your tongue if you can't speak without misleading. Close your eyes if you are going to "look innocent" and appear kind, but at heart really seek to get the better of your neighbor. Build a walkway that has solid foundations, so you can be sure-footed. Don't bend to the right or swerve to the left in your life: just avoid with a passion doing what is wicked—this is the only direction to take! (4:24–26).

You wonder, if it's this clear, why God's people always seem to be headed in different directions, often at variance with one another. Some say they lean to the right, others feel inclined a little left. These believers crusade against "dirty books" as the evil that will do our families in; other believers lambast the stiff formality of worship services and scholastic theology as "the Lie" made flesh. Renewal groups turn judgmental, if they last; and mainline churches pitter-patter along, guardians of an accommodating tradition that homogenizes in the name of Christ. Why do all we who believe in the Lord and can read Proverbs 4 not see eye to eye, walk in step, beat heart to heart, and talk without guile to one another?

Every Christian knows the answer. Each one does what is right in his or her own eyes because followers of Christ are still sinful. Even Peter and Paul had different priorities in the Newer Testament (cf. Galatians 2–3), and factions are indigenous to the spread of the gospel (cf. Acts 18:24–28), and the millennium of theocratic peace awaits the return of Christ (cf. 2 Thessalonians 1:3–12).

But *Proverbs* says that those who live before the face of the LORD God hate what is evil, shun sin, eradicate factions, unite on priorities, and enjoy a work communion that makes unbelievers jealous of such joy! (cf. Proverbs 8:12–21, 32–36, Psalm 133, 1 Corinthians 1:10–17, Philippians 1:12–18).

I'm not certain why, but there seem to be different visions of the christian life on earth that persist historically and are compatible only next to one another. (1) The Nazarene, Rechabites, and believing progeny of John the Baptizer who prefer to be culturally ascetic or loners on pilgrimage here below, feel uncomfortable with (2) royal Solomonic splendor and faith-life dominated by a high and mighty established Church. (3) Franciscan simplicity, the eighteenth-century Methodist circuit riders who preached the Word in *deeds of charity* to the forgotten dregs of society, along with prison chaplains and those on the front lines of third world or urban ministries today, often tend to be impatient with (4) a reflective, Pauline Reformation that cherishes argued thoroughness, theory, and long-range conversion of cultural and institutional structures themselves as our reasonable, historical service.

That is, to this day, some Christians (1) take the book of Acts as the test model for a life of faith in our century, while other Christian communions (2) find themselves highlighting and celebrating the Psalms, with responsive chants, liturgical dances, and fragrant incense as the high point of each week. Certain Christians (3) run into battle girded with the pages of James, while still other believers (4) labor through the ponderous paragraph-long sentences of Romans, eight chapters, followed by three chapters of historical debate, followed by more chapters disquisitioning on feuds, gifts, government, customs, doubts, and mission policy.... And there is so much bloodletting among brothers and sisters of Christ because, in general, each hates evil in others so much a person smashes at it despite the cataracts obstructing one's own perception (cf. Luke 6:39–42), and because, specifically, each in one's own brand of Christianity thinks of ourselves as holier than the other.

It is very important, I believe, that disciples of Christ within these deep-going, differing tendencies, variously amalgamated with long Christian traditions, learn to pray for one another's testimony to Jesus Christ's lordship in our age, to judge one another compassionately by the fruits each is enabled by the Holy Spirit to bear, and not to hinder but to reinforce the other's Anabaptist, Roman-Anglo-catholic, Methodist, or Reformed christian service. Proverbs 4:20–26 is not a full-blown directive toward such housekeeping among the saints, but this paragraph of *Proverbs* lays down a crucial orientation: don't you bear to the right or lean to the left; instead, **take the only true direction—build wisely what redeems, and keep yourself! from evil in walk, word, and look** (4:24–26).

That means we should get rid of the common practice of lining up people's stand on issues as right or left, as if a minimum deviation from dead center puts you on the track of life. To veer to the right in your economics or to the left in your politics are both wrong. There is no biblical sanction for a right-wing hardline on church discipline, or a left-wing softline on school pedagogy. For a child of God to be just a little bit leftish revolutionary is like being a little bit pregnant, and for a Christian to abide undissolved pockets of rightist conservatism in his or her way of life is like still drinking specks of arsenic in your tea. As *Proverbs* tells it, God's folk should turn neither to the right nor to the left. That doesn't mean they must just barge straight through like bulls in china shops. We may have to jump over a wall with our God (cf. Psalm 18:29), dig out from underneath a prison we've been put in (cf. Isaiah 42:5–9), or detour around the walls of Jericho until the Lord knocks them down; but the only true direction for God's people—whatever their brand—is the way of wise obedience that refrains from evil, also the evil of being leftish or rightist.[7]

A Newer Testament reading of Proverbs 4:20–26, intensified by the revelation of Matthew 5:17–48, if obeyed, might lead to many persons closing their mouths (so they don't lose their tongues). And in the ensuing quiet, especially if many people also closed their eyes (to avoid looking innocent), people of God might begin to reach out and touch one another in a communion of saints. And if we would stand still long enough to get our bearings of common obedience and diverse tasks, we could move ahead in preparing the way of the Lord.

[*VANGUARD*, August–September 1978, 11–12]

---

7   The Septuagint translators of Proverbs *added* a verse after 4:26, which says: "God knows what the right-hand ways are like, but those on the left are inveterately perverse. God self, however, will make your tracks orthodox, and shall guide your comings and goings in peace." Such a gloss increases my wariness of Septuagintal theologizing, because the addition here confirms the error of believing that God is partial to right-wing causes. *Proverbs* wants to free us from working in categories of both "right" and "left."

21. Holiday Spirits in a Disjointed World

26 Give me your heart, my boy, my girl,
  Let your eyes light up when they see the road I point out,

27 because if you go whoring, you walk into a bottomless blackhole;
  what's strange and uncreaturely will trip you into a
    constricting pit

28 —that's right! loose living kidnaps you by surprise,
  and self-indulgence multiplies double-crossers in society.

29 Who do you think has pain? Who feels queasy in the stomach?
  Who acts bitchy? Who is tied up in knots of complaints?
  Who has body bruises for no reason at all?
  Who walks around red-eyed?

30 Those who dawdle over too much wine
  and develop the habit of testing the taste of mixed drinks—
    that's who.

31 Don't squint at the wine in your glass
  observing fondly how red it sparkles,
  how its reddish twinkle picks up the glint in your eye:
  strong drink slides smoothly down [the gullet];

32 only afterwards does the snake bite and spit out its poison
  like an asp.

33 Then your eyes will see terrifying, unheard of things
  and your innermost heart will promise mixed-up matters in
    perverse confusion.

34 You will sense yourself sunk down deep in the sea,
  like a nauseated seasick person tossed about complete with a
    migraine headache.

35 "Somebody hit me, but it didn't hurt!" [you will boast];
  "Somebody struck me down," [you'll say,] "but I couldn't care
    less...
  When I come to, I'll seek it out, devour it all over again!"

19 Listen closely, my boy and girl, so that you become wise;
  let your heart be set in the right direction:

20 don't be found clinking glasses with those who tipple wine,
  don't sit down with those who stuff meat into their bellies,

21 because drunks and gluttons ravage themselves,
  and to live in a stupor is to wrap yourself up in shabby togs
    indeed.

22 Instead, keep on paying attention to your father who got
    you born.
  Don't look down your nose at your mother when she turns old.

23 See to it that you acquire what is truly trustworthy and never
    dispose of it:
  wisdom, discipline, insight—that's what I mean.

24 The father and mother of a child who does what is right can really
  enjoy a festive holiday,

and those who have borne a wise son or daughter
can be thoroughly glad in their offspring.
²⁵ I hope you make your father and your mother happy—
may those who gave you birth be able to shout with laughter!
(Proverbs 23:26–35, 19–25)

Biblical writing rings true to our experience (if we are able to hear it naked before the Lord). But the Bible never just "mirrors life," adding a list of do's and don'ts to keep, if you want to reach heaven. The Bible is more like a two-edged sword than an informative essay or interesting tract.

The *Proverbs* paragraph before us is a good test of how to read the Bible so as to meet God and repent, thanking the Lord for the way of life God spells out, or how to read it wrong, as bad news.

The riddle about social drinkers (23:29–30) and the vivid snapshot depicting a connoisseur of red wine gone alcoholic with hangovers (23:31–35) illustrate the main injunction of the passage, to stay free from "living it up" in godless fashion (23:19–21, 26–28). Instead, keep the faith of your parents alive, says Scripture, so that old and young together, you may celebrate with hearty laughter what is truly joyful (23:22–25).

One way to mistake what one reads here is to think the Bible prohibits drinking wine and eating meat. The trouble is that teetotalers and vegetarians cannot inherit the kingdom of heaven upon grounds of abstinence: it takes *deeds* of faith to be accounted righteous (James 2:14–26). Besides, Christ must have missed the cue then, since his first miracle was to make so much wine for the wedding feast in Galilee (John 2:1–11), and he later told with approval in his story about the roasting of a fatted (grain-fed) calf to celebrate the return of a repentant, prodigal son (Luke 15:11–32).

Another way to cripple the good news of Proverbs 23:19–35 is to misread it as a stern rejection of *excessive* drinking and eating. There's nothing redemptive about moderation; pagans did it all the time. And to take the focus of "too much," opens the wide door of calculating casuistry beloved by every scholastic exegete: so long as you don't experience nausea under the table, you're okay my boy; and if you hold your liquor well, dear woman, fill 'er up! Only habitual drunkards and perennial gluttons make the gross list of those who forfeit the kingdom of heaven (cf. Galatians 5:21, Ephesians 14 5:18). So long as you avoid going overboard too much or too often, you're home free on this count, and the passage doesn't apply to you....

Not so, I believe. Proverbs 23 holds today for those who never taste strong drink or overeat, and speaks directly to those who only indulge "moderately." Because the greed and covetousness Holy Scripture exposes here clings as close to us *Vanguard* readers as our underwear. Underneath our christened public propriety lies a contentment with affluence or a canker to have at least enough amenities, like the neighbor, to do our thing ("for the glory of God"); or we suffer debilitating guilt-feelings that we are not destitute or poorer than our neighbor, which can be a kind of inverted work-righteousness. Any way we examine ourselves, we do well to hear this paragraph of *Proverbs*, because it sets us straight on the stupidity of idol worship and reveals the certainty of a future for those who eat and drink, talk and think, love and do business, to show the presence of the true, covenanting God.

How? And what's so good newsy about that "old story" (1 Corinthians 10:23–11:1)?

Proverbs pokes fun at the pseudo-glamor of sin. Mixed drinks are drunk by mixed-up people (23:29–30). Those who are mesmerized by the look and taste of the very best red wine receive its stigma in their bloodshot eyes (23:31). People who dress themselves up in luxurious food undress their native humanity (23:20–21). That is, with exquisite irony our *Proverbs* passage describes how the self-indulgent return to their counterfeit pleasures like dogs go back to their vomit (23:35, cf. 26:10). And the Good News of it all is that whoever sees through the bubble of seduction (23:27–28), and shucks it to accept the discipline of the Lord's discipleship, will be blessed with lasting excitement and wonder (cf. 23:17–18 and 24:1–6).

That promise holds good for every reader today who does two things: (1) recognize that *our* consumptive habits are acts of prostitution, and (2) adopt the policy of giving away our lifetime (cf. Ecclesiastes 11:1–6).

It's very difficult to admit that one's own personal indulgences might be catalogued in God's library under "Whoredom." We are willing to label another person's "weakness" for sweets or smoking, clothes or a cruise, as spendthrift in our day of the weakening mission dollar overseas, but a person is not called to live a stingy, cheerless life, are you? You don't have to be a Nazarite (Numbers 6) or Rechabite (Jeremiah 35) to be saved, do you? Can't one have a few peccadilloes?

But the point is: we are caught in a web that does more than compromise our christian lifestyle. Every Swift Premium ad and Ballantine IPA billboard, Air Canada commercial, or No Frills food store is intent upon swallowing us into the black, bottomless hole of "loose living," which is a living death of debt, inequality, hate and selfishness. You'll know what Proverbs 23:28 means if your son or daughter is kidnapped by a cigarette or turned into a double-crosser (say one thing but do another) by booze or ruined for love by "sex." Maybe we have such difficulty recognizing pimps when we see one, because they're almost all legal.

Should we then do as Paul once did (cf. Acts 21:18–26), abstain from the good things of the earth to honor the absence of our bridegroom (cf. Mark 2:15–22), to show solidarity with the suffering neighbor (cf. 1 John 3:17–18), and to win those almost persuaded for Jesus Christ?

Perhaps, as proof of genuine repentance and understanding, and as a necessary biblical act of cultural exorcism, if it can be done without judging your neighbor (cf. 1 Timothy 4:1–5). But for those who are able to castrate themselves from the hedonistic materialism that seems to weasel its way into our very bones, and *can* let go of the wine and meat so biblically assumed for festivities (cf. 1 Corinthians 6:12–30, 7:29–32), and are driven by the holy (Good Samaritan) spirit of give-it-away! rather than "give-it-up": God will bless you with holiday spirits indeed!

The right way to read Proverbs 23:19–35 is to hear it in the context of section 23:17–24:22 whose refrain is:

Don't let your heart get worked up, envying to be like those crooked-to-God.
Instead, be driven the whole day by waiting attentively upon Yahweh—
if that is kept there, there is future [to your work]!
and your excited expectation will never be defused.
(23:17–18, 24:14, 19–20).

And then obey the Word (23:23 as focus) with the Newer Testament outreach of 2 Corinthians 9:6–15: God intensely loves a cheerful, ready giver. And the Good News of Proverbs 23 includes the notice (23:24–25) that believing parents and believing children will laugh themselves holy in this kind of insightful, disciplined, wise doing of what is upright.[8]

To receive an unexpected good gift elicits joy spontaneously—surprise, openness and thanksgiving. Since the secular Western civilization we inhabit programs our human giving to mean "getting," we will need a special dispensation of God's Grace and much imagination to find ways and means to give away things and ourselves unexpectedly, and to give in Christ's name without expecting or hoping for returns somehow. Because our "consumer society" rules out sheer biblical giving and always measures giving in terms of what you yourself get out of it, our societal patterns act to kill holiday joy to the world, and cruelly feed competitive envy, also within the home (and even in churches where ministries that are shortchanged need to wrestle one another for the year-end dollar).

But Proverbs 23 offers hope to all those who listen closely: shun "painting the town red" with your friends or going on an emotional binge "once a year," for such license is not taking a holiday, but is stepping into a fearful blackhole of self-massage, lonely remorse, or helpless confusion. Instead, thanks giving is the core of a true holiday that will rest in the love and spirit of the Lord Jesus Christ whose glorious, "unexpected" Coming we dearly anticipate (Revelation 22:20).

[*VANGUARD*, November–December 1978, 14–15]

---

8 Those whose natural parents do not fear God should maybe also adopt some who do, and begin a progeny of wise children themselves.

D.
GOD'S WORD FROM ARABIAN AGUR AND
JESUS CHRIST'S BROTHER JAMES

FOOD FOR LIFE IN PROVERBS 30 AND JAMES 3

Before the Bible existed, God told Adam and Eve what God wanted, as they took care of God's garden. God spoke directly to Cain and Abel, Noah, Abraham, the Egyptian Hagar and Ishmael (Genesis 16), Isaac, Jacob, Joseph, Moses, Joshua, and many other leaders of God's chosen people, to help them follow the way God formed us creatures to be together in God's world.

God gradually articulated the LORD's will through the ministration of priests in the line of Aaron, who helped you offer grain and animal sacrifices to rid yourself of sin. And the LORD God equipped special prophets to turn up who quoted God to people, "Thus says the LORD." God later anointed kings and queens to rule God's folk, according to the LORD's way of just-doing.

God also used wise women and wise men to make the LORD's will known to people somewhat differently: telling stories, offering counsel to leaders (2 Samuel 15:31–37, 16:15–17:23), and by fashioning and even writing down poetry for readers to mull over. The wise woman of Tekoa, for example, was hired by General Joab, the way you would employ a therapist or a labor negotiator today (2 Samuel 14:1–24), to make up a story to reconcile King David to Absalom, much as Nathan earlier had told David a story to convict him of his sin with Bathsheba (2 Samuel 12:1–25). "The wise" were storytellers and philosophical poets.

So, next to priests, prophets, and kings, the men and women who held the office of being "the wise" were educated, literate teachers whose poetry, dramatized stories, parables, and riddles made God's will known to students and listening people in a thoughtful, roundabout artistic way. God's Spirit used "the wise" to book the back-and-forth dialogue of *Job*, the questioning monologue of *Ecclesiastes*, the chorus of voices named *The Song of Songs*, and the book we call *Proverbs*. Much of rabbi (teacher) Jesus' ministry on earth with his parables and cryptic sayings also comes out of the Older Testament tradition of "the wise," whom the LORD often used to explicate God's revelation in God's creatural handiwork.

Young King Solomon was a wise man who knew about the strangest animals, countless herbs, and foreign trees, and could make comparisons that startled your imagination. Solomon debated with the wisest of Egypt, Africa, and Arab countries, says the Bible (1 Kings 4:29–34). In those days "the wise" held contests, like "Once upon a time, so and so," or "There are three things, no four, that make a person vomit, for example," and then the idea was to see who could tell the best, the most insightful compacted, poetic epigram that surprised you with its wisdom worth noticing and living by.

"There are three things that make a church service memorable, no, four, really, you'll not soon forget:

singing psalms you can throw your voice into,
a sermon that seems too short,
somebody's honest testimony that made you cry, and
hearing a child's unaffected laughter. . . ."

Chapter 30 of *Proverbs* is a Holy Spirited edited collection of certain wise sayings by a descendent of Ishmael (if the "Massa" [mentioned in the NIV footnote] is the one referred to in Genesis 25:12–18 and 1 Chronicles 1:28–31). I read chapter 30 in three loosely connected paragraphs: verses 1–9, a kind of Ecclesiastes-Job struggle with and request to God; verses 10–17, a graphic restatement of a few of the Words God pronounced at Mount Sinai; and verses 18–33, several standard riddles that declare the glory of God's creation, the chaos sin brings, the good news of animals, and a warning on vanity and violence.

This is the Word of God given for disciplining us in right-doing (cf. 2 Timothy 3:16–17).

Sayings of Agur Jakehson, from (the Arabian tribe of) Massa

^{1b} So says the strongman:
"My patience is worn out, God! God, my patience is worn out,
I am exhausted."
² That's right! Am I too stupid to be considered human?
I don't have human insight?
³ So I have not learned **wisdom**:
I do not **have intimate, experiential knowledge of what matters are holy**?
⁴ [Okay,] who has gone up to heaven and come down again!?
Who has (ever) collected the wind in his or her fists?
Who can squeeze the (world's) waters into a piece of cloth?
Who (in the world) has fastened down securely the ends of the earth?
What's the person's name?
What's that person's child's name—do you really know?

⁵ **Everything God speaks proves to be true.**
God is a safe place for those who run to take refuge

-142-

with God.

6 Do not add onto the words spoken by God
   lest God set you straight, and you be found out to be a liar.

7 There are two things I'd like to ask of you, [God].
   Don't withhold them from me before I die:

8 **(1) Keep deceit and misleading talk far away from me;**
   (2) Do not give me either poverty or riches
   —let me eagerly eat food that is just enough for me

9 lest I become over-full and disavow [your bounty] and say,
      "Who is this LORD God?"
   or lest I become so poor I have to steal, and do violence to the
      name of my God.

[A: Wisdom means knowing what is true and holy to God.]

10 Do not bad-mouth a servant to his or her master
   lest the servant curse you and you be held guilty [for slander].

11 There are people who curse their father and never praise their
   mother

12 **people who in their own eyes are morally lily-white,**
   but as a matter of fact have never been washed clean of their
   own excrement!

13 There are people—my! how they raise their eyes and arch their
   eyebrows!

14 people—whose teeth are swords, whose jawbones are knives
   that butcher and eat away the poor from off the face
   of the earth, swallow down the needy of humankind.

15 The twin daughters of the leech are: "Come on, give! Gimmie still
   more!"

16 That's right, there are three things that never stop craving—
   four things, you could think of, that never say, "Enough":
      the grave,
      a woman's womb unable to bear a child,
      the parched earth without water, and fire
   —they never say, "That's enough."

17 A young person's eye that mocks a father and
   deals contemptuously with motherly requests:
   that young eye will be gouged out by black ravens of the ravine,
   and shall be eaten by young birds of prey.

[B: Fools bear false witness, dishonor parents, rob the poor, and covet for MORE.]

18 There are three things too marvelous for me,
   four, you could say, I simply do not know how to experience:

19   the way of the eagle in the heavens
      the way of a snake on top of a rock,

the way of a ship in the middle of the ocean, and
the way of a young man **in** a woman able to bear a child.

(14) Overnight scnow sculpture, Toronto

20 I could also mention: the way of an adulterous woman [or man]
who eats up [sex], wipes off the mouth, and says, "I didn't do
anything wrong."

21 Under three things earth has been quaking,
under four things, you could say, the earth is simply unable
to bear up:
it can no longer stand being under
22 a male slave who suddenly becomes king;
a godless fool glutted with too much food;
23 a disdained woman who suddenly comes to be in charge;
a servant girl who is dispossessing her very mistress.
24 There are four things, really, that are so tiny on earth,
but wow! are they ever more shrewd than the other
wise creatures:
25 the ants are not a mighty people,
but they prepare their food in the summer ahead of time;
26 rock-badgers are not particularly strong as a species,
but they set their homes up on a crag;
27 locusts have no king at all,
but they march out, all of them together, in orderly rows;
28 a lizard you can grab with your hands,
but it hangs around in kings' palaces.

29 There are three things I've noticed that are stately in their walk,
four, you might say, that are supremely confident in the way
they move:
30 the lion, most powerful of beasts, which never turns its back
on any other animal;
31 a strutting rooster, or a he-goat, and
a king passing in review before his people.

³² **If you have been rash, however, in trying to make yourself
    look good,**
   if you have been thinking up (things), hand to mouth,
³³ **[realize]:**
   when you press milk, you get curds;
   when you press a nose, you get blood; and
   **when you press somebody's whole face hard, you get a
       real fight.**

**[C: God's world is marvelous instruction; so beware of sudden
        power, vanity, and violence.]**

(Proverbs 30)

There is a lot to digest here, but I've spelled out in summing-up
captions the A, B, and C we could focus on briefly, so we can top off
Proverbs 30 with the Newer Testament passage in James about "wisdom."

Wiseman Agur begins by admitting that his struggles to become
wise by himself have been fruitless; he is not the Almighty Creator God
of Isaiah 40! "Wisdom," verse 3, "is intimate experiential knowledge of
what is holy" (cf. also Proverbs 9:10). The Hebrew word for "knowledge"
there is the one used for human sexual intercourse ("Adam **knew** his wife
Eve and she conceived and bore Cain, saying 'I have begotten a man with
the help of the Lord,'" Genesis 4:1). You are wise, says Proverbs 30, only
when you genuinely, thoroughly **know what God wants done, what is
holy and true to the Lord.** And the point is: God alone is the source of
wisdom (cf. Job 28, Proverbs 2).

Agur quotes David from Psalm 18:30 (cf. 2 Samuel 22) in verse
5: "God's Word and promises weather the ups and downs of history;
God always comes through; God is a safe place to run to for refuge." So
take God straight, on the rocks, trust the Lord for direction. And don't
finagle with what God has said and tells us is the way to walk our daily
life, or you will misrepresent the Lord! Therefore, please, God, pleads the
wiseman Agur (v.8), keep me and my tongue from being tricky, and give
me and my family or friends just enough manna good for each day so I
know who is in charge of our lives.

Then comes a section that restates some of the ten commandments,
plus a vivid indictment of fake wise people (vv.12–14), as sharp as Jesus
in Matthew 23 about those God-believers who are whitewashed tombs
full of rotting bones: moralistic do-gooders who keep the law's P's and
Q's, but deep-down ruthlessly trample on the weak and needy neighbor,
are really godless fools.

So the prohibitions depicted in the paragraph of verses 10–17 are
enunciated in the context of verses 1–9, where God says our human talk
and walk is not to be deceitful, but must be couched in a heart transparently holy before God and true to one's neighbor. Obeying God's com-

mandments has to be an act of trusting thankfulness, or going through the motions is a farce.

The last section of Agur's little anthology that God's Spirit has provided for us (vv.18–33) exemplifies the acute observation and artistic flair of the Bible's "wisdom literature."

God's world is amazing! The soaring sweep of a mighty eagle in the air; the slithering scramble of a snake without legs over a hot rock; a lowly lizard sneaking into the dining hall of royalty; a lion, rooster, he-goat, and king (president/prime minister) parading around before his hens.

You notice Agur is not preachy. He doesn't allegorize what he sees and make it have a "heavenly" meaning. Like a good landscaper or carpenter or therapist, the wiseman Agur has a sharp eye, reads body language, and calls a spade a spade with **metaphorical**, poetic intensity!

It's too marvelous, says verse 19, "the way of a young man **in** a woman able to bear a child"! Extraordinary! says verse 20, the way a fornicator gorges on sex, wipes off the mouth afterwards, and says, "Next…" (I could have mentioned that the Hebrew word in Proverbs 30:12 I translated "excrement" [NIV has "filth"] has an exact common four-letter word equivalent—hypocrites have not wiped themselves clean, says the Bible.)

I'm just trying to say *en passant* that the Bible has literary guts, rough tenderness, and a fresh, surprising insight into our daily lives in God's world. Naturally. Because God braided us in our mother's womb (Psalm 139). God keeps our tears in a bottle (Psalm 56:8). God wants us human creatures to be playfully at rest in God's world (Matthew 11:28–30; cf. Proverbs 8:30–31).

If you have been trying to make yourself look good by putting down others, say verses 32–33, remember:

> when you churn milk, you get curds;
> when you twist a nose hard, you get blood; and
> when you smash somebody's whole face, you get a real fight.

since "losing face" incites hateful resentment that lasts a long lifetime.

Agur's wise reflections tip us off on how God wants us humans to live in creation: joyful about the glory of all God's creatures, from ants to rocks and from wind patterns to zinnias. And God's Word dearly wants to protect us from our vanities, so that we become wise and adopt the light **yoke** of…Christ's gentleness.

That last remark brings us to the Newer Testament completion of Proverbs 30 in James' paragraph on wisdoms (3:13–18). God's Word says there:

> Is there a wise man or woman among you? one who knows what he or she is doing?
> All right, let that person **show it by** their **daily deeds dealing wholesomely with others in the gentleness peculiar to wisdom.**

But if you have ruthless enthusiasm and ambitious rivalry in your heart, do not boast [about your wisdom], do not lie against the truth. Such "wisdom" has not come down from heaven: it is utterly earthbound, emotionalistic, demonic. Wherever jealousy and selfish ambition exist, there you will always find upheaval and every kind of mean skullduggery.

Wisdom from heaven is first of all worshipful; it will also produce shalom. True wisdom is willing to wait, is able to be talked to, is full of mercy and good fruits, not hypocritically hiding something, but open-whole-hearted.

Those who produce shalom, in that spirit of rich wholesomeness, sow the fruit of doing what is right [before God].

[D: Breathe the Gentleness Peculiar to Wisdom as You Enact the Lord's Peace.]

God's Word of James' paragraph deepens Agur's instruction on the discipline of becoming wise to God's will, by spelling out further the differences between the truly wise and the pseudo-wise guys.

God-honoring wisdom is "show" as much as "tell." If you are only a "hearer" of God's will, but do not embody what God wants done in your thought, spoken words and other deeds, then you, as mere auditors, are deceiving yourselves, says James 1:22–24. Wisdom is only evident in action.

But if you "show" your clever knowledge in order to get an advantage for yourself, show-off your "wisdom," play the subversive activist who knows better than others, who wants a following, who proudly pushes things through, such zealous "wisdom" is demonic, says the Bible, and fulminates disorder, dirty, crooked underhandedness (James 3:16)— virtually a state of war that kills people who are neighbors, if not brothers and sisters—to one another (James 4:1–10).

True wisdom, however, given by God's Holy Spirit to us often wishy-washy humans (James 1:5–8), shows up by our begetting deeds, speech, and a steady perspective that bespeaks the generous gentleness of Jesus Christ, the wholeness and peace dear to the triune God. The spirit of genuine wisdom (v.17) is pure-hearted, worshipful, and produces shalom, makes peace, because the wise person's judgments are merciful, considerate, not impatient, sure, without guile. And whenever someone is wise enough to consummate difficult decisions that prove true, are holy, and bear good fruit, then indeed what is right in God's eyes will get done (James 3:18).

Deciding on who to marry or not; deciding which job or profession or volunteer work you find best fits your native gifts; deciding what to do with your leisure time, if you have such an option; deciding what music to listen to or films and videos to see; deciding the tempo, texture, and habits of daily life you can live with: such far-reaching decisions are often set unawares, before we become fully conscious of what we have done and are doing or are having done to us.

Proverbs 30 and James 3 tell us that without godly wisdom we will be prey to making a frantic mess of our lives in our most fundamental decisions, and possibly have a hateful effect on our neighbors and a following generation. We need to become wise **at heart**, in our preconscious stance before God as creatures open to the presence or not of the Holy Spirit, so those unconscious decisions generate shalom.

The LORD God can overrule, bide God's anger, or punish our foolishness anytime God wants, and correct our acting godlessly in our own strength and cunning. That's good to know. But Scripture, in the mouth of the Arabian Agur Jakehson and James the brother of Jesus Christ, is calling us to be proactive on wisdom: learn to be wise, says the Bible (Proverbs 1:1–9).

You don't become wise as a young person or an older person by looking at creation under a microscope and getting an academic Ph.D. You don't learn to become wise by going into a room without windows to pray endlessly for the Holy Spirit to parachute out of heaven and fill your heart to overflowing. You don't become wise by copying over the Ten commandments and the Beatitudes fifteen times, as if you were a student writing lines because you have been delinquent. Since **wisdom is a gift of God**, you can't earn it, demand it, buy it, steal it, or achieve wisdom by studying or doing certain rituals—that's what the Pharisees and Sadducees of Jesus' day thought.

As I understand the thrust of God's Word in *Proverbs* and the letter of *James*, you learn to be wise somewhat like osmosis. To study harder is not enough. To pray harder is not enough. You need to study **prayerfully**, and pray **studyingly**, that is, struggling to let the Scriptures, where God speaks, soften up and direct your heart so that as you examine God's world and come to grapple with and understand our historical troubles in this good creation, we back into wisdom, as it were.

(15) Author with favorite flower, 1980s

You stand there admiring a brightly colored, fresh sweet pea flower on the vine after a rain shower has passed, with Psalms 104 and 148 tintinnabulating in your head, and you can't help but think and say wisely, "Thank God! Only God could make a sweet pea (or strawberries to pick yourself)!" Or you are faced with a convoluted mash of bitter emotions in the break-up of a marriage where abuse and hurt expectations have a long hidden history, and as the Psalm laments and Job's agonies resonate in your subconsciousness, you wisely say, "No one is guiltless; go and sin in frustrated anger no more" (cf. John 5:1–16, 8:1–11).

That is, becoming wise is like catching the mumps or a bad cold. Suddenly the light of God's Word in Scripture you have been immersed in, and the creatural order or disorder you are examining in God's world with a heart aching to know God's will, quietly grateful to have been freed from the power of sin by the Holy Spirit's presence following up the death, resurrection and ascension of Jesus Christ for sinners (cf. Romans 6:12–23): suddenly God's Word, the Spirit's leading, and creational revelation clicks, jells, and makes you contagious with "wisdom from heaven." We need faithfully to search communally the integral holy Scriptures given to us, and grapple unafraid as a communion of saints with the glories and turbulence in creation, if we would grow in the gentling healing and wholesome directed shalom that wisdom from God affords. To become wise is not an achievement—and then you've got it!—but is a continual process of being humbly attentive to the creatural word of God and the Holy Spirit Christ has sent, while directed by the penetrating, no-nonsense, rich biblical revelation.

To put it sharply in conclusion: I understand our Scripture to say it is simplistic to think that "Jesus is the answer to all our problems; accept Jesus as Savior and you become a wise person, knowing what is true and holy to God." Proverbs 30 and James 3, in the matrix of the whole Bible, say: "Jesus' historical sacrifice and triumph over death, the wages of sin, makes it indeed **possible** for us human creatures who repent of 'doing it our way' and who become adopted children of God, **to undergo the discipline of probing what the Rule of Jesus Christ a-coming means for directing our lives into shalom**, whether it be landscaping, studying, making music, raising children, or doing the dishes.

Wisdom is not like instant coffee: heat the emotional water, spoon in some grains of intellectual truth, mix, and serve as a tonic for what ails you. No, godly wisdom has to brew in the crucible of rigorous Scripture knowledge, a prayed wrestling with the Holy Spirit over time, and respect for understanding creatural foibles in detail—what makes family ties tick or constrict, what promotes economic responsibility or greed, what distinguishes education from indoctrination.... That is, wisdom takes effort to be seasoned by tough life decisions, because godly wisdom is not opinionated, is not judgmental **or** lax, but is **firmly flexible with gentleness in its ministry of always moving toward**—God protect us!—**the norm of producing shalom among our neighbors**.

Would to God that the Israeli generals and the Fundamentalist Muslim "suicide bomber" network and the Western VIP fix-it advisers embroiled in the terribly complicated Palestine history of hatred and war atrocities for generations could somehow hear the good news of Proverbs 30 and James 3 **and act upon the LORD's call for WISE just-doing**. Exacting "justice"—the retribution we have coming to us!—that has not a jot of pure-hearted gentleness but is ruthless with bitter ambition will continue to be demonic and destructive, world without end, says Scripture.

I know, God's injunction to exercise gentle wisdom holds for me too, for us as people in today's world. Do those who are called to exercise authority believe the **meek** shall inherit the earth? Do **we** act in our daily life at school, the office, in recreation, "hanging out," as if that Word of God Jesus Christ calls us to hear about "the meek" (Psalm 37:1–11, Matthew 5:5) shall indeed prove to be true (Proverbs 30:5)?

Proverbs 30 and James 3 is asking us, much as the letter God had Paul write to the Romans says, to present ourselves bodily as a living sacrifice, holy and pleasing to God, not conformed to the "Gimmie" world, but to be transformed by the renewing of our whole consciousness, so we may test out what is the good, mature, wise will of God (Romans 12:1–2). Jesus himself spelled out the message of A, B, C, D in a simple invitation:

> Come to me all you who are tired out and overburdened, and I will give you rest. Take my yoke upon you [says Jesus] and learn from me [and my Rule in God's world], because I am **gentle and humble** at heart: then you shall find genuine rest for your selves. You see, my yoke is "sweet," and my burden is light. (Matthew 11:28–30)

PRAYER: Dear LORD God,

Thank you for the wise sayings of Agur, which can speak to us many, many generations later. We pray, Lord, that You will make all those gathered under the umbrella of your grace to be as a congregation of such diverse persons and interests and abilities wise.

Teach us to take careful looks at the ants and roosters and pileated woodpeckers, Arabian sheiks, members of Congress, and Canadian MPs and checkout persons at No Frills, in advertisements and cemeteries, and those with bloody noses. Help us to stop, look, and listen to our world as we persistently search the Scriptures to find out what "following the Christ" means for us, whether we are 13 years old, 30, or aged 70.

And as we take time to examine our surroundings and to understand the Scriptures, please get us down on our knees, literally and metaphorically, to plead for your Spirit to fill the deepest crevices of our heart.

We pray this, LORD God, in the name of the savior of the world, Jesus Christ. Amen.

(Toronto, July 2002)

PROVERBS 10:1–22:
FROM POETIC PARAGRAPHS TO PREACHING

As a Christ-believing amateur in scholarship on the book of Proverbs, I have been protected from much wrong-headed professional study in "wisdom literature" because I naively took seriously the canonic shape in which Proverbs has been accepted by the church. As a great-grandchild of the historic Reformation, my Bible reading is one that assumes "the Bible be read as sacred Scripture." This we do in the communion of the saints, living and dead, carefully trusting the text will lead the community of faith enough to find definite direction in "the entire manner of service which God requires of us."[1]

Such a trusting experience is crankled by practically all Proverbs commentators—from the higher critical Crawford H. Toy (1899) to the more recent Protestant evangelical Derek Kidner (1964).[2] They treat the text like a collection of individual sayings, loose from any defined context—a kind of anthology of nuggets of wisdom arranged in apparently random fashion for our benefit and admonition. The assumed contextlessness of the sayings collected in Proverbs 10–29, however, easily makes their interpretation arbitrary, truistic, or opaque (not exactly a fertile source for a twenty-minute Sunday sermon that would bring Bible-exposited Good News).

A brief history of exegesis
The background to this state of affairs is fairly well-known. In 1924,

---

1   *Belgic Confession,* articles 2–7; cf. Brevard S. Childs, *Introduction to the Old Testament as Scripture* (Philadelphia: Fortress, 1979), 27–106.

2   Crawford H. Toy, *A Critical and Exegetical Commentary on the Book of Proverbs* (Edinburgh: T. & T. Clark, 1899); Derek Kidner, *Proverbs* (Downers Grove: InterVarsity, 1964).

First published in *Reading and Hearing the Word from Text to Sermon: Essays in honor of John H. Stek,* ed. Arie C. Leder (Grand Rapids: Calvin Theological Seminary and CRC Publications, 1998), 181–200.

Adolf Erman claimed that Proverbs 22:17–23:11 was derived from the Egyptian instruction of Amenemope. Later, Johannes Fichtner argued that biblical wisdom was derived from the ancient Near Eastern eudemonistic teachings that the Hebrews gradually nationalized with Yahwist references.[3] Subsequently, scholars sought to track these refinements, which they claimed moved from teaching a mundane "folk" wisdom, to the more acceptable, pious "theological wisdom."

The influential result was William McKane's decanonization of proverb sentences into three groups: advice for living a successful life, admonitions against harmful deeds to society, and Yahweh God-talk.[4]

As late as 1979, R.N. Whybray suffered the same geneticistic approach and kept reading Proverbs as an attempt by a Yahwist editor to be "bringing 'secular' wisdom under the umbrella of Yahwism."[5] Claus Westermann still holds to the presence of unresolved opposites of "profane" and "isolated propositions about God" in Proverbs, even though he admits that this has kept biblical wisdom from playing a central role in the proclamation of the church.[6]

Udo Skladny set the record straight, as I see it. He argues that the earliest original calling of biblical proverbial wisdom is for people to respect and follow the Lord's order for everyday life, which is first of all ordering to be trusted (*"eine geglaubte Ordnung"*) and obeyed truly as the Lord God's will, full of blessing.[7] Likewise, Zimmerli affirmed that "wis-

---

3   J. Fichtner, *Die altorientalische Weisheit in ihrer Israelitisch-Jüdische Ausprägung* (Giessen: Töpelmann, 1933).

4   William McKane, *Proverbs* (Philadelphia: Westminster, 1970), 10–13, 415.

5   R. N. Whybray, "Yahweh-sayings and Their Contexts in Proverbs 10, 1–22, 16" [1979] in *La sagesse de l'ancient testament*, ed. Maurice Gilbert (Leuven: Leuven University Press, 1990), 162. Later on he writes, "it would seem we have to acknowledge three stages: a) a morally 'neutral' attitude ('old wisdom'); b) a moral attitude which expresses itself in terms of an immanent force making for just reward; c) a recognition that this just reward is not simply immanent but directly due to the personal will of Yahweh" (165). In a later work (*Wealth and Poverty in the Book of Proverbs* [Sheffield: Sheffield Press, 1990], 68, n. 1) Whybray modifies his earlier formulation: "I should no longer use the term 'secular.' . . . The 'Yahweh-proverbs' may be said to represent a theological development in so far that they reflect a tendency to *clarify* Yahweh's involvement in all that happens; but—contrary to a widely held view—there is in my opinion no reason to suppose that the absence of reference to Yahweh in the majority of these proverbs necessarily implies a lack of recognition of that involvement."

6   Claus Westermann, *Forschungsgeschichte zur Weisheitsliteratur* 1950–1990 (Stuttgart: Calwer Verlag, 1991), 46–47.

7   Udo Skladny, *Die ältesten Spruchsammlungen in Israel* (Göttingen: Vandenhoeck & Ruprecht, 1962), 89–91.

dom theology is Creation theology."[8] It is a false start to pit secular proverbs against sacred proverb glosses and to spend time guessing at probable stages of compositional genealogy. Such a split orientation fosters treating Old Testament "wisdom" as a topic foreign to "salvation history."[9]

The purported derivative nature of biblical wisdom sayings, culturally dependent upon comparable Egyptian and Mesopotamian "wisdom," is no longer considered compelling today by various specialists.[10] But McKane's wrenching apart of what is canonically given operates as a smokescreen that leaves exegetes uncertain as to what is actually given for us to read in the booked Proverbs. This is especially true in the contemporary atmosphere of wanting "living proverbs" fit for quick reading in the fast lane.

The effort to center the discussion of the proverb on its presumed oral folk wisdom origins also pushed scholarship in the wrong direction.[11] Through this approach the booked Proverbs (especially those in Proverbs 10–24) came to be considered an anthology of atomistic *logia* treating a miscellany of topics arranged at most by catchwords (Boström's paronomasia) or grouped loosely around similar themes. Perhaps Proverbs 25–29 signals a firm move from oral to "transcribed" proverbs (25:1), that is,

---

8 Walther Zimmerli, "Ort und Grenze der Weisheit im Rahmen der alttestamentlichen Theologie," in *Gottes Offenbarung. Gesammelte Aufsätze zum Alten Testament* (München: Chr. Kaiser Verlag, 1963), 302. This essay is translated as "The Place and Limit of the Wisdom in the Framework of the Old Testament Theology," in *Studies in Ancient Israelite Wisdom,* ed. James L. Crenshaw (New York: KTAV Publishing House, 1976), 314–326.

9 That is, as the biblical story of the exodus to the promised land. Patrick Skehan (*Studies in Israelite Poetry and Wisdom* [Washington: Catholic Biblical Association of America, 1971], 23) argues that "to ascribe a primitively 'secular' character to the origins of any phase of human life in ancient times, in or out of Israel, is to go against all that we know of ancient man. . . . The 'secular' basis for the supposition is altogether gratuitous in afflicting some unidentifiable group of ancient sages with the misfortunes of the modern agnostics." Childs (*Introduction to the Old Testament as Scripture,* 553) writes, "As sacred scripture the book [of Proverbs] was not to be read according to a history of development in the concept of wisdom, rather from a fully developed confessional standpoint."

10 The Egyptologists K. A. Kitchen, "Proverbs and Wisdom Books of the Ancient Near East: The factual history of a literary form," *Tyndale Bulletin* 28 (1977): 69–114; "Egypt and Israel during the First Millennium B.C.," *Vetus Testamentum Supplement* 40 (1986): 107–23; Jutta Krispenz, *Spruchcomposition im Buch Proverbia* (Bern: Peter Lang, 1989); John Ruffle, "The Teaching of Amenemope and its Connection with the Book of Proverbs," *Tyndale Bulletin* 28 (1977): 29–68.

11 See, for example, the work of Otto Eissfeldt, *Der Maschal im Alten Testament* (Giessen: Alfred Töpelmann, 1913).

literary deposits by education court scribes.[12] But the presumption that the book of Proverbs is a largely unedited compilation of now contextless oral one-liners continues to dominate wisdom scholarship.[13]

Recently, however, this atomistic approach has been questioned by a qualified and tentative attempt to find unifying edited contextuality within the Proverbs text, a *Sitz in Text*.[14] Already in 1968, Hermission carefully treated the sayings of Proverbs 10–15 with considerable cohesion, paying particular attention to how their aesthetic quality intimated a connecting order.[15] In 1988, Van Leeuwen argued: "If the text presents us with larger, unified blocks of proverbial material, the exegete possesses a much surer basis for interpretation than if only a random accretion of isolated proverbs exists."[16]

That is precisely the thesis of this article, which is dedicated in thanks to John Stek. He has always served Christ's body with his Old Testament scholarship, dedicating an incredible amount of his lifetime to carefully annotated translation (NIV study edition) of the Bible, and giving insightful lectures and valuable syllabi on Old Testament books to theological students at Calvin Seminary, in Toronto, and elsewhere over many years.

I state my thesis as follows:

> Expect poetic paragraphs within the booked Proverbs 10–29, because the artful comparisons (מְשָׁלִים) and oblique riddles (חִידֹת) are rooted historically and professionally in the office of wise leaders recounted in the Bible and have been written down by God-breathed educated literary scribes.

---

12 So R. B. Y. Scott, "Solomon and the Beginnings of Wisdom in Israel," *Festschrift for Harold Henry Rowley. Supplement to Vetus Testamentum III*, eds. M. Noth and D. Winton Thomas (Leiden: Brill, 1960), 272–274.

13 McKane (*Proverbs*, 414) and Westermann (*Forschungsgeschichte*, 46) assert that didactic instruction like Proverbs 1–9, the longer and later artistically worked pieces, has a tradition separate from the original popular aphoristic tradition.

14 Brian Watson Kovacs (*Sociological-structural Constraints upon Wisdom: The spatial and temporal matrix of Proverbs 15:28–22:16* [Dissertation Vanderbilt University, 1978], 308) writes, "the catchword and paronomastic patterns which connect various proverbs simply cannot be adventitious nor accidental. Groupings of sayings must be accounted for, along with disruptions and incursions into the text." See also Raymond C. Van Leeuwen, *Context and Meaning in Proverbs 25–27* (Atlanta: Scholars Press, 1988), 37, and Duane A. Garrett, *Proverbs, Ecclesiastes, Song of Songs*. The New American Commentary (Nashville: The Broadman Press, 1993). In a series of articles in *Vanguard* (1972–1979), I exposited Proverbs 25–29 as an anthology of gnomic poems.

15 Hans-Jürgen Hermission, *Studien zur israelitischen Spruchweisheit* (Neukirchener Verlag, 1968), 180–181.

16 Van Leeuwen, *Context and Meaning in Proverbs 25–27*, 6.

Finding the poetic parameters in Proverbs 10–29 so as to discern the unified paragraphs[17] will open up the book of sayings for good preaching.

CONTEXT AND TASK

Before demonstrating this thesis with Proverbs 10:1–22, I will sketch the historical and literary setting, and then present evidence that "the wise" men and women in Israel had a special task and way of presenting a word from the Lord to God's people. These matters are critical for a proper reading of the booked proverbs.

The Literary Setting

Since the superscriptions of Proverbs 1:1, 10:1, and 25:1 suggest c. 950–700 BC[18] to be the historical parameters for the bulk of the written material, then Proverbs should address not nomads but settled city dwellers who were becoming fairly prosperous and secularized. There was a strong farming community at the time, but the younger generation was leaving the countryside to make its fortune in Jerusalem, where the building of the temple and the royal palace were causing a construction boom. Along with the extremely high inflation rate caused by Solomon's enormous deficit financing (1 Kings 9–10, esp. 9:10–14, 10:27), the labor force's shift from herding sheep to city work upset a traditional lifestyle and the accompanying faith-commitment. Freedom from parental control and moving outside the country confines of cultic worship and rituals of sacrifice also increased the importance of education for the next generation.

These dates for Proverbs also cover Ahab and Jezebel's appropriation of Naboth's familial homestead and Jehu's subsequent rough-and-ready retribution (1 Kings 21, 2 Kings 9). The prophets Elijah, Amos, Isaiah, and Micah proclaimed God's justice during the generations when the wise sayings and admonitions would be particularly relevant. And good kings like Hezekiah needed to train young scribes and princes to carry out godly civil administration in the outlying districts of Judah away from the courtly precincts, where judgments in civic disputes would be given orally.

It took Christa Kayatz's 1966 dissertation[19] under Gerhard von Rad

---

17 It may be useful to think of something like the various Psalms (although in Proverbs the poetic paragraphs are epigrammatic poems for speaking, not songs for singing).

18 This dating is also supported by Kitchen on external historical-literary grounds. Cf. Kitchen, "Proverbs and Wisdom Books," 102, 108–110, and "Egypt and Israel," 119–23.

19 Christa Kayatz, *Studien zu Proverbien 1–9. Eine form- und motivgeschichtliche Unter-suchung unter Einbeziehung ägyptischen Vergleichsmaterials* (Neukirchen-Vluyn: Neu-

to overturn earlier authorities' (e.g., Eissfeldt, Kittel, Sellin, Gressmann) post-exilic dating of Proverbs 1–9. She argued that Proverb's 1–9's familiarity with ancient Egyptian wisdom literature undermines the hypothesis that later Hellenistic sources account for biblical motifs present.[20] With Childs,[21] I hold that the Masoretic text version the church has come to live with leads it to read Proverbs 10–29 in the light of Proverbs 1–9. So the artistically nuanced Proverbs 1–9 provides a clue to the poetic compositional character of chapters 10–29, since that is the way "the wise" formulated God's word.

If Proverbs 1–9, like Proverbs 31:10–31, exemplifies the kind of poetic paragraphs booked by "the wise," then Proverbs 1–9 not only provides, as Van Leeuwen writes, "a worldview and hermeneutic introduction to the short sayings and admonitions which follow,"[22] but also suggests the poetic format normal for biblical proverbial literature. The prevalent notion that "each proverb is an independent unit that can stand alone and still have meaning," and that "textual context is not essential for interpretation," is wrong, and invites a myopic reading of Proverbs. Garrett significantly adds, "Context, however, sometimes qualifies or gives a more precise meaning to a given proverb."[23] But even Garrett's attempt to "collect" proverbs into groups needs, I think, to be driven more radically by the realization that what we have here first of all are poetic paragraphs. In poetry the chicken comes before the egg—the paragraph whole determines the sense of the separate lines. One must accept that literary critical point in order to read and exhort from the booked Proverbs in a way that "plows the word of truth rightly" (2 Timothy 2:14–19).

The Historical Setting:
The Place and Task of Wise Counselors in Israel

Leadership in Israel: Priests, Prophets, and Kings
After God covenanted with Israel at Mount Sinai, Moses ordained Aaron and his sons to care for the tabernacle and the ark (Leviticus 8). They were

---

kirchener Verlag, 1966).

20 Roland E. Murphy ("Assumptions and Problems in Old Testament Wisdom Research," *Catholic Biblical Quarterly* 29 [1976]: 413) still maintained, "It is generally agreed that Prv 1–9 is a later addition and introduction to pre-exilic collections of wisdom sayings." Westermann (*Forschungsgeschichte*, 46) also still thinks Proverbs 1–9 is late. These earlier traditions of thinking about Proverbs die hard.

21 Childs, *Introduction to the Old Testament as Scripture*, 552–555.

22 Raymond C. Van Leeuwen, "In Praise of Proverbs," in *Pledges of Jubilee*, eds. Lambert Zuidervaart and Henry Luttikhuizen (Grand Rapids: Eerdmans, 1995), 313, n. 12.

23 Garrett, *Proverbs, Ecclesiastes, Song of Songs*, 46.

in charge of sacrifices for propitiation and for thanksgiving to offset the people's sin, they gave liturgical leadership, and they were set aside for the important protocol of moving the ark (Numbers 10:33–36). Levites were officially consecrated to assist in such priestly tasks in Israel (Numbers 1:47–54; 3:5–13).[24] After Joshua's death, the regularly ordained priests of Aaron and Eleazer's line tended the ark at Bethel (Judges 20:24–28), but do-it-yourself priesthoods during the days of Israel's judges (Judges 17) showed how Israel's priesthood could deteriorate to the nadir of the abusive sons of Eli, and end shamefully with Ichabod (1 Samuel 2:12–17, 22–25; 4:1–22).

The angel of the Lord (מַלְאַךְ יהוה) had brought crucial messages from God since the olden days—to Hagar (Genesis 16:7–16), to Abraham about to sacrifice Isaac (Genesis 22:9–19), to Moses at the burning bush (Exodus 3:1–4:17), to Balaam and his ass (Numbers 22:21–25), to Gideon (Judges 6:7–10), and to Samson's prospective parents (Judges 13). The prophet Samuel was trained by the old priest Eli during a time when the Lord God, says scripture, was not speaking much to Israel, and when revelatory visions were infrequent (1 Samuel 3:1). The Bible tells of an unnamed seer in Gideon's day who already used the typically prophetic phrase "Thus says the Lord" (כה אמר יהוה) (Judges 6:7–10). Such speaking is what prophets were supposed to do, and that's what judge-prophet Samuel did when he anointed Saul to be the first king of Israel, saying, "I'll sound out to you the word of God" (1 Samuel 9:27). By the time of Elijah, Ahab, Elisha, and Jehoshaphat, there were schools for prophets in Bethel and Jericho (2 Kings 2:1–3, 15–18). When Amaziah, high priest of corrupt King Jeroboam II, labeled Amos "a visionary" (חֹזֶה), Amos was glad to tell him that he had not been to any such school, but to "Hear the Word of the Lord!" (שמע דבר-יהוה) anyhow (Amos 7:10–17).

The kings of Israel were anointed to rule and protect God's people, particularly to administer justice (Deuteronomy 17:14–20; 1 Samuel 8). There seems to be a sorting out of leadership tasks among Israel's first kings. King Saul—anointed one of the Lord (מְשִׁיחַ יהוה)—made sacrifices in Gilgal when Samuel was late, and lost his kingship because they were disobedient sacrifices (1 Samuel 13:2–15; 15:22–23). David tended burnt offerings and peace offerings before the Lord when he brought the ark to Jerusalem to centralize his tribal administration in Jerusalem, the city of God. His priestly dancing pleased the Lord, if not Michal (2 Samuel 6). Young King Solomon sacrificed in Gibeon (1 Kings 3:1–15) and

---

24 As artisans, for example, the charismatic Bezaleel from Judah, and Oholiab from Dan had crucial roles in the construction of the Tent of Meeting (Exodus 35:30–39:43).

later offered a long priestly prayer with untold offerings at the dedication of the new temple (1 Kings 8) without punishment for mixing priestly duties with his royal tasks. King Solomon also exemplified the wisdom of God, with an encyclopedic horticultural and animal knowledge and the ability to ferret out the truth needed for making just judgments (1 Kings 3:16–28; 4:29–34).

So leaders among God's people were anointed to be priests, prophets, and kings. These posts of trust were quite differentiated, even though historical overlapping of duties existed on into the early monarchy. What needs attention, however, if we are to understand the booked Proverbs, is the fact that there emerged a loosely differentiated group of "counselors" (יֹעֵץ) of the Lord, distinct from mediating priests of the Lord in Israel, from oracular prophets of the Lord in Israel, and from the Lord's kings in Israel. They made professional in Israel the kind of guiding, teaching leadership practiced by Moses, the village elders at the gates, and the charismatic tribal judges. These "wise" persons, who served as a core of special advisers to royalty, held a definite office as normal and highly valued in the court of Israel as in the courts of surrounding countries.

Leadership in Israel: The Wise

When Pharaoh's counselors failed to interpret God-sent dreams, the wise-man Joseph because Pharaoh's secretary of state. Scripture reports Pharaoh saying, "This is a man in whom is the Spirit of God; nobody sees through things as you do" (Genesis 41, esp. vv. 7–8, 38–40). Moses was also trained in Egyptian wisdom (Acts 7:17–29; Hebrews 11:23–28; cf. Exodus 2:1–15). That Moses was a highly literate commander-in-chief of God's folk wandering through the desert is evident from the elaborate memorial songs he composed (Exodus 15:1–18, Deuteronomy 32:1–47) and the poetic benedictions recorded in his name (Deuteronomy 33). Balaam, son of Beor at Pethor on the Euphrates, was Balak's highest paid "consultant" or "wise man" (Micah 6:5). King Balak needed advice on dealing with the horde of Israelites camped on his borders. After missing out on the honors Balak had offered him, Balaam proved his credentials as an evil "wise man" (cf. James 3:13–18) by later providing the elders of Midian with an intermarriage policy that would break the Lord's favor upon Israel (Numbers 25; 31:1–20).

Such counselors of royalty—like the princesses (wise women, חֲכָמוֹת) attending General Sisera's mother (Judges 5:29)—held humble positions early among the Lord God's people. To help him rule the unwieldy multitude of Israelites, Moses appointed "wise men, insightful, seasoned persons" selected by the various tribes to head up the civil order and to judge disputes without playing favorites (Deuteronomy 1:9–18; cf. Exodus 18:13–27). The tasks of these "wise ones" was allied with ruling; they did not make laws, but they had important judicial responsibilities.

That there was still a definite place for "the wise" to give counsel in Israel during King Saul's day is clear. It was reported that the Lord was no longer answering King Saul's prayer for direction, either by the Urim (used by the priests for making important decisions—Exodus 28:30, Leviticus 8:5–9, Ezra 2:59–63), or by prophetic seers, or by dreams (the peculiar interpretive task of "the wise," 1 Samuel 28:6). During King David's reign, the established practice of "wise women" in the countryside is matter-of-factly told. Joab requisitioned "a wise women" from Tekoa— Amos's hometown—to act out a kind of morality playlet designed to give the pining David a rationale for recalling his murderer son Absalom (2 Samuel 14:1–24). It was in the office of "wise woman" that a leading woman in the city of Abel debated with General Joab and then convinced her townspeople to throw the head of Benjamite insurrectionist Sheba over the wall to save the town's inhabitants (2 Samuel 20:1–22).

The seer Nathan was King David's confidante. His story of the one little ewe lamb (2 Samuel 11:26–12:15) is a characteristic way for "the wise" to bring fools to their senses, and to give suggestive, persuasive advice to those in power. With considerable eloquence, Nathan got the dying King David to let him and Zadok the priest quickly anoint the boy Solomon to be king to foil Adonijah's bid for the throne (1 Kings 1). This consummate story-telling, roundabout, deferential, yet surprising way to bring God's specific direction to bear on life problems stamps the activity of "the wise." The crucial role Hushai and Ahithophel played at the court of David and at the headquarters of renegade Absalom is comparable to the role of the "wise women" mentioned above. Counsel was highly prized in Israel. "In those days the counsel (עֵצָה) that Ahithophel delivered was as if one consulted the very word of God" (2 Samuel 16:23).

Even King Solomon's prodigious wisdom was backed up by ranks of courtly counselors. They outlived Solomon's apostasy and death and saw their good counsel dismissed by Solomon's son Rehoboam when he formed a new cabinet of more modern "wise men," who led him to speak in a harsh spirit to the people seeking redress (1 Kings 12:1–20). This overturning of good counsel by poisoning advice (עֵצָה), with historic results of a split from David's line, was overseen by the Lord, says Scripture (1 Kings 12:15).

By the time of the God-fearing Hezekiah, the composition of

a courtly council with wise counselors included figures like Shebna, a scribe or secretary, and Joah Asaphson, an historian or record keeper. They knew Aramaic, the international language of diplomacy, and entered into high-level negotiations of royal decisions (2 Kings 18:1–19:7). So "the men of Hezekiah, King of Judah," who were given the precious task of "transcribing" the artful comparisons of Solomon (מִשְׁלֵי שְׁלֹמֹה, Proverbs 25:1), were not underpaid copyists. They were educated, cultured wise men concerned with editing a canon for instructing the inexperienced and for providing "the wise" with disciplined training for setting their consciousness in awe of the Lord.[25]

Even in the run-down court of King Jehoiakim there were polyglot wise men like Daniel, Hananiah, Mishael, and Azariah. When they were taken to the palace of Babylonian Nebuchadnezzar, Daniel and his wise friends proved to be better than any of the Chaldean sorcerers, astrologers, wiseman counselors, and interpreters of dreams, because God's Spirit revealed to Daniel mysteries and made him and his God-fearing friends wise (Daniel 1:1–2:30, esp. 1:4; 2:27–28; 5:10–12).

R. N. Whybray argues for an intellectual tradition in ancient Israel that is "distinct from other traditionalists such as the historical, legal, cultic and prophetic." At the same time he maintains that there is no societal institution carrying this tradition, no school, "no special professional class."[26]

I find the term "intellectual" too disengaged from the determinative faith orientation that was present from the very beginnings of Israel's leadership, even in Abraham's exodus-response to the Lord (Genesis 12:1–9). It is also problematic to over-define terms like "counselor," "teacher," "wise man," and "scribe," as if each excludes the other. Gerhard von Rad, for example, has argued that the biblical words "discipline" (מוּסָר), "discernment" (בִּין), "insightful action" (שֵׂכֶל) "circumspection" (עָרְמָה), and "handiness in knowing what's up" (לֶקַח) are differentiated from the other, but that these differences overlap within the family of "wisdom."[27] Moreover "wisdom" in the Old Testament is not a matter of having a "superior degree of (personal) intelligence,"[28] but of "knowing what God wants done." God can give such "understanding" to the for-

---

25 The word "counsel" (תַּחְבֻּלוֹת) in Proverbs 1:5, reminds one of the phrase "instruction of the Lord" (νουθεσία κυρίου) in Ephesians 6:4.

26 R. N. Whybray, *The Intellectual Tradition in the Old Testament* (Berlin: Walter de Gruyter, 1974), 70, 49.

27 Gerhard von Rad, *Wisdom in Israel*, trans. James D. Martin (London: SCM Press, 1972), 13.

28 Whybray, *The Intellectual Tradition in the Old Testament*, 9, 117.

eign soothsayer Balaam, just as he can call the unbelieving Persian Cyrus messiah (מָשִׁיחַ) among the nations (Isaiah 44:23–45:8).

I have shown how the calling to be "wise" is at home both in the tribal society Moses organized and in the precincts of Solomon's extravagant royalty. "Wise men" and "wise women" exercised a leadership among God's folk that was variegated, fluid, but constant, with certain features that identified its practice as "counsel" (עֵצָה). Differentiation of "the wise" had become commonplace by the time the prophet Jeremiah's adversaries spoke their oath to do him in, when they said, "Come, let's make plans against Jeremiah, as surely as a priest is never without law-guidance (תּוֹרָה), wise man without counsel (עֵצָה), and prophetic seer without the word (דָּבָר)" (Jeremiah 18:18).

After the exile in the day of Ezra and Nehemiah, when kings had forfeited their office among the people of God, the wise men and scribes came to the fore. Ezra was known to Artaxerxes as "priest, scribal scholar in the worded precepts of Yahweh and the ordinances for Israel" (Ezra 7:11). Indeed, that is what scribes in Israel became—Torah specialists. And it needs to be said that when the charisma of wisdom died because there was no vision among God's people, and when "the wise" began to trust their proverbs more than "standing in awe before the Lord God," when these leaders began to put stock in the Abrahamic blood rather than in obeying Yahweh's will, then we see "wise men" like Job's friends and like the scribes of Jesus' day, whether orthodox Pharisee or heterodox Sadducee.

Qoheleth[29] was one of the "wise" teachers in post-exilic Israel who was trained to lead the people in a back-and-forth, speaker-assembly, communal-probing way to determine the right direction to take. Qoheleth is a counselor and folk leader.[30] He speaks words of wisdom, makes artful comparisons, tells riddles and stories to help keep them on the Way of what is right in the eyes of God.

The Imaginative "Yes, but" Pedagogy of "the Wise," and the Literary Configuration of Proverbs 1–9

If you hear Scripture as a true story, as I do, you are startled and impressed by the way young King Solomon distributed the wisdom of God's justice when he told his courtiers to cut a child in half to determine which harlot

---

29 The title of the book Ecclesiastes/Qoheleth designates the official speaker to the people assembled (קָהָל) for a special occasion.

30 This is why in his day Luther translated the title Ecclesiastes/Qoheleth as *Prediger*, that is, "preacher."

was the mother (1 Kings 3:16–28). If such a dramatic ploy was part and parcel of "wisdom" in that day, the contests Solomon held with Egyptian and Babylonian wise men (remember Moses and Aaron's test before Pharaoh's wise men, Exodus 7:8–13)[31] were imaginative, live-wire contests to show wisdom on an international scale (1 Kings 4:29–34).

In fact, Solomon's quasi-dramatic way of bringing God's Word so vividly to bear on life's problems is the very way "the wise" we have discussed above were trained to lead the people in God's directives. I call this parry-and-thrust, parable-telling, decoy method of making a point, the "Yes, but" way of teaching God's will.

This "Yes, but" methodology permeates the artistic literary configuration in the canonically booked section of Proverbs 1–9. There are cohering "my child/my student" (בְּנִי) paragraphs that spin out variations on the central theme, which resonates everywhere:

> To stand still, listening before the Lord God Yahweh gives you a head start in full-bodied knowledge, in wisdom and corrective discipline—exactly what fools despise. (1:7)

These בְּנִי paragraphs sport vivid quotations of tempters (1:11–14; 7:14–20) and provocative alliterative epigrams (1:17; 6:26–28). In counterpoint to these paragraphs, there are stirring appeals by Wisdom in the first person, appealing to the inexperienced to follow the ordinances of Yahweh (1:20–33; 8:1–21). Hymns about Wisdom also highlight the authority, power, and glory of living as children of Wisdom (3:13–20; 8:22–31). These poetic passages act like antiphonal recitations, heightening the one basic thrust of the whole book: live straightforwardly before the Lord, knowing what counts in all kinds of daily life matters.

And there are specially pregnant, capsule summations of the double-edged message permeating the בְּנִי paragraphs (3:11–12; 8:32–36), which festively recapitulate the theme of 1:7. Chapter 5 balances a warning about "the strange woman" and an encouragement to take joy in your wife's erotic love with an interspersed commentary. The structure of chapter 9 is similar. It climaxes the whole proem of chapters 1–9, spelling out the God-breathed point: to live with (Holy Spirited) Wisdom and to know that what God wills shall bring shalom, but to set up a housekeeping with godlessness and to use good gifts illicitly leads to utter ruin.[32]

---

31 ". . . wise men, hieroglyphic specialists, and mumbling magicians"—the narrative pokes fun of them (Exodus 7:11) but recognizes their important official courtly task as Pharaoh's cabinet of advisors.

32 One could schematize the antiphonal artistic structure of chapters Proverbs 1–9 as follows:

The literary configuration one needs to appreciate in order to understand Proverbs 1–9 and (my proposal) the book as a whole is this: think of paragraphs of variegated gnomic poetry, artistically juxtaposed as point and counterpoint, as example and repeated refrain, as graphic vignette and extended metaphor supplementing one another or in polemic contrast. Proverbs 1–9 is like a chorus of stimulating reflections, voices orchestrated on the principle of "Yes, but." The gambit "Yes, but" is the pedagogical tactic of a wise one leading the less experienced person by saying "It seems so, but have you considered this?"

God's revelation booked here in the "wise man and wise woman" format presents arranged paragraphs that need to be studied like poetry. They give an oblique presentation of reflective truth compressed rather than in a direct indicative plus imperative direction (as is the wont of Paul in the New Testament). This "Yes, but" nuanced complexity ranges in the Bible from the chorus of voices lyrically contesting erotic human love called "The Song of Songs" (7:1–9a bespeaks lust, in my reading),[33]

introduction 1:2–6
theme of the whole 1:7

paragraphs on decisive living & temptation by what is "strange" to the Lord	WISDOM passages
1:8–9, 10–19 (with vignette vv. 11–14) 2: 1–22	1:20–21; 22–31, 32–33 appeal of Wisdom
3:1–10, 11–12 3:21–35	3:13–18, 19–20 hymn to Wisdom
4:1–9 on Wisdom as a pearl of great price	
4:10–19 godly Way and godless way contrasted	
4:20–27 obedient heart and bodily acts	
	5:1–6, 7–14, 15–23 strophic caesura
6:1–5 on surety	
6:6–11 on lazy fellow	
6:12–15 on deceiver	
6:16–19 on seven-hated matters	
6:20–21, 22–7:27 (with parable of seduction 7:6–23)	
	8:1–21 appeal of Wisdom
	8:22–31 hymn of Wisdom, in beginning
	8:32–36 closing appeal of Wisdom
	9:1–6, 7–12, 13–18 strophic culmination

33 Cf. my *The Greatest Song: In critique of Solomon*, freshly and literally translated from the Hebrew and arranged for oratorio performance [1967] (Toronto: Tuppence Press, 1988). (I cannot help but wish Duane Garrett, who repeats G. Lloyd Carr's severe judgment [InterVarsity Press, 1984], "that the Song, as it now stands, is unactable" [*Song of Songs*, The New American Commentary, {1993}, 359–60] could once attend one of the many performances I have directed in the last thirty years in Canada, the United States, and Europe. Their error is to force the chorus of voices in the Old Tes-

to the book of Job with speeches permeated by laments, to the dialogical monologue wisdom of Ecclesiastes with refrains of thankful joy, to the teachings of rabbi Christ. Although booked wisdom is not in the "Thus says the Lord" manner of the prophet, and is not an atoning sacrifice offered by the priest, the "Yes, but" Scripture of interwoven poetic paragraphs is still an authoritative kerygmatic word of the Lord that gives healing words of direction.

To show the reach of the "Yes, but" way of "the wise" into the New Testament, one need but notice that Jesus renewed the wise man way of revealing God's will to the people after the intertestamentary commentators and scribes of Jesus' day had dried up its blessing (cf. Matthew 7:28–29). And Jesus "dramatized" teaching in other ways than by using parables (e.g., Matthew 13). Christ's teaching on the hillside epitomizes the living wise man tradition of the Qoheleth-rabbi: "You have heard it said, but I say"; "If your hand causes you to sin, cut it off"—cut the living baby in two! (Matthew 5–7).

Also, Luke reports how Jesus carried out the wise man tradition of unrehearsed interchange with disciples, crowd, and Pharisees, right after Christ's spirited exchange with those who said he exorcised by Beelzebub. Christ had just told the story (Luke 11:24–26) of the unclean spirit that is cast out, returns to find its old hideout clean but empty, gets seven other spirits worse than itself, and returns, so that the fellow is permanently worse off—filled with self-righteous demons!

> Now it happened that while Jesus was speaking these words, some woman or other in the crowd raised her voice and hollered to him, "Blessed is the belly that carried you around and the tits that gave you suck!" But Jesus said, "That's fine, [lady,] but the point is, 'Blessed are those who hear the Word of God and are busy doing it!'" (Luke 11:27–28)

Luke 11:27 (like Proverbs 10:15) is not a text for "Mother's Day" ("May your children be like Christ")! Luke records this incident under the Spirit's guiding to show how superficial the response of Jewish approval often was to rabbi Jesus' teaching, and how Jesus here did a wise man "Yes, but" *au point.*

The woman sensed Christ had done a great deed, and defended his ministry of healing at a very fundamental level, but she didn't have a clue that Christ's exorcism act showed that the glorious rule of God was already begun on earth, and she didn't grab the story (which Mark 3:23 calls a parable) of an exorcised evil spirit returning with seven worse ones.

---

tament text into a Greek/Shakespearian concept of "drama" in order to dismiss "the dramatic interpretation.")

So the lady says, "A son like you makes a mother glad."

Christ corrects her immediately in the next verse: thank you very much, ma'am, for the support, *but* (μενοῦν) more to the point, don't put down self-righteous people in their logical contradictions, not even to be freed from dumb-making devils. The point is that you need to be cleansed from sin in order to do what God wants done. Don't congratulate me, woman. Repent and believe, fear the Lord, love your neighbor, be a steward of God's gift to you on earth.

Poetic Paragraph of Proverbs 10:1–22

Aware of the historical setting and literary penchant of the indirect, polemical way "the wise" make God's will known, one can hear how chapter 10:1–22 presents Wisdom (act *coram Deo,* 1:7, hate evil, 8:13) correcting the worldly-wise street "wisdom" of the day. I contend that 10:1–22 is almost as tightly composed a piece as chapter 2, which is one single ode-like sentence holding the dependent "if, then" balanced clauses together in twenty-two verses that snap shut as a poem should.[34]

Translation[35] and Commentary

1.   A wise son or daughter makes a father or mother's heart merry,

---

34 2:1 My son/daughter if you take hold of what I say. . .
   2:5 *then* you shall catch on to standing still listening before the Lord and truly find a full-bodied knowledge of God. . .
   2:9 *then* you shall get to understand doing what is right, the just thing, and doing things simply the way they are set up to be—what is creationally good. . .
   2:12 snatching you away safe from the way of evil. . .
   2:16 snatching you away safe from the strange woman. . .
   2:20 *so that* you shall be walking on the way of creationally good things. . .

35 The layout of my translation hints at the counterpoint connections that make the whole intelligible. "My son" (בְּנִי) paragraphs are not just referring to teenage boys. בְּנִי has the meaning of "my son, my daughter, my child, my student, my disciple," and can include adults who are humble enough to sit at the feet of "the wise" to receive teaching in God's way. So the translation embraces the fact that בְּנִי is not gender-restrictive. My translation of רְשָׁעִים in verse 3 as "those who like to cut corners" and in verse 6 as "those who don't act straight" may set the teeth of purists on edge. But scriptural words are more than technical terms. The words are not jargon but poetically wrought; so putting the Hebrew into English needs a little play to allow this literary quality of the worded thought to have its force. I always check out my translations with purist Buber who wrenches German into the same refined Hebraicized term every time the word appears, lest one stray beyond aesthetic limits. "Blockhead babbling" in verse 14b is my metaphoric equivalent for פִּי אֱוִיל even though "blockhead babbling" hides the fact that the Hebrew has "mouth of a fool" sounding again the "mouth of the crooked" from verse 11b.

and an insolent, godless child breaks its parent's heart to pieces.

2. Treasures gotten by underhanded dealings are of no use at all: doing what is rightly just, however, saves you from death!

3. The Lord God Yahweh never lets a man or a woman who is actually righteous stay hungry,
but God rams the greedy desire of those who like to cut corners right back [down their throats]!

4. "A negligent empty hand brings on poverty:
the grip of the diligent makes one rich."

5. "A fellow who gathers in at harvest time
knows what he is doing:
a fellow who oversleeps at harvest time is
simply disgraceful!"

6. Genuine blessings halo the head of whoever come through with just deeds,
while the mouth of the people who don't act straight casts up a smokescreen over deeds that violate others.

7. The person who has persevered in doing what is just will be remembered as a gift of shalom, while the good name of those who have been guilty of crookedness shall decompose.

8. A person who is at heart wise simply carries out
[his or her] tasks:
it's the pair of slippery lips that will be smashed to bits.

9. "Who walks in wholesome ways will walk securely
unafraid:
who chooses his paths to be twisty will be discovered
[tied in knots]."

10. An eye that blinks the double-crossing wink
makes bitter trouble;
[I repeat:] it's the pair of slippery lips that will be
smashed to bits!

11. The mouth of folk kept truly just is a bubbling source
of life;
while the mouthing of people who don't act straight
[I repeat] casts up a smoke-screen over deeds that
violate others.

12. Hate rouses bickering, blistering discontent,
while love dresses all kinds of rebellious misdeeds with clothes.

13. You will find wisdom on the lips of an experienced, discerning person,
    but, "You need a stick for the backside of anybody who at heart lacks sense."
14. Judicious men and wise women are thrifty with hard-won knowledge,
    but blockheaded babblings are pregnant with disaster:
15. "Possessions are a citadel of strength to a man of wealth.
    It's poverty that ruins the poor—"
16. [No!] the handiwork and wages of a tried-and-true man or woman is full of life,
    but the income of the crooked fellow only increases his or her sin.
17. When one faithfully follows a nurturing discipline, you are on a pathway of life;
    but to pay no attention to corrective judgments will leave you wandering around lost!

18. Lips of deceit conceal hate,
    and whoever spreads gossip is a godless, insolent fool;
19. wherever there is too much talk, the upstart misdeed will not fail to materialize—
    whoever is more chary of his or her lip movements has more sense.
20. The tongue of a tried-and-true woman or man is as valuable as the choicest silver,
    while the heart of the connivers is worth next to nothing.
21. The lips of a tried-and-true woman or man will nourish many [to new life!]
    Stupidly closed fools, however, because they lack sense at heart, drop dead!
22. It is only the Lord God Yahweh's blessing that makes one rich: all your troubled struggle doesn't add a bit to it.

10:1 gives the usual setting, posing the alternative of "Wisdom or foolishness" in a two-generational context so important to the covenanting Lord. This introductory verse probably doubles as a common subtitle to the paragraphs that follow in chapters 10–15 until 15:33 paraphrases the cornerstone of 1:7 to end the section.

10:2 formulates the theme of the whole paragraph: crooked success is worthless, but right-doing (צְדָקָה) keeps you from a dead end. And 10:3

proclaims the Good News that the Lord provides the one with integrity
(צַדִּיק) with sustenance, but frustrates the greedy wicked. It takes a saving faith to believe this thesis (as Psalm 73 and the book of Job affirm),
because such truth is not observable to the naked eye.

10:4–5 counter the theme and thesis of 10:2–3 with what "people
today say." Imagine verse 4 as the quip of an entrepreneur leading one of
Solomon's trade missions to Hiram's court, and verse 5 as the "wisdom"
of a city foreman to a work crew building the temple or Solomon's gor-
geous palace, that is, as an incentive to country boys displaced in Jerusalem trying to make big money.

But 10:6–7 counters the street-smart sense and half-truth of "indus-
try-makes-rich" (v. 4) and "those who work hard get ahead in the world"
(v. 5) with the wisdom that lasting blessings (בְּרָכוֹת) come to the one with
integrity (צַדִּיק, vv. 6–7) while the wicked (רְשָׁעִים) are deceitfully violent
and short-lived. That is, 10:6–7 reinforces 10:2–3[36] after the false lead
of 10:4–5 by positing that "just-doing versus crooked acts," not "riches
versus poverty," is the framework for thinking and doing wisely.

10:8–11 is a brief commentary on the point of verses 1–3 and 6–7,
to make clear that being wise (חָכָם) consists in following the Lord's ordinances (מִצְוֹת, v. 8) for life. In other words, the voice of a just person,
which brings life (v. 11), is precisely the opposite of being foolish (v. 8)
and wicked (v.11).

Repeating verse 8b in verse 10b and verse 6b in verse 11b corrects
the false courtier's mode of operation and teaches the audience to avoid
the conflagration caused by slippery lips in a competitive workforce, and
a glib tongue at the office or in the neighborhood (cf. James 3:1–12).
Duplicit speech entails actual destruction (vv. 8b, 10b); the death of the
deceitful (v.2) is the antithesis of life (v.11a) for the righteous (צַדִּיק).[37]

Between 10:2–11 and 10:13–22 we find the central verse of this poetic paragraph. Proverbs 10:12 exposes the nature of crookedness (רֶשַׁע) and
of integrity (צַדִּיק) on which one's life or death hangs. Arousing contention
(making this crooked, מְעַקֵּשׁ, v.9b) is hatred in action, while love is action
that covers over the nakedness of your neighbor's wrongs and evil (פְּשָׁעִים).

In the context of 10:1–22, verse 12 is as resounding a statement as
Micah 6:8, which proclaims: "What does the Lord require of you? Noth-

---

36 No wonder the LXX added יהוה after בְּרָכוֹת in v.6. R. B. Y. Scott (*Proverbs,* The
Anchor Bible [Garden City, NY: Doubleday, 1965], 83) repeats Toy (*The Book of
Proverbs,* 203) to second-guess why v. 11b doubles v. 6b. They represent an earlier
generation that read doubling as scribal error rather than as poetic emphasis.

37 The alliteration in verse 9a הוֹלֵךְ בַּתֹּם יֵלֶךְ בֶּטַח hints that it is a known aphorism; so the
converse in verse 9b may be minted fresh for this occasion.

ing but doing what is just, loving to keep your promises, and walking humbly with your God." James quotes Proverbs 10:12 from memory as the punch line that sums up his whole letter (James 5: 19–20). Peter also quotes verse 12 as the crux for life in the end times (1 Peter 4:7–11). He argues that Proverbs 10:12 teaches how the body of Christ should be "economical" (house-holding) and hospitable with its charismata. This is the clue to withstanding great troubles, says Scripture.

Verses 13 and 14 pick up the "wisdom versus foolishness" theme from verses 1 and 8. Verse 15 exemplifies this theme, but not as a plank in a biblical economic policy. Rather, 10:15 is the slogan of God's people on the make in 1 Kings 5–7: "Capital is the stronghold of the wealthy: poverty is the weak spot of the poor." Proverbs 10:15 is the proverbial recapitulation of 10:4–5 run amuck in a policy of Mammon. This policy is immediately corrected by verses 16–17.

10:16–17 pulls the runaway concern for success and trust in money back into the orientation of Wisdom: integrity versus wickedness. These verses explicitly condemn the acquired gain, possessions, and profit of those who are devious as an increase in sin (חַטָּאת, v. 16). They declare that only the word of the righteous (צַדִּיק) brings life, and that only those who follow the discipline (מוּסָד) of Wisdom are walking on the path of life (vv. 16a, 17a). So the creed of security-in-riches (10:15) is indeed the babble of fools (v.14).

10:18–21 provides an almost line-by-line explication of verses 12–17, except for verse 15. Verse 18 links hate (שִׂנְאָה, v.12) to being a fool (cf. vv. 1 and 14). Verse 19 emphasizes what verses 13 and 14 pronounce—too much talk is prone to misdeed (פֶּשַׁע), while the judicious (חשֵׂךְ) are chary of their words. Furthermore, verse 20 exposits verse 16 by saying that the tongue of the righteous (צַדִּיק) is most valuable while the conniver's (רָשָׁע) talk is worthless. Finally, verse 21 echoes verse 17's sentiment that disciplined lips will nourish many; it also sounds the note that fools (אֱוִילִים) who at heart lack sense (בַּחֲסַר־לֵב cf. also vv.13's contrast to v. 8) will wander around in circles, only to drop dead (cf. v. 2).

This poetic paragraph concluding verse, by using the name of YHWH to recall the Good News of verse 3, corrects all the "get rich and be safe" homespun palaver and street-smarts of verses 4, 5, and 15; the blessing of the Lord (cf. v. 6), not hard work, brings riches. Contrary to all the public opinion in boomtown Jerusalem, Judah, and Israel c. 950–750 BC, pulling yourself up by your own bootstraps in the economy, in foreign trade, in the turmoil of civil administration, and in royal court intrigue—scrambling—do not add to one's well-being: riches (v. 4b) are not the fruit of industrious labor; they come only from the hand of the Lord God's blessing upon those with integrity (צַדִּיק, v.6).

The Paragraph and Its Message

Once one grasps that Proverbs 10:1–22 is a tightly knit poetic paragraph, its powerful message of comfort and rebuke becomes evident: curb the drive to reach prosperity by cutting corners, by talking crookedly to be impressive and to get ahead. Say "No!" to such a self-centered, selfish program of clever discontent and fermented strife, because that is hatred in action, and the end of hatred is ruin. Instead, believe that doing your ordained task is the way of genuine life. The compassionate Lord God will surely bless the one who comes through trials, withstands temptations, and deals trustworthily with colleagues and neighbors. Yahweh's blessing of shalom (veritable riches) is not something a hard-working man or woman can achieve. To know in your guts (לֵב) this truth of total dependence upon the Lord is to have a disciplined life and to be wise.[38]

So Proverbs 10:1–22 carries on in detail the very formidable choice with which Proverbs 1–9 faces every new generation: will you succumb to the seduction of what is "strange" to the Lord, the deeply foolish delights that lead to your death in hell (5:15–23, 7:21–23, 9:13–18), or will you hear the cry and accept the invitation of Wisdom to receive the Spirit[39] of knowing what is holy (1:22–33, 3:13–18, 8:4–36, 9:1–12)? Proverbs 10 develops Proverbs 1–9 by explicitly asserting that wisdom (חָכָם) shows up concretely in trustworthy right-doing (צְדָקָה), and foolishness (אֱוִיל) is embodied in crooked deeds (רֶשַׁע). Heart and mouth

---

38 To put the literary structure of this poetic paragraph in a schematic way:
    v. 1 (setting)
    v. 2 theme: crooked success is worthless: right-doings keeps you from a dead-end
    v. 3 good news! the Lord protects the righteous and frustrates the wicked.
       vv. 4–5 People say. . .
          vv.6–7   But the truth is:
          vv. 8–11 commentary on vv. 2–7
    v. 12 response God wants: love your neighbor; never hate.
       vv. 13–14 It isn't so. . .
       v. 15   People say. . .
       vv. 16–17 But the truth is:
       vv. 18–21 commentary on vv. 12–17
    v. 22 good news (deepening the theme): only the Lord's blessing makes you rich.

39 The NIV misses, it seems to me, a crucial place to help the reader see the "spirit" versus "flesh" horizon to the choice Proverbs is proclaiming by mistranslating (רוחי) in 1:23 as "thoughts." The Good News paraphrase is worse: "advice"! Peterson's *The Message* at least reads "spirit." Cf. note to RSV on Proverbs 1:23, "Heb spirit," which is dropped in NRSV.

are intimately linked: a wise heart (חֲכַם־לֵב) carries out God's ordinantial tasks with words of life (vv. 8, 11, 21); a vapid heart (חֲסַר־לֵב) vv. 13–15, 21) arouses and courts death.

This message, which links wisdom to just-doing, is in the forefront of the concern of prophets Amos, Isaiah, and Micah, who are contemporary with the later range of the Proverbs book. Spiritual wisdom is false unless is goes beyond pious sacrifices and regulated worship services and enters into the very bloodstream of society by giving justice to the downtrodden, the lonely, and the destitute, and ending the oppression of societal outcasts (Isaiah 1:10–20; 29:13–24; 58–59; Amos 5–6; Micah 2–3, 6).

The oppositional juxtaposition in Proverbs 9 of the woman Wisdom and the woman Foolishness reappears in Revelation 12 and 17 where the woman with child is saved from the dragon and from the whore of Babylonic culture.[40] Proverbs 10:1–22 ties this fundamental apocalyptic decision, which God already spelled out to Israel in the wise speech of Moses generations earlier (Deuteronomy 30: Choose the life of doing good or the death of doing evil.). Proverbs 10:1–22 reveals that the choice between life and death is made when one's mouth nourishes the neighbor (10:21), or when one's "slippery lips" (10:8b, 10b, 14b–15) murder the neighbor with vain, conniving putdowns.

In Pauline fashion, Proverbs 10 takes the wisdom/folly horizons, depicted by Woman Wisdom (Proverbs 8:12) and Woman Foolishness (Proverbs 9:13; Proverbs 2:16; cf. Ephesians 6:10–13), of Proverbs 1–9 into the tangible courts of gentle speech that sets things straight: a just deed (10:11a, 19, 20a, 21a) or the concealed hatred of ambitious, boastful, insolent talk (10:1b, 6b, 18). Later in James 3:13–18, the Newer Testament clearly proclaims this very difference between godly wisdom and demonic "wisdom" as the difference between what seeds the contention of careers and success and what sows the shalom of restorative justice (δικαιοσύνη, cf. Matthew 5:5–6).

---

40 All the debate about whether "the strange woman" is a real flesh-and-blood woman (the Septuagint treats 2:16–17 as an allegorical personification and translates אִשָּׁה as ὁδός and אַלּוּף as διδασκαλίαν!), and whether capital "W" Wisdom woman is a rhetorical personification or a mythic hypostatization due to Hellenistic Gnostic influence of Sophia, is simply evidence of how learned theologians do not know how to read poetic lines aright. With heavy-lidded eyes they either over-read the poetry into *theologoumena* or they mistake the allusive truth as mere dress-up embellishment. The "strange woman" (like the Babylonian harlot of Revelation) is poetic reference to your corner-store *Playboy* magazine or the Jaguar you covet to have under you, and the "Wisdom woman" is a poetic Older Testament reference, I believe, to the Holy Spirit (Proverbs 2:6, 8:14–18; cf. Isaiah 11:1–3, Micah 3:8, Daniel 5:10–12).

An Open Conclusion

How does one determine where Proverbs' poetic paragraphs begin and end? As Hermission carefully said a generation ago, we are looking for an ordering principle that is not commonly practiced today.[41] However, if we come to the text aware that the tradition of "the wise" in Israel assumed a creational theology of Yahweh's ordinances as fundamental to an obedient people of God, and if we approach the booked sayings as poetic writings, that is, as intentionally composed "Yes, but" wholes (varied wholes perhaps as diverse as the canonic psalms are), finding the paragraphic beginnings and endings in the Proverbs book will be less mysterious.

But exegetes and pastors will have to disabuse themselves of the traditional idea that Proverbs 10:1–22:16 is a collection of one-liner aphorisms and precepts.[42] Garrett's remark is true: "Identifying the small collections of proverbs is essential for the use of Proverbs in the church."[43] But Garrett still seems to work with the idea of Near Eastern paranomastic "collection" and didactic "random repetition" of formulaic sententiae.[44]

With the working presupposition that what we need to find are the artistically refined paragraphs that juxtapose and contrast epigrammatic sayings, we need to edit Proverbs into a format comparable to the Psalms. Proverbs 10:1–22 commends itself as such a literary paragraph for the following reasons.

The name Yahweh appears in verses 3 and 22, and wherever it graces a poetic line one may expect something weighty to be stated, so that a Yahweh phrase initiates the train of thought like a leading paragraph sentence, or it brings the movement of a poetic whole to a conclusion, a kind of caesura.[45] Twenty-two verses is also a natural Hebraic pattern for closure, even if the whole is not an alphabetic acrostic like Proverbs 31:10–31 (or Psalm 9–10; cf. Proverbs 2).

Verse 12, given special attention by the New Testament (James and 1 Peter), and the two flanking four-verse groupings I call "commentary"

---

41 Hans-Jürgen Hermission, *Studien zur israelitischen Spruchweisheit* (Neukirchener Verlag, 1968), 174.

42 Scott, *Proverbs*, 83.

43 Garrett, *Proverbs, Ecclesiastes, Song of Songs*, 47.

44 Krispenz (*Spruchkompositionen im Buch Proverbia*, 161) argues that Egyptian paranomastic use is unlike that in the Old Testament book of Proverbs.

45 I call this the "firefly" indicator, and am using it as one method to discern other paragraphs in Proverbs 10:23–24:34. You catch the trajectory of a firefly in the night by seeing where it lights up. Wherever Yahweh radiates a spot, a hint is given, I think, of where the poetic paragraphic point is headed.

all highlight the importance of couplets verses 6–7 (double blessing) and verses 16–17 (double life) for explicating the theme of verse 2. There is a kind of sustained, ode-like structure to the whole.

The to-be-corrected nature of verses 4–5 and verse 15 is unambiguous when one sees their contextualization by the whole twenty-two-verse paragraph. That one should not accept Proverbs 10:15 as bona fide biblical wisdom is shown by the subparagraph Proverbs 18:10–12, which renders explicit the phantasmagorical delusions that attend those who are vainly rich.[46]

What the apostle Peter said about brother Paul's writings (2 Peter 3:14–16) is also true about the wisdom of Proverbs: too hard to understand. The poetic paragraphs of Proverbs are not popular verse. Every attempt to market them for reading like Benjamin Franklin's "Poor Richard's Almanac"—as quips for punctuating and motivating the sanctified life—misses their sturdy God-breathed point and their lasting proclamation. So long as our versified published Bible translations neglect to conceive Proverbs and to print them in collocated poetic paragraphs, we may be hindering the "simple" readers from hearing God's message.

It will take courage to buck the established tradition of Wisdom literature scholarship, which has served up Proverbs as Egyptian precepts made kosher by a Yahwist editor, and to go against the stream of making the Old Testament gospel simple. But such work has been begun by Stek, Van Leeuwen, and Krispenz. It needs to be carried on so that the book of poetic paragraphs comes to be heard today as giving substance to the living water.

---

46 If one does not have the twenty-two-verse poetic context, one can take verses 4–5 as a straightforward work ethic opposed to laziness, which, of course, will be "complemented" by other admonitions not to trust wealth (11:28, 15:27, 23:4–5, 27:24; cf. Scott 84). Such restraint of Nature by the caution of Grace may scotch the snake of (North American) self-reliance but will not kill it as it biblically deserves.

BUSINESS MATTERS TO GOD

I would have you consider that those who think business is business miss the mark—because business is God's business![1]

In approaching this topic, I want to read almost three chapters of proverbs—we seldom read the Bible in long enough pieces to catch its meaning well. Our focus will be mostly just listening to that Scripture.

Proverbs 22–24, literally translated from the original texts goes like this—the Word of God:

> 22:17 Bend your ear this way, and listen to the words of wise men and
> women.
> Get your heart set for really knowing something.
> 18 It would be good, in fact, if you actually remember these things
> so they are always ready on the tip of your tongue.
> 19 I am pointing out [certain things] for you today—yes, you!—
> so that your trust be existentially in the LORD God Yahweh.
>
> 22 Do not take things away from those who do not have much,
> because they do not have much as it is.
> Do not exact every thing you can at the door of your office
> from those who have troubles,
> 23 because the LORD God shall sue their case
> and cross out the life of anybody
> who puts a double cross on those with troubled lives.
> 24 Do not make friendly deals with an owner of something,
> who gets easily riled.
> Do not pal around with a hot-tempered man lest you pick up
> his habits
> 25 and have swallowed the bait to make your [own] life trapped.
> 26 Do not become one of those glad-handers who stand guarantee
> for shady loans:
> 27 suppose you don't have the money to make payment?
> why have them take your bed from underneath you?
> 28 Do not finagle with the age-old boundary markers of property
> your fathers set up... .

---

1 Trinity Christian College held an overnight retreat for a couple dozen of Chicago businessmen in the late 1960s, to talk with profs about how to structure their commercial operations in a redemptive way, aware of rich and poor, the well-to-do, and people caught in difficult financial circumstances. This meditation on *Proverbs* was given before we turned in for the night to sleep.

[Do you get the point?]

29 **Show me a man or woman fit and dedicated in their job:**
   they gravitate to a place with executives who have a
   royal kind of dignity—
   they do not set up shop with the corner-cutting type
   of people.

23:1 When you sit down for a feed with somebody who has power,
   you had better take thorough stock of what you have got on
   your hands:

2 You put a knife to your throat if you show yourself to be a climber.

3 Do not drool over a rich man's dainties: it is weasel food, fake!

4 Do not strain yourself to get rich—if that is being smart, forget it!

5 What do you want? bloodshot eyes for that business?!
   It doesn't pay.
   Wealth has a habit of growing…growing wings:
   like a huge vulture it soars away through the wide blue skies.

6 Do not go to eat a meal made ready by a covetous eyed fellow;
   [I'll say it again,] Do not drool over that rich man's dainties,

7 because he is like one calculating every thing under his breath
   —that's the way he is.
   "Eat and drink," he says to you,
   but deep in his heart he is not with you at all.

8 The tasty bites you eat you will have to spit out later on, all right, and
   All your fine thank-you words you shall regurgitate.

9 Do not make talk for the ear of a [well-to-do] fool:
   he will just laugh contemptuously to himself at the pious
   insight provided by your conversation.

23:12 Please! Let your heart stay open to the prick of these teachings!
   Let your ear really hear these words of deeply knowing
   [what is at stake]!

13 You are supposed to not withhold
   corrective teaching from a young lad, right?
   He will not die if you strike him a blow; in fact,

14 you might save the young lad from the dead-end of hell
   if you [can] correct him by a blow.

15 [Well, O.K.,] "young lad[s],"
   if your heart becomes [correctedly] wise now,
   my own heart will be genuinely glad;

16 my deepest insides will be joyfully laughing all around,
   if your mouth comes to speak what is right, just, straight,
   before God….

17 **Do not let your heart get worked up, envying to be like those**
   who are "crooked-to-God."
   Instead. be driven the whole day by awe of the LORD God
   Yahweh—

18 **if that is kept there, there is future [to your work!]**
   and your excited expectation will never be defused.

24:1 Do not become challenged, [I said,] envious to be like men
and women who are covetous.
Do not even want to associate with them,

2 because their heart is continually busy concocting things
that deceive and oppress,
and their tongue wags and works a plague of harm.

3 By Wisdom is a household built up, and
it is a sound understanding that makes it sturdy; and

4 only by genuine, knowing insight do its rooms get filled
with truly valuable and lovely possessions of all kinds.

5 A fellow who is wise stands there equipped with strength.
A man or woman of knowing insight is constantly developing
capable power!
You know that—

6 only under prudent direction can you wage yourself a war, and
a successful conclusion can come only after many, many rounds
of careful consultation.

7 [But] Wisdom is beyond the reach of a fool –
the fool had better keep the mouth shut in the door of the
office....

8 People call whoever premeditates wrong-doing a master schemer.

9 Well, that is the nature of sin: the enterprise of a fool...god-less
scheming;
What an outrage [abomination] too to people is [the deceit of]
a scornful talker!

10 If in the day of trouble you show yourself to be faint-hearted,
then your [vaunted] strength is in trouble, all right....

11 Set free those being dragged to their death! And
Oh, no! hold back, hold them back! those being readied for
their execution!

12 If you say later on, "Is that so?! We didn't know anything about it."
Will not the One who puts hearts to the test, will God not see
through you?
The One who watches your heart with care knows [what is
going on]; and
God shall see to it that every man and woman be paid back in
kind according to what the person has done.

13 Eat honey, my young lad[s], for it is good stuff;
honeycomb honey tastes so sweet in the back of your mouth...

14 Just so—and you had better know it!—
so good and sweet is Wisdom for your heart!
[Remember (23:18)?]
If you have found Wisdom, there is future [to your work].
and your excited expectation shall never be defused.

15 Do not try, like some wicked fellow, hiddenly to figure out
how to get the landed goods of a righteous person.
Don't you dare try to ruin his or her peaceful place of rest;

¹⁶ because if a righteous person falls to the ground seven times,
    they [always] get up again;
    But wicked, guilty men and women, in the time of trouble,
    sway and crash to the ground!
¹⁷ (Yet) don't you be happy at the crashing fall of your enemy;
    Do not let your heart start smiling and shouting when your
    enemy stumbling sways,
¹⁸ lest the Lord God see you triumphing, and it be evil in God's
    eyes,
    and God wend away God's [holy] anger from the enemy.
¹⁹ Do not get so provoked at those wicked men or women who
    crookedly damage others.
    **Do not secretly yearn to be like those who godlessly do as
    they please,**
²⁰ **for there is no future inside the wicked person's life!**
    Any light lighting guilty, wicked men or women lights out.
²¹ **Fear the Lord God Yahweh! you people, and respect the ruler;**
    **Do not let yourselves get mixed up with those who think
    and live otherwise,**
²² **because disaster strikes (the impious) without a warning!**
    Nobody even knows what hit them—extinction!
        (Proverbs 22:17–19, 22–29; 23:1–9, 12–18; 24:1–22)

The terrible thing about Scripture is that you can never just leave it
there. Once it has come into your hearing, you have to reply: either talk
back—"Hmm, so so!"—or, respond believingly; trusting your lifetime to its
directive.

Do not be crooked-to-God is the directive of these *Proverbs* passages.
That is, do not separate your doings from the anticipated presence of the
Lord; that's not in line with the way things are set up! Let awe of the Lord
God Yahweh work itself into and through your bread and butter decisions,
life and death judgments, acts of war and peace and poverty—if you want
to have the joy of hope attend your daily life rather than an apprehensive
nervousness.

You misunderstand *Proverbs* if you think it is a book of rules on how not
to make a buck, or on whom not to practice that American invention of a
"business lunch" with, as if *Proverbs* was a tract to make you feel guilty about
dealing in money or being well-to-do. No. God's Word is much different
than a tabulation of do's and don'ts; and it goes much deeper than offering
advice against being crooked-to-men.

These Older Testament Scriptures are after your heart! God's revealing
speech aches to set our heart straight, make the driving force at the very heart
of you a humbled, exciting, for-God's-sake! drive. And what's in the heart
comes out of your mouth, and is printed all over your hands and deeds and
thoughts and lunches, possessions, attitude, questions, style of life....

When a man or a woman's heart is genuinely holy, says the Word of

God, their exercise of justice will be gentle and compassionate, their mode of life will be unencumbered by the jealousy of keeping for themselves whatever they've got, and their business or profession will be conceived and executed as a holy trust, a trust from the Lord.

Woe to those who think business is business: because business is God's business! Woe to those who want to combine business as it is and shaping world affairs along with walking a straight and narrow path: because there is no rest in such a combination, and the path of obedience is as broad as God's world! Woe to those who act as if they are the authority, and may set up the norms as they please, so long as it is above board: because such self-constructed, well-meant law and order lacks the be-in-awe-of-God! Directive—the pearl of great price!—and is utterly unprotected from the terrible calamity of doing hard, above-board work all for nothing!

Blessed are those who become wise! says *Proverbs*, who are convicted by the Holy Spirit that hearted obedience and not financial sacrifices is what pleases our God. Blessed are those who become wise, and are saved from the evil of coveting, because their consciousness is drenched with the happy insight and understanding that every thing they have and get and be! belongs totally to our Lord. Blessed are the wise, for they know that the faithful following Jesus Christ, who practice what they believe, are inheriting now upon the earth the coming of the riches and the power and the glory, the Rule of our LORD God.

With that there is rest for the people of God. And fear for those who bend an ear but do not really hear and understand....

Our professional women and business men's lives are often too cluttered with appointments and things to get done. Our living rooms and dens and offices are over-stuffed with luxuries. And we have too easily too much of that middle-aged authority that stultifies—we have largely lost the exciting edge of a youthful, hoping faith!—it's so hard for us grown-up, responsible citizens to be childlike again.

Proverbs 22–24 is not a manual for tired business men and women hard pressed to relax christianly. But this Word of Life has the power and grace to help us get our sights fixed again and give us a sense, under its hearing, of our being the body of Christ in a world of secular covetousness—not to congratulate ourselves, but to repent, straighten out before God, believe, expect guidance and Light that shall not light out.

> **Do not let your heart get worked up, envying to be like those who are crooked-to-God.**
> **Instead, be driven the whole day by awe of the LORD God Yahweh—**
> **if that is kept there, there is future to your work!**
> **and your excited expectation will never be defused.**[2]

---

2 From my *For God's Sake Run With Joy* (Toronto: Wedge Publishing Foundation, 1972), 37–41.

POSTSCRIPT

A crucial feature of the Bible often not well recognized is that the text is **God-speaking literature**. So it is a mistake to read the Bible as if it be like an old telephone book that gave you precise answers to someone's address and telephone number. The Bible tells **a true story** that begins in *Genesis* with God's creation of all things, and ends with *The Revelation of Jesus Christ given to John*, promising how things will come to a climax.

A person also errs, I think, if you treat the Bible as if it be an almanac of dogmatic facts with reliable predictions. Erudite theologicians have often written commentaries that decipher strange words in the Scriptures, identify obscure phenomena mentioned, and debate intricate grammatical constructions, until the literary verve and confrontational bite of the text has been smothered, and the telling point of God's voiced word gets lost.

Good Bible reading comes to **hear** God's call to stand in awe of the LORD God, that is, give up your vanity—"I can take care of myself!" —and simply accept the gracious invitation to become one of God's adopted children, following the Way of Jesus Christ, praying to become wise under the leading of God's Word and Holy Spirit.

If one accepts the reality that the Bible is God-speaking **literature**, then you need to learn how to read its narrative, honoring its literary, metaphorical character. Especially *Proverbs*, like the *Psalms*, *The Greatest Song*, *Job*, *Ecclesiastes*, prophetic writings like *Amos*, *Isaiah*, *Jeremiah*, *Ezekiel*, and *Daniel*, are largely full-fledged **poetry.**

So one needs to have poetic antennae, an aesthetic imaginative focus in one's reading approach in order to grasp the meaning of what is poetry. One needs to be aware, for example, of wordplay, the suggestion dimension of images, realizing that the elliptical generates unsaid nuances that are still meant. Irony, sarcasm, hyperbole, innuendo, are not nonsense, but are important literary subtleties one should be sensitive to.

Poetry does not make its message less certain, but poetry by its very polyvalent character is open to multiple interpretations; poetry can normally take more than one interpretation to cover its full complex symbolic content.[1] And poetic texts remain ambiguous.[2]

Biblical proverbs, you could say, are aphoristic poetry, brief epigrammatic conundrums somewhat like stripped down Newer Testament parables.[3] Proverbs 1:6 itself describes its Older Testament book as a collection of "artful comparisons" (מָשָׁל), "allusive sayings" (מְלִיצָה), a kind of literary puzzle and "riddles" (חִידֹת).

In their original oral educational form proverbs are heteroglossic, allowing conflicting voices to engage each other in a genuine dialogue, and provoking the reader-hearer's engaged response,[4] weighted toward a tentative emphasis within its penumbra of possible alternatives. For example, Proverbs 26:4–5 is **not** a contradiction so much as a succinct poetic way of instructing us on how to be wise with fools: undercut their proud vanity while not taking their proposal seriously (cf. pp. 57–59 above).

When proverbs are well spoken, they are given context by facial features of the speaker and their relevance apropos the present circumstances. When biblical proverbs become written, they are given context by the edited grouping of their formulations. And it is not always "clear" whether the paratactic juxtaposition is supplemental, critical, intensive, chiastic, oppositional, or what. For example, unlike most expositors who take Proverbs 27:17a as a positive illustration of friendship—"as iron sharpens iron"—I take Proverbs 27:17a as being corrected by 27:17b, thanks to 27:19: good friendship thrives on an open, empathetic face-to-face resonance, not abrasion (cf. pp. 81–84 above), But both readings lay claim to our attention, thanks to multiple variant, other proximate proverbs on friendship in the whole book.[5] After all, human friendship is a many-sided, complex phenomenon.

Current scholars Heim (2013, 2001) and Hatton (2008), Scoralick (1995) and Camp (1985), Whybray (1990) and late Fox (2000), **all** by and large confirm now that the right hermeneutic for reading biblical proverbs must recognize that "compositional units" occur with differ-

---

1 This is why you can rightly get different sermons out of a same biblical text, as well as sermons unsupported by the text.

2 "Ambiguity is very frequently the point of the poetic statement." Heim (2013), 241.

3 The Older Testament parable of Proverbs 7:6–23 is encapsulated in the third strophe of Proverbs 5:15–23. Walter Benjamin puts it this way: "A proverb, one might say, is a ruin which stands on the site of an old story and in which a moral twines about a happening like ivy around a wall." "The Storyteller" (1936), in *Illuminations*, translated by Harry Zohn, edited by Hannah Arendt (New York: Schocken Books, 1969), 108.

4 Hatton, 15, 116.

5 While 27:6 hints at friendly wounds, Proverbs 17:17 and 18:24 and 22:24–25 promote the encouraging, gentle heart-reflective notion of friend.

ent rationales,[6] and the boundary markers and linking devices forming "clusters of proverbs" are of various sorts.[7] Booked *Proverbs* is a lively collage of pronouncements, one might say, made by several circles of women and men made wise by God's Spirit,[8] and anthologized by several Holy Spirit-led editors.[9] So if one denies or neglects these larger, overlapping and complementing contexting features, one runs the danger of reducing the poetically compacted proverbs to disjointed platitudes, trivial truisms.[10]

It is an especially happy matter to have Proverbs 25–29 noted as coming to book with the historically dated provenance of good King Hezekiah's (c.728–637 BC) time (Proverbs 25:1), when written texts were being increasingly important.[11]

Hezekiah's cabinet of advisors included the Secretary of State Shebna (סֹפֵר), the scribe who kept the royal archives, and Joah, the official historiographer (מַזְכִּיר), along with the Financial Minister of the Treasury (עַל־הַבַּיִת) Eliakim (2 Kings 18:13–37).[12] Hezekiah and his wise administrators of Sennacherib-pressured Judah were busy absorbing refugees from Israel due to the Assyrian invasions and the fall of Samaria in 722 BC. Hezekiah wanted to reunite the Israelite divided kingdom;[13] so what better way to move in that direction than to have his wise scribes copy out scrolls of Solomon's proverbs, and then send out teachers with the writings to mediate this Holy Spirited wisdom among "the people of the land" (עַם־הָאָרֶץ), much as King Jehoshaphat had done with his teacher-priests and Levites several generations earlier using the booked *torah* of Yahweh (2 Chronicles 17:7–9). Now the guiding light would be the renowned wisdom that Solomon, son of David, had spoken.

The historical fact that when Hezekiah's great-grandson King Josiah was killed at Megiddo by Egyptian Pharaoh Necho, the vision of

---

6   Ruth Scoralick, *Einzelspruch und Sammlung. Komposition im Buch der Spruchwörter Kapitel 10–15* (Berlin: Walter de Gruyter, 1995), 240.

7   Heim (2001), 24–25, 106.

8   Claudia V. Camp, *Wisdom and the Feminine in the Book of Proverbs* (Sheffield: Almond [JSOT Press], 1985), 182. Just as Hushai and Ahitophel differed on their political counsel, but agreed on fundamentals, I imagine there were coteries of counselors with slightly different strengths and interests, although united in articulating the wholesome guidance of Wisdom.

9   This may explain the several collections of Proverbs: 1–9, 10:1–22:16, 22:17–24:22, 24:23–34, 25–29, 30 and 31.

10 Halton, 11, 47.

11 Isaiah knew how to write down as well as to speak the Word of the LORD (Isaiah 8:1).

12 Tryggve N.D. Mettinger, *Solomonic State Officials: A study of civil government officials of the Israelite monarchy* (Lund: CWK Gleerup, 1971), 19–24.

13 Cf. 2 Kings 18:13. William M. Schniedewind, *How the Bible Became a Book: The textualization of Ancient Israel* (Cambridge University Press, 2004), 80, 86–90.

a reunited independent Kingdom of Judah and Israel in David's line was dashed, until Jesus Christ picked up the promise for non-Jews too (Matthew 1:1, 10:46–52; Romans 9–11). Yet Proverbs 25–29 remains a treasured gift of God for disciplining our compromised lives with Holy Spirited wise counsel for governing the tasks before us in following the Way of the LORD's shalom.

[written in May 2017]

(16) Handwritten manuscript of "Postscript," 2017

APPENDIX

"If I were to state simply what I believe is the key to understanding the Bible, so I could avoid scrutinizing it like a Pharisee or Sadducee scribe (cf. Luke 11:52, John 5:36–40), I would say something like this: one needs to realize that the holy Scriptures are God-speaking literature given to us historically for our learning by faith the one true story of the LORD's Rule a-coming, and the contours of our obedient response. I believe the holy Scriptures come at us as the compelling Word of the LORD, and that it faces us whole, bodily men and women in our concrete life activity today with the overall directive to praise the LORD! repent and get adopted!, love your neighbor as yourself, and reconcile all creation back to God in Jesus Christ! It is to this ministry of thankfulness for what God has done for fallen creation in Jesus Christ that the LORD calls us through the Scriptures (cf. 2 Corinthians 5:17–21). Every reader and hearer either heartfully accepts and concretely obeys this pregnant directive, in the guiding strength of the Holy Spirit, or lets it pass by, as a fool.

"So there are four elements fused in my biblical hermeneutical method, you might say: (1) find the passage's thread in the whole true story narrative of history as God reveals it; (2) discern the literary configuration of the passage you are reading; (3) win a sense of the historical matrix in which the section was booked; (4) listen intently, on your knees as it were, to the convicting enlightening direction-message.

"People have different Bibles depending upon what they assume (1) to be—what is the main, true story of the Bible. (I go to Acts 1:3 for my lead.) One must always remember that no correct formula and not even the right perspective for Bible reading guarantees you sound exegesis every time. We believing men and women readers are fallible. The Bible's kerygmatic nature (4) defies a paint-by-number kind of exposition. Each portion of Scripture has to be prayerfully wrestled with in the communion of the saints under the leading of the Holy Spirit as to its historical matrix (3) and its literary contours (2) within the defining limits of (1) and (4). (I begin with Luke 24:44 and Hebrews 1:1 for orientation on the kind of narrative and the reality of historical date to the biblical text.) The final understanding of a passage—detecting the point of the piece, in the context of the whole Bible, for our lives now—is always an understanding of

Scripture that is an accountable, existential understanding that shall bear good fruit in season, or hurt people with its misleading lie. (I struggle to be responsible for the blessing promised in Proverbs 1:2–6 and 2 Timothy 3:16–17.)"[1]

Following this briefly stated hermeneutic, one could summarize along those lines what listening to the Older Testament book of *Proverbs* means:

(3) Most of *Proverbs* was booked by wiseman King Solomon and his counselors (1:1, 10:1) and edited later by the wise counselors of King Hezekiah (25:1). That dates the booked text c. 950–700 BC. The milieu of the book is the wisdom practiced by educated Egypt (remember Joseph) and Near-Eastern (Arab) countries (cf. 1 Kings 4:29–34).

(2) Tight paragraphs of epigrammatic poetry are edited into pericopes that contrast real-life vignettes of tempting wayward paths offset by warning counsel and the strong voice of Womanly Wisdom. This rabbinic format of "**Yes** it is so, **but** consider what is a wise alternative" characterizes the pedagogical nature of God's instructing proverbial Word.

(1) Proverbial חכמה (wisdom) translates God's תורה (*torah*) given to Moses and the wandering tribes of Israel into an educational form geared to a developing urban settlement life, a society with wise counselors concerned with the daily life decisions of God's people, next to priests concerned with purity and sacrifices in God's house, and distinct from evangelizing prophets calling rulers and backsliders at large to repentance. (Cf. rabbi Jesus' ministry and a Newer Testament book like the letter of *James*.)

(4) Proverbs 9 epitomizes the choice people have: to hear and respond to Woman Wisdom (= the Holy Spirit) and her good food and drink, OR, follow the siren of illicit Foolishness and go-getting stealth (Σάρξ). יראת יהוה (to stand in awe of God) is the beginning of חכמה; to be led by the Spirit of merciful just-doing is to choose LIFE and becoming τέλειος (mature). (Cf. Deuteronomy 30:11–20, Joshua 24:14–15, Matthew 5:48, 56:33).

---

1   From the 1979 Preface to *How to Read the Bible to Hear God Speak* (Sioux Center and Toronto: Dordt College Press and Tuppence Press, 2003), xii–xiii.

LIST OF ILLUSTRATIONS

AP—reproduced with the artist's permission
CS—photograph by Calvin Seerveld
CSU—© status unknown
PD—in the public domain

(1) Egyptian Coptic woman (c. 1950), photographer unknown. CSU

(2) Abattoir, photographer unknown. CSU

(3) Bible song, Leviticus 19:15–18, Psalter Hymnal #154 (1985), Calvin Seerveld.

(4) Duane Michals, *The Return of the Prodigal Son* (1982), 5 gelatin silver prints 13x18 cm. Henry L. Hillman Fund. CSU

(5) "Someday we will all die" is often attributed to Charles M. Schulz of *Peanuts* fame, but Peanuts Worldwide informed us that this image is "an unofficial meme that has been available over the internet but never appeared in the Peanuts strip nor was authored by Charles Schulz."

(6) Peter Smith, *Leaving* (1984), wood engraving, 103 x 127 mm. Collection of Inès and Calvin Seerveld. AP

(7) Saul Steinberg, in *The New Yorker*, 25 November 1961. CSU

(8) David Versluis, *Enlaced: A Burning Bush* (2013), Dordt University, Sioux Center, Iowa, COR-TEN, H 18 x W 8 x D 8 ft. AP

(9) Jean Siméon Chardin, *La Pourvoyeuse* (c. 1739), 47 x 38 cm, Musée du Louvre. PD

(10) Gaston Lachaise, *Standing Woman* (cast 1930), 187.6 x 81.3 x 45.1 cm, Metropolitan Museum of Art, New York. PD

(11) Johannes Vermeer, *De Kantwerkster* (1669–70), oil on canvas, 24 x 21 cm, Musée du Louvre. PD

(12) Käthe Kollwitz, *Woman with dead child* (1903), Kunsthalle, Bremen, Germany. © 2019 Artists Rights Society (ARS), New York / VG Bild-Kunst, Bonn.

(13) Henry Moore, *Reclining Figure* (1929), brown Horton stone, 83.8 cm, Leeds Art Gallery, U.K. Reproduced by permission by the Henry Moore Foundation. CS

(14) Overnight snow sculpture in Toronto. CS

(15) Author with favorite flower (1980s).

(16) Handwritten manuscript of "Postscript" (2017).

INDICES

Pertinent Bible Passages

TRANSLATIONS OF SELECTIONS FROM PROVERBS